Date

OLD & MIDDLE ENGLISH TEXTS
General Editor G. L. Brook

The Owl and the Nightingale

Edited by
ERIC GERALD STANLEY

MANCHESTER UNIVERSITY PRESS
✳
BARNES & NOBLE, NEW YORK

First issued 1960
by Thomas Nelson & Sons Ltd

This edition 1972
© E. G. Stanley
issued by
MANCHESTER UNIVERSITY PRESS
316–324 Oxford Road
Manchester M13 9NR

ISBN 0 7190 0513 2

Published in the U.S.A. 1972 by
Harper & Row Publishers, Inc.
Barnes & Noble Import Division

PRINTED IN GREAT BRITAIN BY
BUTLER AND TANNER LTD, FROME AND LONDON

CONTENTS

ACKNOWLEDGMENTS

I wish to express my gratitude to the British Museum and the
Bodleian Library for allowing me to consult the manuscripts in
their care, and for supplying me with photographic reproductions
of MS Cotton Caligula A.ix, and MS Jesus College 29. For a
multitude of points of detail and for much help involving general
principles I am indebted to Professor and Mrs A. S. C. Ross and
Mr R. W. Burchfield. What I owe to Professor C. S. Lewis, and
Mr G. T. Shepherd and Dr D. S. Brewer, I am precluded by the
terms of our association in NMRL from expressing to the full,
yet cannot allow the opportunity to go by without saying that it
is far more than any editor has reason to expect from the General
Editor or the Editorial Board. I also wish to thank Mr K. W.
Humphreys, the Librarian of the University of Birmingham, and
his staff for their great courtesy to me at all times. To the staff of
Thomas Nelson & Sons Ltd, and especially to Dr Katharine Davies,
I am deeply grateful for the care with which they have produced
this book. Finally I must not omit to thank the Faculty of Arts of
the University of Birmingham for some grants of money from
the Research Fund, as a contribution towards my expenses.

ACKNOWLEDGMENTS

In this second impression some misprints, factual errors, and ambiguities contained in the first have been removed. These corrections have benefited from Professor R. M. Wilson's review [*MLR* 56 (1961)] and friendly criticism, and especially from Professor E. J. Dobson's copious review [*Notes and Queries* 206, Nos. 10, 11, 12 (1961)]. My Notes to the following lines are among those which have been corrected with Professor Dobson's criticism in mind : 323-8, 453, 614, 917-20, 955, 978, 1229f, 1400, 1432.

Additions of my own and the discussion of new work on the poem must wait for a more thorough revision than is possible at present. I only wish to mention one or two of the most outstanding suggestions made since the first impression went to press : Professor Dobson's view that J's *þu clechest euer among* ' You seize with your jaws at recurrent intervals ' (cf. *MED* s. *clēchen*) is to be preferred to C's and avoids the difficulty at line 82 ; Professor C. E. Bazell's emendation of line 1644 to *þu anst wel . . .* ' You grant fully ', ' you admit ' (quoted by Professor Dobson) ; and Professor A. A. Prins's emendation of *Vor þeg* at line 1724 to *Vor-þe* ' because ' (with a full stop or semi-colon at the end of the line (*Mélanges de linguistique et de philologie : Fernand Mossé in memoriam*, pp. 417-19).

Professor Dobson's views on the rhymes of the poem I find less convincing. Of the two writers of ME rhyming verse whose work survives in holograph, Dan Michel and William Herebert, neither rhymes with the philological exactness required by Professor Dobson (cf. Wallenberg, p. 306 ; Carleton Brown, *Religious Lyrics of the 14th Century* : *under on mon* 14[5f], *kynedom þorn* 15[31f], *kunde bunde munde* 19[2-9]). What we know of the history of rhyme in Latin and the vernaculars (including English) shows that rhymes were not aimed at in the beginning, nor always achieved later. ' I dare almost affirm, that the Difficulty of finding Rhymes, has been the unlucky Cause that has frequently reduc'd even the best of our Poets to take up with Rhymes that have scarce any Consonance, or Agreement in Sound ', says Edward Bysshe in his *Art of English Poetry* (1702). Before I follow Dobson's absolute acceptance of rhymes as ' one of the most valuable tools of ME. textual criticism ' I wish to see the reliability of the tool demonstrated.

ABBREVIATIONS

(a) Grammatical and linguistic abbreviations

>—becomes
<—(derived) from
acc.—accusative
adj.—adjective
art.—article
conj.—conjunction
cpd.—compound
dat.—dative
def.—definite
Fr—French
gen.—genitive
Gmc—Germanic
imp.—imperative
ind.—indicative
indef.—indefinite
inf.—infinitive
interj.—interjection
intr.—intransitive
ME—Middle English
MnE—Modern English
MnFr—Modern French
n.—noun
neg.—negative
nom.—nominative
num.—numeral
obj.—object

OE—Old English
OFr—Old French
OIcel—Old Icelandic
OK—Old Kentish
ON—Old Norse
p.—past
pl.—plural
p.p.—past participle
Pr—Primitive
prep.—preposition
prepos.—prepositional case
pres.—present
pres. p.—present participle
pron.—pronoun
refl.—reflexive
s.—sub (verbo), under the heading indicated
Scand—Scandinavian
SE—south east(ern)
sg.—singular
subj.—subjunctive
SW—south west(ern)
tr.—transitive
v.—verb(o); vv.—verbis
voc.—vocative
WS—West Saxon

(b) Other abbreviations

Anglia—*Anglia, Zeitschrift für englische Philologie*
Anglia Bbl.—*Beiblatt zur Anglia*
Archiv—*Archiv für das Studium der neueren Sprachen und Literaturen*
S. T, R. O. d'Ardenne, *Iuliene*—Bib. 67
Atkins—Bib. 15

Bib.—Bibliography; i.e. pp. 41-6 of this edition. The number refers to the item of the Bibliography
Bloomfield—Bib. 49
Börsch—Bib. 19
Bradley—Bib. 4
Breier—Bib. 20
B.T.—Bib. 2

B.T. *Suppl.*—Bib. 3

C—MS Cotton Caligula A.ıx

Cawley—Bib. 47

Dickins and Wilson—Bib. 18

Dobbie, *A.S. Poetic Records*—Bib. 68

Dobson, *1500–1700*—Bib. 55

E&GS—English and Germanic Studies

E&S—Essays and Studies by Members of the English Association

EDD—Bib. 6.

EETS (E.S.)—Early English Text Society (Extra Series)

EETS (O.S.)—Early English Text Society (Original Series)

Eggers—Bib. 24

Einenkel—Bib. 56

EStn—Englische Studien

ESts—English Studies

C. T. Flower—Bib. 103

Gadow—Bib. 13

Grattan—Bib. 16

Hall—Bib. 14

Hässler—Bib. 23

Huganir—Bib. 21

J—MS Jesus College Oxford, 29

JEGP—Journal of English and Germanic Philology

Jordan—Bib. 54

Liebermann—Bib. 101

LSE—Leeds Studies in English and Kindred Languages

Luick—Bib. 52

MÆ—Medium Ævum

Mätzner—Bib. 10

MED—Bib. 5

MLN—Modern Language Notes

MLR—Modern Language Review

Neckam—Bib. 86

Napier, *OE Glosses*—Bib. 64

NED—Bib. 1

O&N—*The Owl and the Nightingale*

C. T. Onions—Bib. 17

Pollock and Maitland—Bib. 102

RES—Review of English Studies

RS—The Chronicles and Memorials of Great Britain and Ireland during the Middle Ages (' Rolls Series ')

Sievers-Brunner—Bib. 53

Skeat—R. Morris's *Specimens of Early English*, revised by W. W. Skeat, 1886

A. H. Smith—Bib. 7

Stanley—Bib. 51

Stenton—Bib. 100

Stevenson—Bib. 8

Stratmann—Bib. 11

Sundby—Bib. 63

TLS—The Times Literary Supplement

Wallenberg—Bib. 66

Warnke, *Quellen*—Bib. 89

Wells—Bib. 12

Irene Williams—Bib. 65

Wright-Wülcker—Bib. 69

YWES—The Year's Work in English Studies

INTRODUCTION

THOSE who have considered *The Owl and the Nightingale* as a work of literature have written of it with so full a measure of praise that one comes with relief upon Thomas Wright's introduction to his edition of 1843, where he simply calls it ' a curious poem '. That it is, and it is more than that. More than any other English poem written before the four-teenth century it makes an immediate appeal to the modern reader. The Nightingale delights ; and the crab-faced Owl disapproves of our delight, of our frivolity, and of the Night-ingale's lascivious promptings. We are allowed to listen to the debate of the two birds, not asked to judge between them. For we are not to be trusted ; we might well decide in favour of the plausible Nightingale, though on more sober reflection we should perhaps admit that it is to the Owl that the victory ought to have gone. The disputants have chosen a better judge than we are, one Nicholas of Guildford, wise, just, and learned, yet not inhuman. Alas, we shall never know for whom he finds. The poet too appears impartial. Let us likewise reserve judgment, at least till we have heard the case.

THE MANUSCRIPTS

We know of three MSS of *The Owl and the Nightingale* [O&N] : MS Cotton Caligula A.ix [C], in the British Museum ; MS Jesus College 29 [J], deposited by the College in the Bodleian Library, Oxford ; and a now lost MS listed in the medieval Catalogue of the Library at Titchfield Abbey (a house of Premonstratensian Canons) ; [see R. M. Wilson, Bib. 26].

C consists of two parts, originally separate. The first is the earlier version of Laȝamon's *Brut*, and the second con-tains poems in French and English and a French prose Chronicle up to the accession of Henry III in 1216. O&N is the first English poem in the second part ; it has no title.

Palaeographers date the MS as of the first half of the thirteenth century, obviously after 1216. A facsimile of a page of the MS is to be found in Atkins's edition of O&N. An account of the contents of the MS [and of J] is to be found in Carleton Brown's *English Lyrics of the XIIIth Century*, pp. xxii-xxv [he uses the old pagination of J].

J also consists of two parts, originally separate. The first is a Latin Chronicle written on paper in the fifteenth century ; the second contains all the poetic works, both French and English (including O&N), found in C [with the exception of one English poem, the omission of which is explained by the loss of a leaf in J]. There are considerably more poems in J than in C. Among the poems in J but not in C is a version of *The Proverbs of Alfred* [cf. Introduction, p. 34]. Palaeographers date the MS as of the latter half of the thirteenth century, rather late in that period [cf. A. C. Paues, *Anglia* 30 (1907), 222]. A facsimile of a page of the MS is to be found in Wells's edition of O&N. An account of the history of J is given by C. L. Wrenn in *E&S* 25 (1939), 101-15. The MS was at one time in the possession of the seventeenth-century bibliophile Thomas Wilkins. It is almost certainly his hand that wrote at the end of the poem immediately preceding O&N (i.e. at the end of the poem *The Passion of Our Lord*, reprinted in EETS (O.S.) 49, pp. 37-57) the following note, under the signature *Tho. Wilkins* :

> On parte of a broaken leafe of this MS. I found these verses written, whereby the Author may bee gues't at.
> > (viz.)
> > Mayster Iohan eu greteþ. of Guldeuorde þo.
> > And sendeþ eu to Seggen. þat synge nul he no.
> > Ac on þisse wise he wille endy his song:
> > God Louerd of Heuene. beo vs alle among.
> > > AMEN.

[Master John of Guildford greets you then, and sends to you to say that he will not sing. But he will end his song in this way : God, Lord of Heaven, may he be among us all. Amen.]

These verses are written (as was not unusual at the time) in imitation of the medieval hand, the first letter, a medieval capital M, being written over an erased normal seventeenth-century capital M. Wilkins does not say where he found the *broaken leafe*. It may have been one of the leaves of the MS now lost; it may have been a fly-leaf. There is little to connect it with *The Passion of Our Lord*, and even less to connect it with O&N. The language of the verses is that of the English poems in J ; the metre is that of *The Passion of Our Lord* (and of a number of other poems in J), but not that of O&N [see Koch, Bib. 28]. The *broaken leafe* will be referred to again (p. 20) in connexion with the authorship of O&N.

The interrelationship of the texts of O&N in C and J is discussed by Wells in the Introduction to his edition, pp. xiii-xvi. J is not a copy of C (though it is later), as is proved, *inter alia*, by lines 86 and 770ff which are omitted in C but not in J. That C is not a copy of J follows from the palaeo-graphical dating of the texts, and is supported by a number of errors in J which are not in C, e.g. the omission of lines 734 and 1308. Since the two texts agree in a number of errors (e.g. at line 1711 there is a new paragraph in both MSS in the middle of a sentence—see footnote) they must have had a common antecedent containing these common errors. A text containing major scribal errors cannot have been the author's text in his own hand. There is no way of telling how many intermediate copies there may have been between the author's and the common antecedent of C and J, nor is there any way of telling how many intermediate copies there may have been between the common antecedent and the extant texts.

THE TREATMENT OF THE TEXT

In *Nelson's Medieval and Renaissance Library* works of early literature are to be presented to the modern reader in a single text, not a conflate of many texts, nor many texts printed parallel with an expressed preference for one. Ideally the modern reader should be able to approach the work as an educated contemporary reader might have done. A reader may forget the existence of MSS other than that chosen by the editor as the basis for his edition ; but the editor cannot, and must not. He must use the evidence of the variant readings to correct and elucidate the chosen MS, for an inferior MS may contain readings that make sense, where the chosen MS makes none ; and a doubtful reading in the chosen MS may be explained by a differently doubtful reading in another MS.

In the case of O&N the choice of the MS on which the edition is to be based is easy. Only two MSS are extant, C and J, of which C is the earlier, and the scribe of C seems the more conservative and faithful. He uses two systems of spelling [see pp. 7, 10], presumably because he is faithfully copying a MS written by two scribes, each using a different system of spelling. The scribe of J is more thoughtful; but in scribes thinking may be as dangerous as not thinking. A scribe copying mechanically (like the C scribe) will often blunder, but he will also often copy what cannot have made sense to him, so that the original sense may be recovered. A thoughtful scribe (like the J scribe), wishing to write sense, will regularise and modernise, and at times even ' emend ' what he thinks is nonsense in his exemplar, thus perhaps weakening the sense of the original which he failed to understand, and often wiping out, beyond hope of recovery, such traces of the original good sense as may have existed still in his exemplar. Thus, such readings as C's *soƷe* 184, *mistempe* 1353, *mannenne* 1725, may preserve traces of original readings lost in J's *sope*, *misnyme*, and *mankunne*. Since the J scribe ' emends ' some of the most discussed readings in the poem (like *brcche* 14, *bov ne rind* 242, *an oper pes* 748, and *wrouehede* 1400) ; and since he frequently leaves out, for no apparent reason, such little words as *wel*, *eure*, *no*, *Ʒet*, etc. [see Introduction, p. 38, and cf. Atkins, p. xxvii], he has been generally considered less reliable than he really is. Editors have not always acknowledged sufficiently in how very many cases (as the footnotes show) C's blunders have been corrected by reference to J's better readings, and that in a few cases J preserves more archaic forms than C [cf. 184 note].

This edition takes C as its basis, and refers to J only for correction and elucidation of C. If a reader of this edition of O&N wishes to compare himself with a medieval reader of the poem, it is with an original reader of the C text that he must seek comparison; but he must remember that he is reading a C text punctuated to conform to modern practice, and corrected by editors and commentators over the last hundred and twenty years with the help of a great volume of material, medieval and modern, among which the work of the J scribe has not been the least trustworthy.

THE LANGUAGE OF THE COTTON MS

A fuller survey of the language of the extant texts of O&N is provided by Breier ; and in the following very brief account only those linguistic features will be considered which have a bearing on the dialect of the C text, and its spellings.

There are in C two spelling systems, as has already been mentioned. The first, covering lines 1–900 and 961–1183, will be referred to as Ci ; the second, covering lines 901–60 and 1184–end, as Cii. Since the whole of the poem in the Cotton MS is in one hand, the two spelling systems reflect the spellings of an earlier MS (presumably the exemplar of C) written in two hands, differing from each other in spelling (as Ci differs from Cii).

Phonological features

Vowels (development in positions of reduced stress is usually ignored in this discussion).

OE short *a* before nasals (other than in lengthening groups) >*a* or *o*, e.g. *man, mon*. In ME *o* is a feature of the West Midlands. OE short *a* before nasals in lengthening groups >*o*, e.g. *honde* ; but this is not confined to one dialect, since, when the MS was written, all areas except the North and North Midlands had *o*. See under OE long *ā* below.

OE short *æ* > *a*, e.g. *apele*, as in all dialects except SE and a part of the West Midlands, which have *e*.   OE long *ǣ* [< WGmc *ā*], a feature of WS (and some other Saxon dialects), was *ē* in Anglian and Kentish ; when shortening takes place, *ǣ* > *æ* > ME *a* ; *ē* > *e*.   C always has *a*, e.g. *raddest* ; such ME forms are not confined to the SW.

OE short *o* is *o*, e.g. *orfe* ; but Cii's *walde* (besides the more common *wolde*) is a feature of the West Midlands (and of the North).

OE short *y* retains its sound *ü* in the dialects of the West Midlands and the SW, but is written *u*, e.g. *sunne* 'sin'; forms with *i*, like *kinge* and *hiȝte* [< *cyning*, *hyht*] are due to the unrounding influence of the neighbouring sounds.

OE *ā* > *ō*, e.g. *mose*.   By the time C was written this change had taken place in the whole of the South and much of the Midlands, especially the West.

OE *ǣ* is usually written *e*, but occasionally in Cii *ea*, e.g. *dede*, *deale* (954).

OE *ē* is written *e*, e.g. *deme*.   In WS and OK *ē* may develop from *eg* before *d* or *n*.   See 349 note.

OE *ȳ* retains its sound *ü* in the West Midlands and the SW, but is written *u*, e.g. *hude*.

OE short *ea* before *l* + consonant is confined to WS and OK, and traces of it are rare in C, e.g. the exceptional *belde* 1715, and *iweld* [for which cf. S. T. R. O. d'Ardenne, *Iuliene*, pp. 136f, s. *wealden*, *wealdent*].   As in ME generally, the usual forms in C [e.g. *alle*, as well as lengthened *olde* (besides very rare *alde*)] are derived from unbroken *a*.   OE *ea* before *r* + consonant > *a*, e.g. *arme*, *harde* [probably unlengthened, cf. Orm's *harrde* (where *rr* indicates that *a* is short)] ; but *ea* > *e* [occasionally written *ea*] when lengthened, e.g. *erde*, *eardingstowe*.

OE short *eo* is monophthongised to an *ö* sound [œ], which is retained in the West Midlands and the SW.   In C it is usually written *o*, but Cii also has *eo*, e.g. *storre*, *steorre*, *houene*, *heouene*.

OE *ēa* is monophthongised to an open *ę̄* sound, usuallv written *e*, but in Cii occasionally *ea*, e.g. *gret*, *deaþe*.   When *i*-mutated, PrOE *ēa* > *ē* in all areas except WS where the development was to *īe* (> *ȳ*). There is hardly a trace of WS forms in C; cf. *ȝeme, ihere* [but *ihire* 312 (? < *gehȳran*)].

OE *ēo* is monophthongised to a long *ö* sound [œ :], which is retained in the West Midlands and the SW. In C it is usually written *o*, but Cii also has *eo*, e.g. *þode, þeode*.

There are some traces in C of PrOE diphthongisation of vowels by preceding palatal consonants, e.g. *ȝiue* beside *ȝeue*. The geographical distribution of this development is uncertain.

Of the diphthongs formed in late OE and ME when vowels were followed by *ȝ, w*, and *h*, only OE *weg* > *wei* or *wai* is of interest. The sound-change from *ei* to *ai* seems to occur very early in this word; although Jordan, § 95 Anm., puts it as late as the second half of the thirteenth century. See 1509f, note.

Consonants. The chief differences between Ci and Cii involve the spellings of consonants. Both Ci and Cii have *þ*, but in Cii *ð* is occasionally used finally. Ci has *ȝ* for the guttural and palatal spirants [< OE *h* and *g*], Cii has *h* more often than *ȝ*.

Initially in words of native origin *þ, s*, and *f* were voiced in the South and in the SW Midlands; but in the spellings of O&N this is apparent in the alternation of *f* and *u* (or *v*) only, e.g. *fare* and *uare, forþ* and *uorþ*.

In early ME *h* was lost before *r, l*, and *n* in all areas except Kentish, e.g. *rape, lauedi, nesche*. Loss of *h* before *w* is a feature of some East Midland and West Midland as well as SE texts; in Ci *hw* > *w* (very rarely *wh*), Cii has more *hw* than *w* spellings, e.g. *wi* (once *whi* 150) or *hwi*.

THE ORTHOGRAPHY OF THE COTTON MS

In C the letters *thorn* and *wynn* often present difficulty. As Grattan says, ' In their extreme forms these letters are entirely distinct from one another.' Often the scribe dots *wynn* to avoid confusion. Even so, there are many cases when the two letters appear to be identical in form, though

Grattan believed that microscopic investigation reveals a difference in the direction of the down-stroke. There are, however, far too many cases of confusion of *thorn* and *wynn*, even in their extreme forms, for Grattan's thesis to be convincing. It seems that the scribe himself was often indifferent to the direction of the down-stroke, and did not attempt to distinguish the two letters. The present edition, therefore, does not reproduce the state of the MS with regard to these two letters, but prints lower case þ or capital Þ for *thorn*, and lower case or capital *double-u* for *wynn*, as required by the sense, and in conformity to the modern practice of capitalisation. [It may be felt that an exception has been made in the case of the word *noþt* ; reasons for retaining this spelling are given in the note to line 1256.]

In C the form of the letter *y* is indistinguishable from *thorn*, and also at other times from a dotted *wynn* ; but *y* does not come often, and there is only one example where the similarity of *y* and *thorn* causes difficulty (see 1494, note).

Not infrequently *d* is written for final *t*, and *t* for final *d*. It is difficult to be sure to what extent *t* for *d* reflects a sound-change [cf. Luick, § 713] in the case of a scribe whose Anglo-Norman scribal habits lead him to write *d* for *t*. For examples and details see Breier, pp. 20f and 32, and Wells, Bib. 62.

A number of times final þ (or ð) appears as *d* or *t*. The verbal inflexional ending *eþ* or *eð* is often written *et*, and *wiþ* is often written *wit*. The spelling *d* for þ or ð might be due to the scribe's failure to understand or copy the obsolescent ð of his exemplar ; the distribution in C of such spellings complicates that assumption, for the letter ð is found only in Cii, whereas *d* spellings come in Ci [*quad*, 117 ; *haued*, 119, 167 ; *nabbed*, 536 ; *god*, 647 ; *kumed*, 683 ; *totorued*, 1119] as well as Cii [*wened*, 901 (a line the inclusion of which within Cii depends on the interpretation of this form) ; *fulied*, 1239 ; *sulied*, 1240 ; *kumed*, 1246]. If these spellings are to be regarded as the result of failure to understand or copy an original ð (and not merely, and perhaps more plausibly, as a possible Anglo-Norman spelling peculiarity), not the scribe of C, but the scribe of his exemplar must be held to blame. Cf. Breier, pp. 30f; Wells, Bib. 62 ; Jordan, § 203 Anm.

Metathesis of *r* occurs a number of times in C. See the note to *þurste* 249 (and cf. Jordan, §§ 165, 168 and Luick, § 714).

Initial *h* is omitted in the following words : *attest*, 255 where the omission has been corrected subsequently ; *is*, 403, 571, 1483 ; *it*, 1090 ; *e*, 1475. This is probably not a reflection of the pronunciation ; whereas the loss of initial *h* of the second element of a compound may well reflect a possible pronunciation : *godede*, 582 ; *swikelede*, 838 ; *licome*, 1054 ; *utest*, 1683 ; as well as the sandhi *attom*, 1527. Initial *h* is added unetymologically a number of times, often in *hule*, *houle*, and also in *hure*, 185 ; *hartu*, 1177 ; *his*, 1498, 1761 ; and *hunke*, 1733. Cf. Breier, pp. 21f ; Wells, Bib. 62 ; Jordan, § 195.

In the present edition MS *double-u* has been represented by *vv*. In Ci this may represent two letters *u*, either of which may be consonantal or vocalic. Thus *vvole*, 8, stands for *uvole* (with the *o* presumably miswritten for *e*) ; and in *vvl*, 31, 236, *vvle*, 35, and *ivvrne*, 637, *vv* stands for *vu*; in this elucidation *u* has been used for the vowel, *v* for the consonant. [Cf. Breier, p. 25, and Wells, note to line 8.]

After *w*, and less frequently after *vv*, a *u* may be omitted, as for example in *wrþ*, *vvrs*, which stand for *wurþ* and *vvurs*. It is unlikely that an *i* could be similarly omitted, and *wse*, 54, and *wte*, 440, are probably errors. For examples see Breier, pp. 24f ; Wells, Bib. 62.

Groups of three consonants are not infrequently simplified (see the note on *drunnesse*, 1399).

The following examples of loss of final stops after *n* and *l* may indicate a lack of precision in the pronunciation of some consonant groups, though this is certain only in the frequent spelling *an* for *and* ; and probable in *chil* for *child*, 1315, 1440, and *am̃on þe* for *among þe*, 164 (exactly parallel to *strenþe* for *strengþe*, 781, 1674) ; while the omission of *d* in *solich*, 1025, and *sele*, 943, is probably a blunder.

Twice, *þungþ*, 1473, and *þing* for *þincþ*, 1694, *nc* (or *nk*) has been written *ng*. These may be inverted spellings in a text which has traces of unvoicing of *ng* to *nk*, e.g. *strncþe* for *strengþe*, 1226. Cf. Wells, Bib. 62 ; Luick, § 713 ; Jordan, § 193.

Final *m* is occasionally written *n* in positions of weak stress : *fron*, 135, 1614 ; *an*, 364, corrected to *am* (see footnote) ; *hon*, 881 ; *hin*, 890 ; *sun*, 1397 ; *wisdon*, 1482 ; *sundel*, 1598. See Wells, note to line 881.

The sound written *sh* in MnE is most frequently written *sch* in C ; *sh* is not uncommon ; and *s* and *ch* are also found. The following are spellings with *s* : *sewi*, 151, *fleses* (where the sound may well be *s*, not *sh*), 895, *solde*, 975, 977, *solich* (for *scholdich*), 1025, *wrþsipe*, 1099. The *ch* spellings may be haplographic, *s* being omitted after an *s* or *f*, which is similar in form to long *s*, or dittographic after *ch* ; for examples of *ch* spellings see 933f note. The spelling *hs* (*fihs*, *flehs*, 1007) presumably represents the sound *x*, not *sh*. [Cf. Breier, pp. 22f ; Wells, note to line 1402 ; Wells, Bib. 62 ; Jordan, § 181 ; Luick, § 691 Anm. 5.]

Paragogic *e* is common between certain consonants, e.g. between *r* and *ʒ* or *h* as in *areʒþe*, *arehþe* ; between *r* and *m* as in *harem* ; before *w* as in *narewe*, *falewi* ; after *v* (the consonant) as in *steuene*, *lauedi* ; between *s* and *m* as in *bisemar*. See Luick, §§ 446-9 ; Breier, pp. 26f ; Wells, Bib. 62.

For the spelling *þ* for *h* (the fricative) see the note to line 1256. It is not impossible that *þunch* (for *þuncþ*), 1649, 1651, is an inverted spelling ; and similarly perhaps *floh* (for *floþ*), 920 (see note).

For the spelling *s* for *h* (the fricative) see the notes to 242 and 1751.

The fricative *h* is written *ch* in *sichst*, 242 (see note), and *þurch*, 1401.

Omission of the fricative is found in such verbal forms as *suþ*, 246, *biluþ*, 1557 (see note) ; in *nout*, 1275, 1426 ; and in *þa*, 1544, where the omission is due to haplography before the *h* of *heo*, and is, therefore, purely scribal.

The spelling *u* for *w* is found a number of times initially :

vel, 95 ; *uel*, 537 ; *uise*, 961 ; *uisest*, 973 ; *uere*, 1306 ; *ueneð*, 1554. After certain consonants *u* is written for *w* with some regularity ; e.g. after *s* in *suich* (frequently), *suiþe*, 376 ; *sviþe*, 377 ; *svete*, 358 ; etc. ; after *t* in *tuengst*, 156 ; *atuitest(u*, 597, 751 ; etc. ; and after *c* in *cualm*, 1157. Similar spellings in *Ayenbite of Inwyt* (cf. Wallenberg, pp. 246f) may be an indication that in certain positions, especially after *s* and *t*, *w* > *v*. [Cf. Breier, pp. 33f.]

Some obviously erroneous spellings involve confusion of letters. Some of these come several times, especially *r* for *t* and *t* for *r* (see the footnotes to lines 1449, 1471, 1106, 1221, 1222, 1341, 1342). The wrong expansion of the contraction which may stand for either *þat* or *þar* probably accounts for erroneous *þar* for *þat* (cf. 918, 970). See Breier, pp. 35–43, Atkins, pp. xxxi-xxxiii.

Abbreviations and contractions in C

The usual contractions used in ME MSS are to be found also in C, where they are, however, used sparingly. [Except for the ampersand, they have been expanded silently in the text.] The words *þat* and *þer*, *þar*, are often contracted, *þurh* occasionally. A contraction mark is frequently used for *er*, less frequently for other *r* combinations, and for *m* and *n*.

The use of capital letters in C

It is not always easy to distinguish capital letters from small letters in C, but it appears that the scribe wished to begin each line with a capital letter. Larger capitals are used at the beginning of a paragraph, and the initial *I* with which the poem opens is some seven lines long. Proper names are, of course, not capitalised.

The punctuation of C

At the end of most lines [there are some one hundred or so exceptions not at all accurately recorded by Grattan] there is a stop. Stops also occur, meaningfully, at times in the middle of lines. See the note to 1271–80.

Corrections in C

There are many corrections in C. Where it seemed clear that these were by the C scribe they have normally been accepted into the text silently; but in some corrections, though they are obviously contemporary, the colour of ink or other details raise a doubt whether they are the work of the C scribe. They are regarded as his work by Sir W. W. Greg in his important discussion (Bib. 35) of Atkins's edition. In the present edition they have been recorded as contemporary corrections in the footnotes, but have not been admitted into the text. Among them are the alteration of *an* to *and* in lines 416-619, and the alteration of *o* to *oe* (? for *eo*) in such words as *wode* 320, *þode* 387. Other corrections are recorded in the footnotes, and are described as later or in a different hand.

STANDARD PARADIGMS OF NOUNS, ADJECTIVES, AND VERBS IN C

The following very brief summary is intended to facilitate the use of the Glossary, which cannot provide a paradigmatic survey of the kind usually called 'the grammar of a text'. Since the Glossary lists every form, it should, however, be used as 'the grammar', especially for minor declensions of nouns, 'irregular' comparison of adjectives, 'irregular' formation and comparison of adverbs, numerals, articles, pronouns, possessive adjectives, the principal parts of strong verbs, 'irregular' weak verbs, preterite-present verbs, defective verbs, and the verb 'to be', all of which form exceptions to the standard paradigm of their class, in so far as that can be established. A full 'grammar' is provided by Breier, pp. 90–150.

The grammatical term *the prepositional case* has been used here and in the Glossary to describe that case of nouns, adjectives, and pronouns which is used after prepositions. It is derived from the OE dative case, but it may be used after prepositions which in OE did not take the dative. [See S.T.R.O. d'Ardenne, *Iuliene*, p. 205.]

Nouns

Note that OE genders are not always preserved in C, and that even in those cases where C indicates the gender of a noun, that gender is not necessarily a preservation of the OE gender [cf. 1434 note]. Nouns may be divided into two classes: those derived for the most part from OE strong masc. and neuter nouns, e.g. **hund, hus**; and those derived for the most part from OE strong fem. nouns, and from weak nouns of any gender, e.g. **schonde, eȝe**.

Adjectives

Adjectives have final **e** except when declined strong in the nom. sg. with nouns of any gender, or in the acc. sg. with neuter or masc. nouns.

	CASE	NOUNS		ADJECTIVES			
				strong			weak
		<OE masc. and neuter strong	< OE fem. strong, and all weak	masc.	neuter	fem.	all
sg.	nom.	-, (e)	e, (-)	-	-	-	e
	acc.	-, (e)	e	-, ne	-	e	e
	gen.	es	e, es	e	e	e	e
	dat., prepos. }	e	e	e	e	e	e
pl.	nom., acc. }	es, (e), (- neuter)	e, (en, ene wk. neuter)	e	e	e	e
	gen.	e	e	e	e	e	e
	dat., prepos. }	e, (es)	e	e	e	e	e

When the stem of a noun or adjective ends in a vowel inflexional **e** is dropped.

Before the initial vowel of the word following, inflexional **e** may be elided.

jo-stems, *i*-stems, and nouns and adjectives which in OE had the suffix *-en*, have inflexional e in every case.

When the suffixes er and e (<OE *-en*) are inflected (e.g. **ere, ene**) the penultimate e may be omitted (e.g. **re, ne**).

es is occasionally written **is**.

The comparison of adjectives

The comparative is formed by adding **er** or **ur** to the stem of the adj. ; inflected forms of the comp. end in **ere, ure,** or **re**. The superlative is formed by adding **est** or **st** to the stem of the adj.

Adverbs

The adverb is formed by adding **e** or **liche** to the stem of the adj. The comparative of the adv. is formed by adding **er, ur, re,** or **ure** to the stem of the adv. ; the superlative of the adv. is formed by adding **est** to the stem of the adv.

Verbs

As in OE, there are four principal parts : I the present stem ; II 1st and 3rd sg. past indicative ; III the rest of the past indicative, and the past subjunctive ; IV the past participle.

The three types of 'regular' verbs distinguished here are : strong verbs, e.g. **singe** ; weak verbs derived largely from OE weak verbs of the 1st class, e.g. **i)here** ; and weak verbs derived largely from OE weak verbs of the 2nd class, which may have either long or short stems, e.g. **fondi, luuie**.

The past participle usually has the prefix **i-**.

est is occasionally written **es** or **ist** ; **eþ** is occasionally written **ed** or **et**.

In contracted verbs inflexional e is dropped or omitted.

Before initial vowel of the word following, final e is elided.

When the stem ends in *d* or *t* the ending þ of the 3 sg. pres. ind. is dropped (eþ is not). When the stem ends in *st* the ending **st** of 2 sg. pres. ind. may be dropped (not **est**).

The endings of the past of the 1st weak class are **de, dest, d,** when the stem ends in a voiced sound, and **te, test, t,** when the stem ends in a voiceless sound.

	STRONG	WEAK (I)	WEAK (II)		
			long	short	not typical (long or short)
I pres. ind. 1 sg.	e		i		
2 sg.	st, est		est		
3 sg.	þ, eþ		eþ		(iet, ieþ)
pl.	eþ			ieþ	eþ
pres. subj. sg.	e		i	ie	e
pl.	e, en		i		
imp. sg.	-		e		
pres. part.	inge				
inf.	e, en		i	ie, ien	
II p. ind. 1, 3 sg.	-	de, te			
III 2 sg.	e	dest, test	edest		
pl.	e, en	de, den			
p. subj. sg.	e				
pl.	e, en				
IV past part.	e, en	ed, d, t	ed		

THE PROVENANCE OF THE OWL AND THE NIGHTINGALE

The dialect of C is, as emerges from an analysis of its sounds, SW, or SW Midlands. This is supported by such morphological evidence as *heo* (=Ci's *ho*) the fem. pron. ' she '; *hi* nom. and acc. pl. ' they, them ' ; and syncopated pres. forms like *ilest*. But there are in C two spelling-systems, and in some ways Cii seems closer to West Midland dialect forms than Ci : thus Cii's *þah* is not found in southern dialects, Ci's *peȝ* is.

Here and there the forms of C are not typical of SW or SW Midlands ; thus *he* for *heo* ' she ', and, more significantly, *hi*, nom. sg. fem. ' she ' ; *hi* as a nom. is only SE, see 9f, note ; the form of the verbal noun *wnienge* is SE, see 614, note, and similarly *heriinge* 981.

ME texts are very often not preserved in the dialect in

which they were written. We must turn to the rhymes for
evidence of the original dialect, for a rhyme, perfect in the
original dialect, may be spoilt by translation. Extreme cases
of that occur in the rhymes *wise/ire* 1029, *singinge/auinde* 855,
worse/mershe 303, etc. (see 277 note) ; all these rhymes con-
firm the evidence of SE origin provided by *hi* and *wnienge*.
Even further evidence is provided by C's garbled *mannenne*
and its rhyme with *þenne*, a rhyme which, with such related
rhymes as *kunne/honne*, is discussed in the note to ·1725f.
Possible dialect words pointing to SE origin are mentioned
in the note to 1166f.

Whenever there is unambiguous rhyme evidence it points to
the South East ; often when a rhyme seems impure, it may
be turned into a true rhyme by translating it into Kentish ;
though there are cases (see 277, note) which cannot be resolved
by translation into any dialect. The confines of the ME
dialect of Kentish are not readily determined. It is the
dialect of Canterbury, obviously, and the dialect of William
of Shoreham in Kent is closely related to that of Dan
Michel of Canterbury. Two place-names are mentioned in
the poem : Guildford, where Nicholas comes from, and
Portesham, where Nicholas lives. There are no early ME
texts written in the unalloyed dialect of Surrey or of Dorset.
Dorset was not close to the Kentish dialect area, but Surrey
was ; and there is nothing known to make it impossible that
the original dialect of O&N was that of Guildford. This is
the view which most recent commentators have held : H. C.
Wyld, W. A. Craigie, J. W. H. Atkins, J. R. R. Tolkien,
C. L. Wrenn, C. T. Onions, J. H. G. Grattan, S. T. R. O.
d'Ardenne, B. Sundby, and others. The older view that the
poem is a product of Dorset [see *NED*, s. *thyvel*, Breier,
Hall] is no longer accepted ; [and S. M. Kuhn's very
tentative suggestion, *Language* 27 (1951), 420–3, that the
place-names of the border of Gloucester and Oxford (and
possibly neighbouring counties to the east and north) should
be investigated to establish the provenance of the poem, was
made after a conscious rejection of such evidence as there
is in the rhymes].

THE DATE OF THE OWL AND THE NIGHTINGALE

The internal evidence for the date is good. From lines 1091f (see note) it emerges that the poem was written after the death of Henry II in 1189. Since King Henry is not referred to as 'old King Henry', or by some similar distinguishing mark, it is clear that the poem must have been written before the accession of Henry III in 1216. All other evidence agrees with a date of composition between 1189 and 1216 [cf. the note to 1016].

Attempts have been made to date the poem more precisely within that period. None of them seems entirely convincing.

F. Tupper [Bib. 44] lists cases where details in the poem correspond with what Alexander Neckam wrote. But much of what the poem has in common with Neckam was general know-ledge, and even where it was not there is no proving whether the poet took his knowledge or his stories from Neckam direct, or that they were working in the same tradition [cf. Huganir, Bib. 46]. In any case Neckam's *De Naturis Rerum* has not been dated more precisely than 1187–99, so that, even assuming that it was used by the poet, there would be no gain in precision. As far as the evidence from Neckam goes, the most that could be said is that O&N could have been written at any time after 1187.

If A. C. Cawley is right in his interpretation of the astrology in the poem (see 1145ff, note) the date of composition is early rather than late in the period 1189–1216; 1194–8, when the Justiciar Hubert Walter kept the peace, would fit well; but the wording of lines 1730f, on which this date is based (see note), will not bear such precise interpretation.

THE AUTHOR

The modern author as he sends forth his work to the press has visions of extending the circle of his friends far beyond that of his acquaintants. He assumes a reader's curiosity in his person, and is not reluctant to feed it with selected details of his life. A few authors, Chaucer among them, there were in the Middle Ages, who were ready to tell of themselves. But before printing was invented the circle of readers was small, perhaps known to the author, who would, therefore, not feel the need to sign his work. Also parchment was dear, and the author of a vernacular work, not immediately didactic, might think that he was squandering for vain amusement materials that might be better used for a better end. Far from feeling an urge to have his name noised abroad, he might well wish to shrink into anonymity. As for posthumous fame he might reflect that it is better not to be remembered, than to be remembered for so slight a product of an idle moment. Had he written a serious work he might have asked his readers to pray for him.

Two names have been adduced for the authorship of O&N; both are of Guildford men, and the dialect of Guildford could, as we have seen, be the original dialect of the poem. One of the two, John of Guildford, wrote the prayer on the lost ' broaken leafe ' in J ; but there is no reason for connecting the prayer with O&N [see pp. 4f]. The metre of the prayer is not that of O&N, and the pitiful rhyme *þo/no* (where *þo* exists merely to supply a rhyme for *no*) is feebler than any in O&N. Only the wish to find an author for the poem has led to the speculation that the author might be John of Guildford. [That speculation is given some support by Celia Sisam, *RES* (N.S.) 5 (1954), 337-43.]

That wish is so strong that critics have seized on the only other name connected with the poem, that of Nicholas of Guildford, and have fathered the poem on him. K. Huganir (p. 141) says that ' probably today [1931] the majority of students accept Nicholas as the poet' ; R. M. Lumiansky [*Philological Quarterly* 32 (1953), 411–17] makes Nicholas's wish for preferment the central theme and purpose of the poem. But, in spite of Atkins's excellent discussion (pp. xxxviii-xlvi) of the problem, and his guarded support of Nicholas as author, doubt remains as strong as it was in 1907, when Wells (p. xxix) wrote : ' Probably we are safest in agreeing with Wülcker in ascribing the poem " to an unknown poet who wrote the work in honor of Nicholas of Guildford," or at least to an unknown poet who in his poem did honor to his friend.'

The reason for doubting that Nicholas is the author is not that, if he were, he would be praising himself too much, as Wülcker and ten Brink thought. If he were writing to gain preferment he would have to state his merits, and bring them to the notice of his superiors in an acceptable manner. Nicholas's indirect praise of himself (if that is how the poem is to be interpreted) would not give offence. Nor would the revelation give offence, that in his youth he had had a taste for the lighter side of life (lines 202–5). We are told that he has mended his ways now, and so is fit for preferment.

The reason for doubting that Nicholas is the author is in the poet's charge that Nicholas's superiors abuse their power and corruptly and nepotistically make over the emoluments from ecclesiastical offices to those unfit to discharge them. Tact stands high among the poet's characteristics as revealed in his writing : he must have known that, if his superiors were to see O&N, his vague accusations would lead to resentful repression, not advancement. [See Tupper, Bib. 44.]

The most likely view is that the unknown poet sent his poem to Nicholas, his friend, a learned cleric, esteemed by all the world for his sound judgment. In spite of his merits he only has one living, and hopes for advancement. Since both sides in the dispute, and the Wren himself, acknowledge his ability to tell right from wrong what better compliment could be paid to him than that he should judge between the Owl and the Nightingale ?

Nicholas is not a rare name in the twelfth and thirteenth centuries ; and there has been more than one Nicholas connected with Guildford (cf. K. Huganir, p. 151). Gadow (pp. 12f) says that Nicholas of Guildford was probably a well-known cleric of the bishops of Salisbury (of whose diocese Guildford formed part), occupied with legal affairs. Such a one signs himself *Nicholaus submonitor capituli de Gude-ford* in a Godalming inventory of 1220, and a *Nicholaus capellanus archidiaconi* witnessed a document of 1209.

Neither, or one, or both of these signatures may be by the hand of the Nicholas mentioned in the poem.

THE OWL, THE NIGHTINGALE, AND THE
SUBJECT OF THEIR DEBATE

The Owl and the Nightingale is written in a style of civilised, literary colloquialism. There is an element of direct and honest obscenity, not of sniggering obscenity, half-concealing, half-revealing ; but of vulgarity there is not a trace. The tone is light, yet much of the matter is serious. Though the poem is not a formal allegory, the Owl stands for the solemn way of life, and the Nightingale for the joyous way of life. The case to be put before Master Nicholas is, which is the better of the two birds ; and this implies the question, which of the two is the better way of life. The poet maintains the balance between them ; earlier in the poem he seems to lean towards the Owl (cf. 30–6, 667f, and see notes), but in the end he does not reveal either his own or Nicholas's judgment. The reader who strives to follow the poet's meaning will remember, as he reads the Nightingale's case, that it is not enough, and as he reads the Owl's, that it is not everything.

The argument is far from neat; it ranges over many aspects of many subjects. Throughout the poem the Owl is seen as representative of all that is sombre ; thus the Owl's song is woeful (220, 225f, etc.), whereas the Nightingale's is joyous (971–94, etc.). Song is the first subject of their debate (11): the Nightingale's varied art (20–4, 142, cf. 319f) might seem to give her superiority, but the Owl defends her own more solemn tones (310–18). Song is the most important of the birds' general characteristics debated by them. Next come their appearance and habits. The Owl, splendidly hawk-like in her own eyes (269–71, 1675f), seems hateful in appearance to the Nightingale (71–80) ; her comments invite the Owl's animadversions on the Nightingale's miserable figure (561f, 577–82). The ways of the Owl and her young are filthy in their nest (91–138, cf. 626–38), but the Nightingale's choice of her nesting site by the privy does not give her much to boast of (584–96), and cannot easily be defended (957–70). Similarly the Owl's food (87f, 591, cf. 603–8) seems no viler than the Nightingale's (597–602). The poet (32) agrees with the Nightingale's statements how all the world, and especially little birds, hate and fear the Owl (61–70, 221–4, 1165–8), even after her death (1139–44). The Owl has to concede that this is so (277–80), but sees in it her special usefulness as a scarecrow and as a decoy-bird (1607–30, cf. 1111–38). The use to which the Owl's body is put after death leads ultimately to the Nightingale's claim of victory in debate over her (see pp. 26f) ; but as long as the debate lasts it is because of her usefulness that the Owl hopes to win ; for she claims that, while the Nightingale has only her song with which she is of use (556–82, cf. 707–14 to 836), and even that is tedious (331–48), she, the Owl, helps mankind with eating mice (which her excellent eyesight—363–84, cf. 240–3—enables her to see in the dark, 608), and helps them especially, though they do not always appreciate it, by warning them of impending disasters (329f, 925, 1261–8). She sings in the miseries of winter (523–40), and not only in pleasant parts of the world like the Nightingale (903–24). This leads to a general discussion of astrology and prophecy (1145–1330, see note). As Hässler says (pp. 94–7), the habitation of the birds is symbolic ; the Owl's old tree-stump overgrown with ivy that is green throughout the year (25–8, 615–22, cf. 640–54) symbolising her sombreness, and the Nightingale's bough with blossoms all around her (15f) symbolising the Nightingale's joyousness. The Nightingale sees the Owl as full of the miseries of winter, while she herself is part of the joys of summer (412–62), and is answered by the Owl's accusation that the Nightingale is full of the lechery of summer, in song and deed (497–500), and when she has glutted her lust her boldness and songs are gone (501–22). Furthermore, her songs entice people to the lusts of the flesh (895–99) ; the Owl reminds the Nightingale of how she was punished when she last led a wife to commit adultery (1045–66). The Nightingale rebuts the accusation that she encourages adultery; all she did was to cheer up the wife out of pity for her (1083–5). She sings of legitimate love (1331–48), and she is not to blame if her teaching is abused (1349–86). Adultery is hateful to her, regardless of whether it is wives or husbands who commit that sin (1467–1510). In fact, if she has the choice, the Nightingale will rather encourage maidens in love than wives (1417–44). The Owl, on the other hand, is the confidante of wives, cheering those loyal wives whose husbands are away, and praying for the death of cruel husbands (1519–1605).

Many of the problems discussed incidentally by the birds stood at the intellectual centre of the age, religious and moral problems to which there are sides but no solutions. In the three MSS that contain, or are known to have contained, O&N, all the other works are of a religious or didactic nature. It is fitting that O&N should be among them, for it too is didactic, though informally; and what it teaches is that there is a place in the world for both solemnity and lightheartedness, that when an Owl and a Nightingale survey the great problems the side taken by the one is irreconcilably different from that taken by the other.

The most important of the questions debated incidentally concerns the nature of divine worship. When O&N was written the traditional manner of worship was coming into conflict with that new spirit and new way of serving God which in the course of the thirteenth century gave impetus to and received strength from the religious movement associated especially with the Franciscans [cf. André Wilmart, *Auteurs spirituels et textes dévots du moyen âge latin*, 1932, p. 63]. The new way was joyous praise of God in songs that give a foretaste of the bliss of heaven (716–42); the older devotional approach was through weeping lamentation, mindful that this world is a vale of tears, where death comes in the end to sinful man (856–74). It is in simple terms such as these that the problem is debated by the disputants. Another great subject discussed incidentally by the birds is the nature of love: to what extent love is sinful, the love of maidens, love in marriage, adulterous love, and homosexual love. A further important problem of the age was the permissibility of prognostication, especially with the aid of astrology, but this occupies a less prominent place in the poem. Again, a question much debated at the time, whether one virtue exercised with great sincerity could weigh as heavily as many virtues exercised less sincerely, is perhaps touched on by the Nightingale in her pleas (707–836, see note).

The manner of discussion is (except for a brief survey of the sins, 1395–1412) largely anecdotal, and no attempt is made to find serious answers to the serious questions raised. The reasons why the poet has handled such serious things so lightheartedly are obvious enough. If he had had something fundamental to communicate on these subjects he would have written in Latin. He would hardly at this date have thought the debate a suitable form ; and certainly not a debate between birds. Moreover, the disputants touch on these subjects only incidentally. Thus, their discussion is not directly about worship and love, but rather about the part played by the birds in helping man in worship and in love ; for the subject of the debate is which is the better of the two birds, and the answer to that is to be found in the way in which they serve mankind and God.

Throughout the poem the poet stresses that the purpose of the birds' existence is to help man. Man has dominion over the fowl of the air ; and the debate of the two birds turns on their service to man, as it turns on man's service to God.

O&N, though it stands alone in early Middle English literature, must not be seen in isolation. It belongs to that genre of debate in which the two disputants are creatures, animate or inanimate. H. Walther, in the standard treatment of all the various kinds of debates in medieval Latin literature [Bib. 85, p. 15], lists among the debates between creatures : sun and moon, crab and rainbow, coast and sea, mountain and valley, gold and lead, silver and iron, frog and crab, chicken and pigeon, etc. Hässler, in an admirable section of his book [Bib. 23, pp. 21f], has drawn attention to the relevance of the Latin dialogue between *Winter and*

Summer to O&N as a whole and to lines 489–94 (see note) in particular. [A brief summary of the debate is given in the Appendix, pp. 167f.] The relevance lies in the close association of the Owl with winter and its forbidding hardships, and of the Nightingale with summer and its attractive, perhaps speciously attractive, delights. Hässler also relates O&N to the Latin debate *Wine and Water*, in which the argument (often supported by scriptural references) stresses the sober gifts of Water, and the wilder joys of Wine. Wine has the last word, ' Whenever a man must leave me he does so without pleasure ; but when he returns to his cup he sings *Gloria in excelsis Deo!* ' All the inhabitants of heaven flock together and acclaim Wine ; the poet wakes up, before he has had a chance to hear God's judgment. [A fuller account is given by J. H. Hanford, *PMLA* 28 (1913), 315–67 ; cf. Walther, pp. 46–53.] The similarity between the sobriety of Water and the seriousness of the Owl, and between the giddy delight of Wine and the lighthearted joyousness of the Nightingale is obvious.

The relevance to O&N of these debates goes even further than that. Their ends are similar. At the end of O&N the Nightingale proclaims herself victor and is acclaimed by the birds that flock together, just as Wine is acclaimed. But the poet of O&N preserves his impartiality, the case has not yet been brought before Nicholas of Guildford, and we are not told for whom he will find. Similarly, the poet of *Wine and Water* wakes up without hearing God's judgment. God may, like Theologia at the end of *Winter and Summer*, urge reconciliation ; for each symbolises one side of creation complemented by the other. It is unlikely that he will find for Wine, for there is something of a trick in the way Wine got the heavenly hosts to acclaim him ; and there is something of a trick in the way in which the Nightingale gains what she claims is the victory. The point at which she does so (1635ff) is immediately after the Owl has pleaded how much more useful than the Nightingale she is to mankind, for when dead she still serves man. It is a feature of all debates of this kind that, as Hässler says (p. 25), the criterion by which the disputants are to be judged is their usefulness to man. The Owl has made a mistake ; the subject of the birds' dispute is, strictly speaking, the usefulness of their existence ; but death is the end of existence, and it is, so the Nightingale pleads, only in death that the Owl is useful to mankind. That is what the Nightingale had alleged at line 1138, and at line 1617 the Owl has in effect conceded her opponent's charge. Earlier in the poem (471f) the Owl had shown that she was afraid of *plaites wrenche*. She had every reason to be, not because hers was not a sound case, but because of what the poet calls the Nightingale's *wise tunge* (1071).

These tricks, wrinkles, *cautelae*, were not merely a feature of literary debates, but they were part and parcel of contemporary legal cases, as is shown by the evidence of actual cases and of manuals of procedure [see C. T. Flower, pp. 464–7 ; and F. W. Maitland, *English Historical Review* **12** (1897), 625–58 ; cf. F. de Zulueta, *Mélanges de droit romain dédiés à Georges Cornil*, 1926, p. 652]. Indeed, the connexion between literary debates and the procedure in courts of law is close, and not due to chance.

Though the ultimate origin of the particular genre of debate to which O&N belongs, the debate between creatures, is unknown, much is known of the history of debates in general, and their development is traced by Walther. The early history has little bearing on the more immediate background of O&N. In the Middle Ages debates owed their popularity to the place they had in the educational system. There was great emphasis on rhetorical training, and pupils were asked to assume rôles in disputation with each other. Disputation was used to practise pupils in logical argumentation. Whoever silenced his opponent, by forcing him into a position that he cannot argue himself out of, gains victory in the debate. Also at a higher level of education, in the training of lawyers, use was made of disputation. In this type of fictitious litigation the disputant who used language best, and who could best blind his opponent by tricks of logic, was the victor, applauded by his teachers and his fellow-students.

Some of the Latin debate poems that survive are strictly legal, and a few of them may have served to impress upon the students the formalities of pleading, or perhaps definite legal principles. Presumably their authors had been brought up in the law schools, where once a week there was held a *disputatio ordinaria* in which the magister and his scholars took part, and in which the subject matter of the lecture courses held during the week was turned into disputation.

The poet of O&N may not himself have been trained in a legal school, but he is certainly influenced by the style of the Latin debate poems that are the products of such schools. As regards the legal element in O&N, two points must be made. First, both Atkins and Hässler have perhaps made too much of it ; for in O&N the legal element seems incidental rather than central : secondly, whatever the extent of the legal element may be, and no one would deny its existence, it seems to be based on the practice of the ecclesiastical courts and not of the lay courts.

A debate could have a legal subject ; there is, for example, the Latin debate which turns on the legal rights of the raised Lazarus to the property which was his before death, the counter-claimant being Mary Magdalene, the possessor of the property after her brother's death. The subject matter of O&N, however, is not legal. Even so, the poet has imparted to his work a sufficiently legalistic flavour (especially strong in two passages, 541–55 and 1087–1101) to give the impression of pleading. He has done so by introducing legal tags and terms into the framework of the debate, which in itself is of course like the pleas and counter-pleas of advocates, and which like a law-case is to be settled in the end by a judge. If, as Atkins thinks, the poet had modelled the dispute throughout its various stages closely on the form of a law-case, we should have expected far more technical details, and not merely terms that must have been familiar to the layman. All the following terms (except *bare worde*) are taken [as R. M. Wilson, *Sawles Warde*, 1938, pp. x-xi, says], from OE law rather than from contemporary French legal terminology. *Speche*, ' law-suit, plea,' (13, etc.) ; *tale*, ' charge ', or merely

' discourse ' (140) ; *mid riȝte dome,* ' with just judgment ',
(179) [cf. A. S. Napier, *Wulfstan : Sammlung der ihm
zugeschriebenen Homilien,* 1883, pp. 253[20], 254[8-9, 20]] ; *fals
dom,* ' improper decision ' (210); *bare worde,* ' an assertion
by the plaintiff, unsupported by witnesses and not requiring
a reply from the defendant ' (547) [=Fr. *nude parole,* Latin
simplex dictum] ; *bicloped,* ' sued at law ' (550) ; *forbonne*
(1093, see note) ; *niþe & onde,* ' malice ' (1096, cf. 417–19)
[the most common plea of *exceptio,* barring the plaintiff's
action, was the defendant's plea that the plaintiff was moti-
vated by malice, *odium et atia* (cf. C. T. Flower, p. 372] ;
fordeme lif an lime, ' to condemn life and limb ' (1098) ; *rem*
(1215, see note) ; *skere,* ' exculpate oneself ' (1302) [cf. F. E.
Harmer, *Anglo-Saxon Writs,* 1952, p. 479] ; *sakè* (1430, etc.),
the original meaning was ' dispute, cause at law, crime ', but
in *wiþute sake* the meaning has been weakened to ' blame ';
at bedde & at borde (1492, see note); *ut(h)est(e* (1683, see
note ; 1698) ; *þes, griþbruche* (1730, see note ; 1734).

Trial by battle, referred to at 541, 656, and 1197 (see
notes), is, of course, a post-Conquest institution. These
references cannot be interpreted literally, for there is no
suggestion of battle. Atkins's statement, that the use of
legal vocabulary in the poem is consistent, certainly does not
apply here, especially if it is borne in mind that trial by battle
is an ordeal of the secular courts only, not the ecclesiastical
courts, whereas lines 745f provide strong evidence that the
legal element in O&N is not secular but ecclesiastic. The
offer made by the Nightingale in these lines to take the case
to Rome is in exact conformity to canon law procedure ; the
impetration of a papal writ was looked upon as a regular
first step in English canon law litigation, the Pope being the
last arbiter in ecclesiastical disputes [see Stanley, pp. 36–9].

There is every indication that the reference to trial by
battle is not to be taken literally ; there is no indication that
the Nightingale's offer to take the case to Rome is meant
metaphorically. It may be that the poet has chosen canon
law procedure for his poem because that is what he and his
intended audience are most familiar with ; but that need not

concern us here. The Nightingale's use of canon law procedure in the poem is important because it stresses the birds'
association with the Church ; for, though the Nightingale
is not ordained (see 1177–82, and 1311), and the Owl, however often she may go to church (1211), is not of the Church,
both birds often assert their love of the Church and their
service to the Church. Thus the Nightingale claims that the
purpose of her song is to help priests with singing the
canonical hours in joyous anticipation of heaven (707–42,
cf. 849–51) ; and her opponent concedes, perhaps ironically,
that the Nightingale with her voice might teach the inhabitants of the barbarous North how angels sing in heaven
(915f). The Nightingale claims that the very love-tidings
which she brings are the songs of the Church (1035). The
Owl loves the Church (609), and keeps churches free from
mice and evil creatures (607–12). She not merely sings the
hours (26, 323–35), and helps with conductus singing at
Christmas (481–4), but she feels that the Nightingale's way
of singing is not priestlike (900–2), whereas she is conscious
that hers is the orthodox form of song (854–92, see note).
Both the Owl (335–62, 879–86) and the Nightingale (716–20)
at times adopt a homiletic style.

The fusion of animal and human elements is the principal
charm of the genre, and this fusion is admirably handled by
the author of O&N. Throughout their dispute the birds are
debating about their nature as birds, but obviously that they
are debating is contrary to their nature. Physically they are
birds—in their appearance, in their habits, in the sound of
their voices even. Yet that they speak is human, and what
they say is human ; their hopes, their aspirations, their
ethical standards, their way of thinking with its mixture of
logic and want of logic, their abuse, their low imputations,
the emotive colouring of their pleas, all these are human.
The reader recognises his own characteristics in those of the
birds, and this recognition gives force to the didactic element
in the poem. The exploitation of the implicit contrariety,
that animals look and behave like animals on the one hand,
yet have human attributes on the other, is at the heart of the

type of literature to which O&N belongs. It is also the pivot of the beast fable, a genre closely akin to that of the debate between creatures ; but in the beast fable the moral is usually explicit ; in the debate it is to be inferred.

The birds abuse each other about their nature as birds, and all the time the standard is man. Thus, when the Nightingale accuses the Owl of the filthy ways of her young, the Owl replies that if her young are unclean in their nest they are following the noble example of human children, and that the convenient arrangements of her nest are in imitation of those of human dwellings (625–54). Human ways, as the highest in creation, are not only the criterion ; they are what the Owl, aware of the lower place of birds in the divine order, consciously aims at. The dirty ways of young owls is a natural characteristic; the Owl's defence of them is the result of her human habits of thought and speech. The poet has endowed the disputants with human habits in that he has consciously chosen a literary form in which animals are anthropomorphised. He reinforces the effect by making relevant beast fables (like that of the Falcon's nest, 99–138) part of the history of the disputants themselves.

Throughout the poem the poet is making use of parallel literary material. Such literary associations are what the historian of literature treats of under the head of ' sources and analogues '. When it leads to a better understanding of the author's literary antecedents, and of how he has handled the material familiar to him, the study of the sources and analogues of a text is profitable. But if such study leads to a discussion of the author's originality, it is usually not profitable, for the result is the inversion of good sense. Mere novelty is all too easily praised for its own sake. Literature is looked upon as a flower that bears its brightest blooms when its roots are shallowest ; the richer an author's mind is, the better read, the better stored with learning, the less original, in the superficial sense of ' unindebted ', he is likely to be. What he observes in nature reminds him of what he has read in books : what he has read in books he discerns in nature. Personal observation and book-learning are not mutually exclusive, but complementary. It is no more profitable to say that the poet must have got his reference in line 413 (see note) to the hen's frenzied behaviour in the snow from direct observation (though it is likely enough), than to say that the poet's references to the Owl's big head (74, 119) should be compared with the fifty-third of Bozon's *Contes Moralisés*, which turns on the bigness of the owl's head—the size of the owl's head must have been common knowledge. Of the poet's learning there is good evidence in O&N; whether or no he was a keen observer of nature there is no means of knowing for certain. No one will think of him as a bird-watcher, yet few will think of him as one who kept his eyes shut. The poem gives the impression that its author was a man of wide sympathies, a man who has seen something of the world and yet was not without the kind of learning valued among the religious.

It is perhaps worth mentioning some of the things which the poet may have derived from books. It is not suggested that he read the very books named here; they are named only to give some idea of the kind of literature that may have been available to him. From works like Neckam's *De Naturis Rerum* or Marie de France's *Fables* (cf. No. 3) the poet might have taken the habitation of the Owl on a tree-stump, of the Nightingale in the thicket, of the frog (86) under the cog-wheel of a mill [cf. K. Huganir, Bib. 46, and Hinckley, Bib. 39]. From Neckam he might have learnt also that foxes are treed (see 816 note). His knowledge that night-birds like the Owl have hooked talons (1676) he might have derived, directly or indirectly, from Pliny's *Natural History*, Bk. x, 16; and the same source would have told him that owls are dim-sighted in the day-time. Some version of Pliny may have provided him with the information (factually untrue, it seems) that the nightingale's song ceases when its lust is satisfied (see 507f, and note). Pliny (Bk. x, 16 and 43) describes the terrifying screams of the owl, and the great variety of music that pours forth from the nightingale, revealing in its tiny throat all the devices which human skill has contrived in the elaborate mechanism of the flute (cf. 20–22). He may be drawing on Pliny, Bk. x, 95 [cf. Appendix, p. 167], for the hostility between the little birds and the owl, and how they mob the owl; though he might also have had these facts from Isidore of Seville's *Etymologies* [edited by W. M. Lindsay (1911), XII, vii, 39]; or from Neckam, pp. 102f. References to the song of the birds are, of course, to be found everywhere in ancient and medieval literature. The cry of the owl is a sinister omen, but the nightingale's song brings joy.

SOME ASPECTS OF THE POEM'S RHETORIC

The form which the debate takes is influenced by the rhetoric of pleading in a court of law [cf. pp. 22ff]. No charge should remain unanswered; however, the poem is not sufficiently disciplined in argument for that to be true in every case, and at times, for no apparent reason, the answer seems to be delayed (see 936ff, note). In some cases the answer echoes the very words of the accusation; thus the Nightingale's charge that the Owl's song is *zozelinge* (40) is answered by the Owl's description of the Nightingale's song as *writelinge* (48; cf. 914).

The giving of instances, which, of course, has a special place at law in the adduction of precedents, is a feature of formal scholastic disputation in general. The birds make frequent use of instances (though not at all forensically). Thus, the Nightingale tells the fable of *The Falcon and the Owl* (99–138) to give force to her point that the Owl's nest is foul; she tells the fable of *The Cat and the Fox* (809–36) to exemplify that her one talent may be worth more than all the Owl can claim; the Owl tells a well-known story of the Nightingale (1049–66; see Appendix, pp. 165f) to show that the Nightingale is famed for leading wives into sin, and the Nightingale turns the story to her own advantage (1075–1108). The Owl has a story of an unhappy marriage (1521–1570) to illustrate her sympathetic relations with ill-used wives. She puts the story of the hare (373–84) to a different use, telling it, not so much as a direct parallel to her eyesight as to refute the Nightingale's logic that those who can see at night must be blind by day.

All the time the disputants state, in support of their assertions, what is well-known and universally accepted. That is the purpose of their use of proverbs. Similar use of proverbial truths is made in all scholastic disputation, as well as in pleading in a court of law. An example of a forensic proverb used in O&N occurs at 943f (cf. note). Many of the proverbs are ascribed by the disputants to King Alfred, who in the later Middle Ages was accredited in England with a store of proverbs extant as *The Proverbs of Alfred*, which are probably referred to by Ailred of Rievaulx (died 1167) and the late twelfth-century *Annals of Winchester*, and possibly by Marie de France, who in the Epilogue to her *Fables* (Warnke, p. 328) gives Alfred as her source [of the *Fables*, not merely of their morals]. The attribution to King Alfred of a collection of proverbs is discussed in Helen P. South's edition of *The Proverbs of Alfred*, 1931, pp. 43-63, and in O. Arngart's edition, pp. 4-6. Only a very few of the proverbs quoted in O&N, and not always those referred to by the birds as his, correspond with any in *The Proverbs of Alfred*, and the chief reason for ascribing them to him seems to be that his name will lend authority to what the birds assert. It is perhaps worth noting that similar use of proverbs is made in the Anglo-Norman debate, Chardry's *Petit Plet* between an old man and a young man (their attitudes corresponding roughly to those of the Owl and the Nightingale), a poem extant in C and J ; for there the disputants quote proverbs, and they ascribe them to Cato [whether or no they occur in the collection that bears his name, the *Disticha Catonis*, which was very popular throughout the Middle Ages], exactly as Alfred is invoked in O&N [cf. Koch, Bib. 28].

Hässler has provided a fairly full analysis of the figures of rhetoric used in O&N. In an edition little is to be gained from the names of the figures ; but everything is to be gained from recognising the conscious use of rhetorical devices in the poem. Various methods of enforcing a point, or giving some grace to a statement by repetition, are among the most noticeable devices ; thus, there is repetition of various kinds in the following lines : 7–10, 21–4, 29f, 56f, 152, 196, 272, 453–60, 479f, 526, 528, 687–700, 1219–21, and 1251–3, and lists like 1151–61, 1189–1216, etc. Antithetical statements serve a similar purpose : cf. 219, 226f, 229–32 (combined with repetition), 317, 979. At times chiastic order is introduced, e.g. 197f. Comparisons of many kinds are common ; those in lines 80, 286, 317–22, 357–62, 413, 421–9, 1021–4, are among the more remarkable, but there are many others. Some of these comparisons, e.g. that at 1325–8, should perhaps be regarded as the kind of extended comparisons found in *exempla*.

The range of styles found in O&N has no parallel in early English verse. The homiletic tone of such passages as 355–62 and 716–20 is in contrast with the lyrical tone of 433–62 or the description of the inhospitable northern land-scape at 999–1014. The poet makes the dispute lively in its argumentativeness, e.g. 955–8. The exposition of the sins is ended in a rhetorical question immediately answered, 1395–1412. And there are such colloquial cries as *Hong up þin ax* 658, and *Drah to þe* 1186. The poet knows how to handle a fable, and perhaps it is possible to detect in the rebuke of the parent and the cries of the little falcons the cadence of nursery dialogue (113–22).

Of the poet's choice of vocabulary little need be said. As is to be expected of an author capable of variations in style, the poet has a wide vocabulary, on which he draws to give fitting expression to his variety of matter. In addition he uses non-technical legal language to give a superficial appear-ance of forensic pleading to the arguments of the birds. And he even makes up words to fit an occasion, like *galegale*.

VERSIFICATION

There are two schools of thought on the versification of the poem ; first, those who [like Holthausen, Bib. 38, and Gadow] assume a strict octosyllabic four-stress line, with frequent feminine endings and some obvious licences, like the omission of the initial unstressed syllable or inversion of the initial stress in the line, and who, finding the extant texts of the poem less regular than their theory requires, subject the poem to a heavy course of otherwise unnecessary emendations ; and secondly, those who [like Schipper, Koch (Bib. 28), Breier in *EStn* 42 (1910), 306f, Wells, and most later writers] accept the poem as it has survived, showing within the general framework of the four-stress line some considerable freedom.   The second seems the preferable view ; first because it saves otherwise unnecessary emendations [cf. Gadow, pp. 21–6, and Holthausen, Bib. 38] ; and because a free system of four-stress verse may have developed from the native metre.

In the majority of lines the basic pattern of the octosyllabic four-stress line is used :

$$x \, ' \, x \, ' \, x \, ' \, x \, ' \, (x)$$

Thus, *Þat plait was stif & starc & strong* (5) ; often with feminine ending, *Þat alre worste þat hi wuste* (10).   Final *e* is elided before a vowel beginning the next word, *Sum wile softe & lud among* (6), *Bet þuʒte þat he were ishote* (23).

Omission of the initial unstressed syllable of the line,

$$' \, x \, ' \, x \, ' \, x \, ' \, x$$

as in *Þu art lodlich to biholde* (71), is common ; as is inversion of the first stressed and unstressed syllables,

$$' \, x x \, ' \, x \, ' \, x \, ' \, x$$

as in *Schamie þe for þin unrede* (161—*scha-mi-e* is trisyllabic).

Instead of the one unstressed syllable of the standard dip there are occasionally two ; thus, *Þat eure spenþ & euer is iliche* (362—probably with *euer is* elided as if it were written *eure is*).   The matter is complicated by the use of paragogic vowels which may, but need not, be orthographic only.   Thus the first *e* of *Aluered* is not syllabic in *For Aluered seide of olde quide* (685), which is a regular octosyllabic line with feminine ending.   In the opening lines of the poem the words *sumere* and *diʒele* might possibly be similarly elided ; but it is far from certain that it is so. The art of versification is not all in counting and weighing of syllables, and it may well be felt that here a dissyllabic dip preceding the final lift provides a more satisfying rhythm than a monosyllabic dip in a completely regular line ; lines 1 and 2 (like 362) scan probably :

$$\times\ '\ \times\ '\ \times\ '\ \times\times\ '\ \times$$

Occasionally there seems to be an additional stressed (or possibly half-stressed) syllable. In the line *Ah neoþeles þarmide beoþ men acwalde* (1370) Gadow following Stratmann replaces *neoþeles* (which has the support of J) by *ȝet*. The rhythm of the line is, however, much better if left unemended (except that the *e* of *mide* must not be sounded), the additional stress on *-les* marks the caesura and facilitates the enjambment at the end of the line.

Similarly, *A bisemere to preost ihoded* (1311) allows, through its irregularity, clearer understanding of the sense, which requires that *A bisemere* goes with the preceding line, a very marked caesura coming after the phrase. The scansion is either $\times\ '\ \times\ '\ \times\ |\ \times\ '\ \times\ '\ \times$, or, with elision of the first *e* in *bisemere*, $\times\ '\ '\ \times\ |\ \times\ '\ \times\ '\ \times$.

The poet's use of rhythm is subtle, and he is able to use rhythm to make effective his skilful use of rhetoric. Exclamations, apostrophes, and commands are brought to life by leaving off the initial unstressed syllable of the regular line, as has already been suggested. A further example of his skill with metre is his use of two unstressed syllables followed by two stressed syllables to point a chiasmus : *Ȝif riȝt goþ forþ & abak wrong* (877), $\times\ '\ \times\ '\ |\ \times\times\ '\ '$, forcing a pause or inflection of the voice after *abak*.

Complete regularity would have been monotonous, especially in lines as short as those of O&N : enough lines are regular for those that are not, to stand out. There is not space here to analyse whole passages, nor it is necessary ; those who have an ear for verse will recognise, in such passages as 407–11, 955–8, 1275–80, 1407–10, 1417–22, 1655–66, how much the poet has gained by varying the standard line.

It may be worth noting how much superior C is to J in

preserving what is presumably the original freedom of the
metre, as well as its regularity; cf. Gadow, p. 26. J omits
many of the particles and little words that are found in C.
At line 840, where C has *Þat hit þincþ soþ al þat þu seist*, a
regular line, J omits *al* and adds a point after *soþ* to mark the
break: *Þat hit þinkþ soþ. þat þu seyst*; J uses punctuation
to retain the perspicuity ensured by the rhythm of C.

In all this, it has been assumed that the extant copies of
the poem more or less preserve (except for orthographic
alterations, like the addition or omission of final *-e*, cf. *-mide*
1370) the metre of the original, and that that metre was not
rigorously octosyllabic. The free handling of the four-stress
line is felt to be a gain in liveliness, and regularity is felt
to be akin to monotony, so that the C text as it stands is
satisfying.

Rhyme and alliteration are aspects of versification that
remain to be considered. Rhyme is an essential feature of
the verse of O&N; alliteration is an added grace.

Of rhyme little need be said. Some of the rhymes that are
not true are discussed in the note to lines 277f. Other
rhymes that should be noted are *dome/to me* 545f, *come/to me*
1671f; such identical rhymes as at 29f, 35, 109, 127, 137,
153, 159, 211, 231, 245, 249, 255, 267, 285, 315, 323, 339,
345, etc., etc. In many of these examples the rhyme involves
different compounds of the same word or suffix, e.g. *Niȝtin-
gale/Galegale* 255, *grislich/ilich* 315; in others a simplex
rhymes with itself in a compound, e.g. *halue/uthalue* 109;
in others the rhyming word is used in different ways, e.g.
clawe noun/*clawe* verb 153. [Cf. Gadow, pp. 26–30.] Such
identical (or 'rich') rhymes are normal in ME, as they still
are in French verse.

Several times a rhyme may be used for more than a couplet;
thus the first four lines of the poem rhyme together, and
similarly, over four lines each time, 221–4, 255–8, 349–52,
455–8, and 1679–82. There seems to be a reason for allow-
ing the opening lines to rhyme together, i.e. they form a kind
of *incipit*; but for the other passages of extended rhyming
no reason suggests itself.

Alliteration is common in O&N; but it is purely orna-
mental. At times it appears, as in regular ME alliterative
verse, over several lines:

> An ise3þ wel bi mine songe
> Þat dusi luue ne last no3t longe.
> Ah wel ich wule þat þu hit wite.   (1465–7)

It is always difficult to be sure how many of the poet's
alliterative lines are merely fortuitous; and it should be
observed that Gadow, in his discussion of the alliteration
(pp. 30f), takes line 1467 to have accidental alliteration.
Alliteration often comes in alliterative phrases, like stif &
starc & strong 5 (cf. 269), knarres & cludes 1001, fihs & flehs
1007, at bedde & at borde 1492, or warp a word 45. Many of
these phrases go back to very early times, others, like þi swore
is smal 73, may just be due to chance.

It may be thought sufficient recognition of the merits of
an author contemporary with Orm to say of him that he has
avoided monotony in his verse; but that would not do
justice to the poet of O&N. His handling of the octosyllabic
line is masterly; his poetry is lively, varied, and often
graceful, qualities heightened by his use of enjambment, and
the ornament of alliteration. The very facility of writing in
octosyllabics makes it difficult to write well in octosyllabics.
An unexpected rhyme is a delight, but a second rhyme-word,
that is no more than a confirmation of the fears roused by
the first, is dreary and open to the kind of attack levelled by
Pope at ' the same unvary'd chimes, With sure returns of still
expected rhymes'. There is much to delight the reader in
the rhymes of O&N (e.g. 13f, 17f, 43f, 69f, 75f, 85f, and very
many more); but it would be foolish to deny that the poet
occasionally suffers from expected rhymes, a weakness which
is rampant among his contemporaries (e.g. 49f, 173f, 253f,
331f, 365f, etc.). He probably forces his rhymes occasionally
by altering the form or pronunciation of words (e.g. 764
1028, 1520, 1523). Yet these are rare faults.

The metrical technicalities of O&N cannot properly be
compared with any poem other than The XI Pains of Hell

(cf. 882 note), a poem which, though very far from being the work of a bungling rhymester, is no masterpiece; it shows the metre of O&N used with mere literate competence. It is a pity that the technical achievement of O&N cannot be analysed by comparing it with later works; for O&N has qualities which are lacking in longer ME verse until Chaucer's time. Among the greatest of these qualities is this, that the poet gives the impression of true ease in writing. It is a studied virtue, and one would give much to know who were his masters, and what was the nature of his training.

BIBLIOGRAPHY

This Bibliography does not in any way aim at completeness. It contains works that have been found useful in compiling the edition, and works referred to in it several times. A fuller bibliography is to be found in J. E. Wells, *A Manual of the Writings in Middle English* (1916) and Supplements.

Dictionaries and lexicographical works

1. *A New English Dictionary*, edited by J. A. H. Murray, Henry Bradley, W. A. Craigie, and C. T. Onions (1888–1933).
2. J. Bosworth and T. N. Toller, *An Anglo-Saxon Dictionary* (1882–98).
3. — Supplement by T. N. Toller (1908–21).
4. Henry Bradley's edition of F. H. Stratmann's *Middle-English Dictionary* (1891).
5. *Middle English Dictionary*, edited by H. Kurath and S. M. Kuhn (1952–).
6. *The English Dialect Dictionary*, edited by J. Wright (1898–1905).
7. A. H. Smith, *English Place-Name Elements*, English Place-Name Society **25** and **26** (1956).

Editions of O&N or of parts of O&N

8. J. Stevenson, *O&N*, for the Roxburghe Club (1838). Only of historic interest.
9. T. Wright, *O&N*, for the Percy Society (1843). Only of historic interest.
10. E. Mätzner, *Altenglische Sprachproben*, vol. i (1867). Lines 701–1042.
11. F. H. Stratmann, *An OE Poem of O&N* (1868). Normalised text of C, improved by emendation from J.
12. J. E. Wells, *O&N*, Belles-Lettres Series (1907). Parallel texts ; useful.
13. W. Gadow, 'Das mittelenglische Streitgedicht Eule und Nachtigall', *Palaestra* **65** (1909). C text, with variants. Careful edition, still useful.
14. J. Hall, *Selections from Early ME 1130-1250* (1920). Well-edited selections.

15. J. W. H. Atkins, *O&N* (1922).   An elaborate edition, full of useful material.
16. J. H. G. Grattan and G. F. H. Sykes, *O&N*, for EETS (E.S.) cxix (1935). A diplomatic edition of C and J. Not always reliable in details.
17. C. T. Onions, ' An Experiment in Textual Reconstruction ', *E&S* 22 (for 1936), pp. 86–102.   Important attempt to reconstruct original text of selections.
18. Bruce Dickins and R. M. Wilson, *Early ME Texts* (1951).   Well-edited selections.

Works on O&N and major studies

19. J. Börsch, *Über Metrik und Poetik der altenglischen Dichtung O&N* (1883). Only useful for isolated points.
20. W. Breier, ' Eule und Nachtigall ', *Studien zur englischen Philologie* 39 (1910).   Important investigation, mainly linguistic.
21. K. Huganir, *O&N : Sources, Date, Author* (1931). Contains useful references. Her views have not found wide acceptance.
22. R. M. Wilson, *Early ME Literature* (1939), ch. vii. Valuable discussion.
23. H. Hässler, ' *O&N* ' *und die literarischen Bestrebungen des 12. und 13. Jahrhunderts* (? 1942).   Important on genre, rhetoric and significance.
24. G. Eggers, *O&N translated into Verse* (1955).   Not literal.

On MSS of O&N

25. C. L. Wrenn, ' Curiosities in a Medieval MS ', *E&S* 25 (for 1939), pp. 101–15. On the history of J.
26. R. M. Wilson, ' The Medieval Library of Tichfield Abbey ', *Proceedings of the Leeds Philosophical Society* 5 (1940), p. 159. On lost MS of O&N.

Studies involving more detailed points of the text and its interpretation

27. E. A. Kock, *Anglia* 25 (1902), pp. 323–5.
28. J. Koch, *Anglia Bbl* 21 (1910), pp. 227–40.
29. J. S. Kenyon, *JEGP* 12 (1913), pp. 572–92.   Valuable textual notes.
30. C. Brett, *MLR* 14 (1919), pp. 7–9.

31. F. Holthausen, *Anglia Bbl* **30** (1919), pp. 242–8.
32. J. W. H. Atkins, *Aberystwyth Studies* **4** (1922), pp. 49–58. Adduces some useful parallels from ME literature.
33. G. G. Coulton, *MLR* **17** (1922), pp. 69–71. Theological.
34. *TLS* (1923), p. 814.
35. W. W. Greg, *MLR* **18** (1923), pp. 281–5. Valuable on editorial policy.
36. C. Brett, *MLR* **22** (1927), pp. 262–4.
37. Bruce Dickins, *TLS* (1927), pp. 250f.
38. F. Holthausen, *Anglia Bbl* **39** (1928), pp. 244–8. Many points ; often interesting.
39. H. B. Hinckley, *PMLA* **44** (1929), pp. 329–59. Largely on date of O&N.
40. H. B. Hinckley, *PMLA* **46** (1931), pp. 93–101. Textual notes ; some useful.
41. C. L. W[renn], *MÆ* **1** (1932), pp. 149–56. Important on provenance.
42. H. B. Hinckley, *PMLA* **47** (1932), pp. 303–14.
43. H. B. Hinckley, *Philological Quarterly* **12** (1933), pp. 339–49. On date of O&N.
44. F. Tupper, *PMLA* **49** (1934), pp. 406–27. Useful notes on date of O&N.
45. G. V. Smithers, *RES* **13** (1937), pp. 467–9.
46. K. Huganir, *Anglia* **63** (1939), pp. 113–34. On date of O&N.
47. A. C. Cawley, *MLR* **46** (1951), pp. 161–74. Important discussion of ' Astrology in O&N '.
48. S. R. T. O. d'Ardenne, in *English Studies Today*, International Conference of University Professors of English (edited by C. L. Wrenn and G. Bullough), 1951, pp. 74–84. Valuable for editing O&N.
49. M. W. Bloomfield, *The Seven Deadly Sins* (1952), pp. 145–8. Briefly discusses the analysis of the Sins in O&N, as part of a general treatment of the Sins.
50. S. T. R. O. d'Ardenne, *Études Anglaises* **7** (1954), pp. 6–21. Useful on rhymes and provenance.
51. E. G. Stanley, *E&GS* **6** (1957), pp. 30–63. Deals at length with points dealt with more briefly in the notes to the present edition.

Linguistic works
    General works on phonology, syntax, and versification
52. K. Luick, *Historische Grammatik der englischen Sprache* (1914–40).

53. E. Sievers, [*Angelsächsische Grammatik*], revised by K. Brunner as *Altenglische Grammatik* (1942).
54. R. Jordan, *Handbuch der mittelenglischen Grammatik*, revised by H. Ch. Matthes (1934).
55. E. J. Dobson, *English Pronunciation 1500-1700* (1957).
56. E. Einenkel, *Geschichte der englischen Sprache : His-torische Syntax*, [H. Paul, *Grundriss der germanischen Philologie*, 3rd edition, vol. vi] (1916).
57. J. Schipper, *Englische Metrik*, I. Teil, *Altenglische Metrik* (1881), § 121.
58. J. Schipper, *A History of English Versification* (1910).
59. C. T. Onions, ' Some early ME Spellings ', *MLR* **4** (1909), pp. 505-7.
60. H. C. Wyld, ' South-Eastern and South-East Midland Dialects ', *E&S* **6** (1920), pp. 112-45.

Specifically on O&N

61. J. E. Wells, ' Accidence in O&N ', *Anglia* **33** (1910), pp. 252-69.
62. J. E. Wells, ' Spelling in O&N ', *MLN* **26** (1911), pp. 139-41.
63. B. Sundby. ' The Dialect and Provenance of the ME Poem O&N ', *Lund Studies in English* **18** (1950). Study based on selected onomastic material.

Incidentally of importance for O&N

64. A. S. Napier, ' OE Glosses ', *Anecdota Oxoniensia*, IV, xi (1900).
65. Irene Williams, ' A Grammatical Investigation of the OK Glosses ', *Bonner Beiträge zur Anglistik* **19** (1905), pp. 92-166.
66. J. K. Wallenberg, *The Vocabulary of Dan Michel's Ayenbite of Inwyt* (1923).
67. S. T. R. O. d'Ardenne, *An Edition of þe Liflade ant te Passiun of Seinte Iuliene*, Bibliothèque de la Faculté de Philosophie et Lettres de l'Université de Liége, **64** (1936).

OE and ME texts referred to incidentally

68. G. P. Krapp and E. V. K. Dobbie, *The Anglo-Saxon Poetic Records* (1931-54).
69. T. Wright, *Anglo-Saxon and OE Vocabularies*, edited by R. P. Wülcker (1884).
14. J. Hall, *Selections from Early ME 1130-1250* (1920).

70. *An OE Miscellany*, edited by R. Morris, EETS (O.S.) 49 (1872).

71. *OE Homilies*, edited by R. Morris, 1st Series, EETS (O.S.) 29, 34 (1867-8).

72. — 2nd Series, EETS (O.S.) 53 (1873).

73. *Ancrene Riwle* (MS Nero A.xiv), edited by Mabel Day, EETS (O.S.) 225 (1952).

74. *Hali Meiðhad*, edited by A. F. Colborn (1940).

75. Dan Michel's *Ayenbite of Inwyt*, edited by R. Morris, EETS (O.S.) 23 (1866).

76. [Orm's] *Ormulum*, edited by R. M. White and R. Holt (1878).

77. Laȝamon's *Brut*, edited by Sir F. Madden (1847).

78. Carleton Brown, *English Lyrics of the XIIIth Century* (1932).

79. Robert of Brunne's *Handlyng Synne*, edited by F. J. Furnivall, EETS (O.S.) 119, 123 (1901-3).

80. K. Böddeker, *Altenglische Dichtungen des MS. Harl.* 2253 (1878).

81. G. L. Brook, *The Harley Lyrics* (1948).

82. *Cursor Mundi*, edited by R. Morris, EETS (O.S.) 57, 59, 62, 66, 68, 99, 101 (1874-93).

83. *The Minor Poems of the Vernon MS*, edited by C. Horstmann and F. J. Furnivall, EETS (O.S.) 98, 117 (1892-1901).

84. G. Chaucer, *The Complete Works*, edited by W. W. Skeat (1894-7).

Works on the literary background and analogues

85. H. Walther, *Das Streitgedicht in der lateinischen Literatur des Mittelalters*, Quellen und Untersuchungen zur lateinischen Philologie des Mittelalters, 5, 2 (1920). The standard treatment of medieval Latin debates.

86. Alexander Neckam's *De Naturis Rerum*, etc., RS (1863).

87. Marie de France, edited by K. Warnke : *Die Lais*, Bibliotheca Normannica, III (1925).

88. — *Die Fabeln*, Bibliotheca Normannica, VI (1898).

89. K. Warnke, Die Quellen des Esope der Marie de France, in *Forschungen zur romanischen Philologie : Festgabe für Hermann Suchier* (1900), pp. 161-284.

90. Nicole Bozon, *Les Contes Moralisés*, edited by L. Toulmin Smith and P. Meyer, Société des Anciens Textes Français [28] (1889).

OE and ME proverbs

91. Proverbs from MS Cotton Faustina A.x. in Dobbie, *A.S. Poetic Records*, VI, pp. cx–cxii, 109.
92. The Riming Poem, in Dobbie, *A.S. Poetic Records*, III, pp. 166–9.
93. *The Durham Proverbs*, edited by O. Arngart, in *Lunds Universitets Årsskrift*, N.F. Avd. 1, 52; 2 (1956).
94. *The Proverbs of Alfred*, edited by O. Arngart, in Skrifter utgivna av Kungl. Humanistiska Vetenskapssamfundet i Lund, 32 (1942–55).
95. *The Proverbs of Hendyng ;* edited by G. Schleich, *Anglia* 51 (1927), pp. 220–77.
96. The ME *Distichs* of Cato, edited by Furnivall ; see Bib. 83, pp. 553–609.
97. *Disticha Catonis*, edited by M. Boas (1952). Source of ME Cato.
98. Proverbs from MS Douce 52, edited by Max Förster in *Festschrift zum XII. allgemeinen deutschen Neuphilologentage in München*, edited by E. Stollreither (1906), pp. 40–60.
99. Proverbs from MS Trinity College Cambridge, O.2.45, edited by Max Förster, *EStn* 31 (1902), pp. 5–9.

General works on the historical and legal background

100. F. M. Stenton, *Anglo-Saxon England*, 2nd edition (1947).
101. F. Liebermann, *Die Gesetze der Angelsachsen* (1903–16).
102. F. Pollock and F. W. Maitland, *History of English Law*, 2nd edition (1898).
103. C. T. Flower, *Introduction to the Curia Regis Rolls, 1199–1230 A.D.*, Publications of the Selden Society, 62 (1944, for 1943).

THE TEXT

The text followed is that of the Cotton MS. Italics indicate alteration of words by emendation. Letters or words added by emendation have been placed within square brackets. Expansion of MS abbreviations and contractions has not been marked. The punctuation, capitalisation, and, to some extent, the division of words conform to modern practice.

In view of the similarity in the Cotton MS of the letters *thorn* and *wynn* (see pp. 9f), no attempt will be made to preserve clear examples of scribal confusion, and these will be silently corrected. The letters *w* and *wynn* are treated as follows: in the text, and elsewhere where the Cotton MS is followed, printed *w* stands for Cotton MS *wynn*, printed *vv* stands for MS *double-u*; for the Jesus MS, wherever its readings are reprinted, in the footnotes, notes, or in square brackets in the text itself, printed *w* stands for MS *double-u*. The letter *wynn* does not occur in the Jesus MS.

Where the printed text departs from that of the Cotton MS the footnotes give the readings of both the Cotton and the Jesus MSS. The *sigla* in the footnotes indicate the edition of the poem in which an emendation here adopted was first introduced; the *sigla* are placed within square brackets where an earlier edition introduces an emendation with which that adopted here should be compared. Where no *sigla* are given in the footnote to a textual emendation, the present edition differs from the earlier editions.

SIGLA USED IN THE FOOTNOTES

C The text of MS Cotton Caligula A.ix in the British Museum

J The text of MS Jesus College 29, deposited in the Bodleian Library

A   J. W. H. Atkins, *The Owl and the Nightingale* (1922)

DW Bruce Dickins and R. M. Wilson, *Early Middle English Texts* (1951)

Ga W. Gadow, 'Das mittelenglische Streitgedicht Eule und Nachtigall,' *Palaestra*, vol. 65 (1909)

GS J. H. G. Grattan and G. F. H. Sykes, *The Owl and the Nightingale*, EETS (E.S.) 119 (1935)

H   Joseph Hall, *Selections from Early Middle English 1130-1250* (1920)

Mä E. Mätzner, *Altenglische Sprachproben* (1867)

Mo R. Morris, *Specimens of Early English 1250-1400* (1867)

Sk R. Morris, *Specimens of Early English*, second edition, carefully revised by W. W. Skeat and A. L. Mayhew (1886)

Ste J. Stevenson, *The Owl and the Nightingale*, Roxburghe Club (1838)

Str F. H. Stratmann, *An Old English Poem of The Owl and the Nightingale* (1868)

We J. E. Wells, *The Owl and the Nightingale*, Belles Lettres Series (1907)

Wr Thomas Wright, *The Owl and the Nightingale*, Percy Society (1843)

INCIPIT ALTERCACIO
INTER
FILOMENAM & BUBONEM

f. 233 r/a

ICH was in one sumere dale ;
In one suþe diȝele hale
Iherde ich holde grete tale
An Hule and one Niȝtingale.
Þat plait was stif & starc & strong,   5
Sum wile softe & lud among.
An aiþer aȝen oþer sval
& let þat vvole mod ut al ;
& eiþer seide of oþeres custe
Þat alre worste þat hi wuste.   10
& hure & hure of oþere[s] songe
Hi holde plaiding suþe stronge.

  Þe Niȝtingale bigon þe speche
In one hurne of one breche,
& sat up one vaire boȝe—   15
Þar were abute blosme inoȝe !—
In ore *u*aste þicke hegge
Imeind mid spire & grene segge.

The Incipit *is from J.*
1–9 *In C* ' *these lines are written in a slightly larger script than the rest*
    of the poem, and thus serve as a kind of heading ' (GS)
7 aiþer] *C* asþer (*cf.* 9 *footnote*); *J* eyþer: *H*
9 eiþer] *corrected from* esþer; *J* eyþer
11 oþeres] *C* oþere; *J* oþres: *Str*
17 uaste] *C* waste; *J* vaste: *DW*

Ho was þe gladur uor þe rise,
& song a uele cunne wise.   20
Bet þuӡte þe dreim þat he were
Of harpe & pipe þan he nere,
Bet þuӡte þat he were ishote
Of harpe & pipe þan of þrote.

    Þo stod on old stoc þarbiside,   25
Þar þo Vle song hire tide,
& was mid iui al bigrowe.
Hit was þare Hule eardingstowe.

    Þe Niӡtingale hi iseӡ,
& hi bihold & ouerseӡ,   30
& þuӡte wel vvl of þare Hule,
For me hi halt lodlich & fule.
' Vnwiӡt ! ' ho sede, ' awei þu flo !
Me is þe vvrs þat ich þe so.

f. 233 r/b
Iwis for þine vvle lete   35
Wel oft ich mine song forlete.
Min horte atfliþ & falt mi tonge
Wonne þu art to me iþrunge.
Me luste bet speten þane singe
Of þine fule ӡoӡelinge.'   40

    Þos Hule abod fort hit was eve.
Ho ne miӡte no leng bileue,
Vor hire horte was so gret
Þat wel neӡ hire fnast atschet,
& warp a word þarafter longe :   45
' Hu þincþe nu bi mine songe ?
We[n]st þu þat ich ne cunne singe,
Þeӡ ich ne cunne of writelinge ?
Ilome þu dest me grame,
& seist me boþe tone & schame.   50

---

21 Bet] *C* Het; *J* Bet: *Str*
25 Þo] *C's rubricator has omitted the capital; the directing letter is in the right place; J* Þo
29 Þe] *C's rubric capital omitted as at 25 (cf. footnote); J* Þe
36 song] *C* fong : *J* song
47 Wenst] *C* West (*omitting* n-*contraction*); *J* Wenestu: *Str*
48 of] *C* os; *J* of

Ʒif ich þe holde on mine *uote*—
So hit bitide þat ich mote !—
& þu were vt of þine rise,
Þu sholdest singe an oþer w[i]se ! ’
  Þe Niʒtingale ʒaf ansvvare :   55
‘ Ʒif ich me loki wit þe bare
& me schilde wit þe blete,
Ne reche ich noʒt of þine þrete ;
Ʒif ich me holde in mine hegge,
Ne recche ich neuer what þu segge.   60
Ich wot þat þu art unmilde
VViþ hom þat ne muʒe from þe schilde,
& þu tukest vvroþe & vuele,
VVhar þu miʒt, over smale fuʒele.
Vorþi þu art loþ al fuelkunne,   65
& alle ho þe driueþ honne,
& þe bischricheþ & bigredet
& vvel narewe þe biledet ;
& ek forþe þe sulue mose
Hire þonkes wolde þe totose.   70
Þu art lodlich to biholde,
& þu art loþ in monie volde :
Þi bodi is short, þi swore is smal,
Grettere is þin heued þan þu al ;
Þin eʒene boþ colblake, & brode   75
Riʒt svvo ho weren ipeint mid wode.
Þu starest so þu wille abiten
Al þat þu mist mid cliure smiten.
Þi bile is stif & scharp & hoked
Riʒt so an ovvel þat is croked.   80
Þarmid þu clackes oft & longe,
& þat is on of þine songe.
Ac þu þretest to mine fleshe,
Mid þine cliures woldest me meshe :
Þe were icundur to one frogge,   85

f. 233 v/a (margin, left of line 69)

[Þat sit at mulne vnder cogge :]
Snailes, mus & fule wiȝte
Boþ þine cunde & þine riȝte.
Þu sittest a dai & fliȝ[s]t a niȝt.
Þu cuþest þat þu art on vnwiȝt.   90
Þu art lodlich & unclene—
Bi þine neste ich hit mene,
& ek bi þine fule brode :
Þu fedest on hom a vvel ful fode.
Vel wostu þat hi doþ þarinne :   95
Hi fuleþ hit up to þe chinne ;
Ho sitteþ þar so hi bo bisne.
Þarbi men segget a uorbisne :
" Dahet habbe þat ilke best
Þat fuleþ his owe nest."   100
Þat oþer ȝer a Faukun bredde ;
His nest noȝt wel he ne bihedde.
Þarto þu stele in o dai,
& leidest þaron þi fole ey.
Þo hit bicom þat he haȝte   105
& of his eyre briddes wraȝte,
Ho broȝte his briddes mete,
Bihold his nest, iseȝ hi ete ;
He iseȝ bi one halue
His nest ifuled uthalue.   110
Þe Faucun was wroþ wit his bridde,
& lude ȝal, & sterne chidde :
" Segget me, wo hauet þis ido ?
Ov nas neuer icunde þarto.
Hit was idon ov a loþ *cus*te.   115
Segge[t] me, ȝif ȝe hit wiste ! "
Þo quaþ þat on, & quad þat oþer :
" Iwis, hit was ure oȝe broþer,
Þe ȝond, þat haued þat grete heued,—

f. 233 v/b

86 *Line omitted in C, supplied from J: Ste*
89 fliȝst] C fliȝt (*under* ȝ *the downstroke of a long* s *erased*); J flyhst: *Mo*
115 a loþ custe] C a loþ vviste; J a loþe custe: *We*
116 Segget] C Segge; J Seggeþ: [GS]
118 oȝe] C oȝer; J owe: *Str*

Wai þat he nis þarof bireued !   120
VVorp hit ut mid þe alre wrste,
Þat his necke him toberste ! "
Þe Faucun ilefde his bridde
& nom þat fule brid a midde,
& warp hit of þan wilde bowe,   125
Þar pie & crowe hit todrowe.
Herbi men segget a bispel—
Þeჳ hit ne bo fuliche spel— :
Also hit is bi þan ungode
Þat is icumen of fule brode   130
& is meind wit fro monne,
Euer he cuþ þat he com þonne,
Þat he com of þan adel eye
Þeჳ he a fro nest leie :
Þeჳ appel trendli fron þon trowe   135
Þar he & oþer mid growe,
Þeჳ he bo þarfrom bicume

f. 234 r/a   He cuþ wel whonene he is icume.'
                Þos word aჳaf þe Niჳtingale,
& after þare longe tale   140
He song so lude & so scharpe,
Riჳt so me grulde schille harpe.
Þos Hule luste þiderward,
& hold hire eჳe noþerwa[r]d,
& sat tosvolle & ibolwe   145
Also ho hadde one frogge isuolჳe,
For ho wel wiste & was iwar
Þat ho song hire a bisemar.
& noþeles ho ჳaf andsuare :
' Whi neltu flon into þe bare   150
& sewi ware unker bo
Of briჳter howe, of uairur blo ? '
' No ! þu hauest wel scharpe clawe,
Ne kep ich noჳt þat þu me clawe.

120 he] *C* hi *corrected from* his; *J* he: *Ga*   þarof] *C* þaros; *J* þarof
144 noþerward] *C* noþerwad (*with* w *corrected from* u); *J* neþerward:
     Ste
149 ჳaf] *C* ჳas; *J* yaf: *We*

Þu hauest cliuers suþe stronge,   155
Þu tuengst þarmid so doþ a tonge.
Þu þoȝtest—so doþ þine ilike—
Mid faire worde me bisvvike.
Ich nolde don þat þu me raddest,
Ich wiste wel þat þu me misraddest.   160
Schamie þe for þin unrede !
Vnwroȝen is þi svikelhede :
Schild þine svikeldom vram þe liȝte,
& hud þat woȝe amon þe riȝte !
Þane þu wilt þin unriȝt spene   165
Loke þat hit ne bo isene !
Vor svikedom haued schome & hete
Ȝif hit is ope & underȝete.
Ne speddestu noȝt mid þine unwrenche,
For ich am war & can wel blenche.   170
Ne helpþ noȝt þat þu bo to þriste :
f. 234 r/b   Ich wolde viȝte bet mid liste
Þan þu mid al þine strengþe.
Ich habbe on brede & eck on lengþe
Castel god on mine rise :   175
" Wel fiȝt þat wel fliȝt," seiþ þe wise.
Ac lete we awei þos cheste,
Vor suiche wordes boþ unwerste
& fo we on mid riȝte dome,
Mid faire worde & mid ysome.   180
Þeȝ we ne bo at one acorde
We muȝe bet mid fayre worde,
Witute cheste & bute fiȝte,
Plaidi mid *foȝe* & mid riȝte ;
& mai hure eiþer wat hi wile   185
Mid riȝte segge & mid sckile.'
    Þo quaþ þe Hule, ' Wu schal us seme,
Þat kunne & wille riȝt us deme ? '
' Ich wot wel,' quaþ þe Niȝtingale,
' Ne þaref þarof bo no tale :   190

---

159 raddest] dd *expuncted in error;* J raddest
184 foȝe] C soȝe; J soþe: [Wr]   185 hi] J he

Maister Nichole of Guldeforde.
He is wis an war of worde.
He is of dome suþe gleu,
& him is loþ eurich unþeu.
He wot insiȝt in eche songe, 195
Wo singet wel, wo singet wronge ;
& he can schede vrom þe riȝte
Þat woȝe, þat þustet from þe liȝte.'

 Þo Hule one wile hi biþoȝte,
& after þan þis word upbroȝte : 200
' Ich granti wel þat he us deme,
Vor þeȝ he were wile breme,
& lof him were niȝtingale
& oþer wiȝte gente & smale,
Ich wot he is nu suþe acoled ; 205
Nis he vor þe noȝt afoled,
Þat he for þine olde luue
Me adun legge, & þe buue.
Ne schaltu neure so him queme
Þat he for þe fals dom deme. 210
He is him ripe & fastrede,
Ne lust him nu to none unrede :
Nu him ne lust na more pleie,
He wile gon a riȝte weie.'

 Þe Niȝtingale was al ȝare, 215
Ho hadde ilorned wel aivvare.
' Hule,' ho sede, ' seie me soþ,
Wi dostu þat unwiȝtis doþ ?
Þu singist a niȝt & noȝt a dai,
& al þi song is " wailawai ". 220
Þu miȝt mid þine songe afere
Alle þat ihereþ þine ibere.
Þu schirchest & ȝollest to þine fere
Þat hit is grislich to ihere.
Hit þincheþ boþe wise & snepe, 225
Noȝt þat þu singe, ac þat þu wepe.
Þu fliȝst a niȝt & noȝt a dai ;

f. 234 v/a

Þarof ich vvndri, & wel mai,
Vor eurich þing þat schuniet riȝt,
Hit luueþ þuster & hatiet liȝt ;   230
& eurich þing þat is lof misdede,
Hit luueþ þuster to his dede.
A wis word, þeȝ hit bo unclene,
Is fele manne a muþe imene,
For Alured King hit seide & wrot :   235
" He schunet þat hine vvl wot."
Ich wene þat þu dost also,
Vor þu fliȝst niȝtes euer mo.
An oþer þing me is a wene,

f. 234 v/b   Þu hauest a niȝt wel briȝte sene :   240
Bi daie þu art stareblind
Þat þu ne sichst ne boℓ ne rind.
A dai þu art blind oþer bisne,
Þarbi men segget a uorbisne :
Riȝt so hit farþ bi þan ungode   245
Þat noȝt ne suþ to none gode,
& is so ful of vuele wrenche
Þat him ne mai no man atprenche,
& can wel þane þurste wai,
& þane briȝte lat awai,   250
So doþ þat boþ of þine cunde :
Of liȝte nabbeþ hi none imunde.'
        Þos Hule luste suþe longe,
& was oftoned suþe stronge.
Ho quaþ, ' Þu attest Niȝtingale,   255
Þu miȝtest bet hoten Galegale,
Vor þu hauest to monie tale.
Lat þine tunge habbe spale !
Þu wenest þat þes dai bo þin oȝe.
Lat me nu habbe mine þroȝe !   260

236 schunet] *C* schunet *altered in a contemporary hand to* schuntet; *J*
    schuneþ
240 *C* eyen *added in a later hand above the line after* a niȝt
242 bov ne rind] *C* bov *altered from* bos, rind *altered from* strind; *J*
    bouh of lynd
255 attest] *C* attest *with* h *prefixed by a later hand; J* hattest

Bo nu stille, & lat me speke,
Ich wille bon of þe awreke ;
& lust hu ich con me bitelle
Mid riȝte soþe witute spelle.
Þu seist þat ich me hude a dai ;   265
Þarto ne segge ich " nich " ne " nai ".
& lust, ich telle þe wareuore,
Al wi hit is, & wareuore.
Ich habbe bile stif & stronge,
& gode cliuers scharp & longe,   270
So hit bicumeþ to haukes cunne.
Hit is min hiȝte, hit is mi wnne
Þat ich me draȝe to mine cunde,—

f. 235 r/a

Ne mai no man þareuore schende :
On me hit is wel isene   275
Vor riȝte cunde ich am so kene.
Vorþi ich am loþ smale foȝle
Þat floþ bi grunde an bi þuuele.
Hi me bichermet & bigredeþ
& hore flockes to me ledeþ.   280
Me is lof to habbe reste
& sitte stille in mine neste ;
Vor nere ich neuer no þe betere
Yif ich mid chauling & mid chatere
Hom schende, & mid fule worde,   285
So herdes doþ oþer mid schitworde.
Ne lust me wit þe screwen chide,
Forþi ich wende from hom wide.
Hit is a wise monne dome—
& hi hit segget wel ilome—   290
Þat me ne chide wit þe gidie,
Ne wit þan ofne me ne ȝonie.
At sume siþe, herde i telle,
Hu Alured sede on his spelle :

272 mi wnne] *C* mi wune; *J* my ynne: [A], GS
280 to me] *C* to ne *with* n *expuncted and later corrected to* m; *J* to
me: *We*
284 Yif] *with* Y *altered from another letter, and* f *altered from* ȝ; *J* Þeyh
293 siþe] *altered to* siþþe (*? by a contemporary hand*); *J* syþe

"Loke þat þu ne bo þare   295
Þar chauling boþ & cheste ȝare ;
Lat sottes chide & uorþ þu go ! "
& ich am wis, & do also.
& ȝet Alured seide an oþer side
A word, þat is isprunge wide :   300
" Þat wit þe fule haueþ imene,
Ne cumeþ he neuer from him cleine."
Wenestu þat haueck bo þe worse
Þoȝ crowe bigrede him bi þe mershe,
& goþ to him mid hore chirme,   305
Riȝt so hi wille wit him schirme ?
Þe hauec folȝeþ gode rede,
f. 235 r/b   & fliȝt his wei & lat hi grede.
    Ȝet þu me seist of oþer þinge,
& telst þat ich ne can noȝt singe,   310
Ac al mi rorde is woning,
& to ihire grislich þing.
Þat nis noȝt soþ, ich singe efne
Mid fulle dreme & lude stefne.
Þu wenist þat ech song bo grislich   315
Þat þine pipinge nis ilich :
Mi stefne is bold & noȝt unorne ;
Ho is ilich one grete horne,
& þin is ilich one pipe
Of one smale wode unripe.   320
Ich singe bet þan þu dest ;
Þu chaterest so doþ on Irish prost.
Ich singe an eue a riȝte time,
& soþþe won hit is bedtime,
Þe þridde siþe ad middelniȝte,   325
& so ich mine song adiȝte.
Wone ich iso arise vorre
Oþer dairim oþer daisterre,

308 hi] C hi *altered to* hem *by a contemporary hand; J* hi: [*Ga*]
317 bold] C blod; J bold: [*Ste*] We
320 wode] *altered to* woede *by a contemporary hand; J* weode
322 prost] *altered to* preost *by a contemporary hand; J* prest

Ich do god mid mine þrote
& warni men to hore note.   330
Ac þu singest alle longe niȝt
From eue fort hit is dailiȝt,
& eure leist þin o song
So longe so þe niȝt is long,
& eure croweþ þi wrecche crei   335
Þat he ne swikeþ niȝt ne dai.
Mid þine pipinge þu adunest
Þas monnes earen þar þu vvunest,
& makest þine song so unwrþ
Þa[t] me ne telþ of þar noȝ[t] wrþ.   340
Eurich murȝþe mai so longe ileste
f. 235 v/a   Þat ho shal liki wel unwreste ;
Vor harpe & pipe & fuȝeles song
Mislikeþ ȝif hit is to long.
Ne bo þe song neuer so murie   345
Þat he ne shal þinche wel unmurie
Ȝef he ilesteþ oure unwille.
So þu miȝt þine song aspille ;
Vor hit is soþ,—Alured hit seide
& me hit mai ine boke rede :   350
" Eurich þing mai losen his godhede
Mid unmeþe & mid ouerdede."
Mid este þu þe miȝt ouerquatie,
& ouerfulle makeþ vvlatie ;
An eurich mureȝþe mai agon,   355
Ȝif me hit halt eure forþ in on—
Bute one : þat is Godes riche,
Þat eure is svete & eure iliche :
Þeȝ þu nime euere oþþan lepe
Hit is eure ful bi hepe ;   360
VVunder hit is of Godes riche
Þat eure spenþ & euer is iliche.

333 leist] *altered from* seist ; *J* lesteþ
340 Þat . . . þar noȝt wrþ] *altered from* Þa . . . þar noȝ wrþ *by a con-*
    temporary hand ; J Þat . . . þe nowiht : *We*
343 song] *C* songe ; *J* song : *Str*
347 oure] *C and J* ouer ; [*Ha, O*]

E

3ut þu me seist on oþer shome,
Þat ich am on mine eჳen lome,
An seist, forþat ich flo bi niჳte,   365
Þat ich ne mai iso bi liჳte.
Þu liest !   On me hit is isene
Þat ich habbe gode sene,
Vor nis non so dim þusternesse
Þat ich euer iso þe lasse.   370
Þu wenest þat ich ne miჳte iso
Vor ich bi daie noჳt ne flo :
Þe hare luteþ al dai,
Ac noþeles iso he mai.
3if hundes urneþ to himward   375

f. 235 v/b

He gengþ wel suiþe awaiwart,
& hokeþ paþes sviþe narewe,
& haueþ mid him his blenches ჳarewe,
& huppþ, & stard suþe coue,
An secheþ paþes to þe groue.   380
Ne sholde he, uor boþe his eჳe,
So don, ჳif he þe bet niseჳe.
Ich mai ison so wel so on hare
Þeჳ ich bi daie sitte an dare.
Þar aჳte men boþ in worre,   385
An fareþ boþe ner an forre,
An oueruareþ fele þode,
An doþ bi niჳte gode node,
Ich folჳi þan aჳte manne,
An flo bi niჳte in hore banne.'   390
      Þe Niჳtingale in hire þoჳte
Athold al þis, & longe þoჳte
Wat ho þarafter miჳte segge ;
Vor ho ne miჳte noჳt alegge
Þat þe Hule hadde hire ised,   395
Vor he spac boþe riჳt an red.
An hire ofþuჳte þat ho hadde

364 am] *corrected from* an *by expuncting* n *and adding the* n/m-*contrac-
    tion;* J an
387 þode] *altered to* þoede *by a contemporary hand;* J þeode
388 node] *altered to* noede *by a contemporary hand;* J neode

Þe speche so for uorþ iladde,
An was oferd þat hire answare
Ne wrþe noȝt ariȝt ifare.   400
Ac noþeles he spac boldeliche ;
Vor he is wis þat hardeliche
Wiþ is uo berþ grete ilete,
Þat he uor areȝþe hit ne forlete :
Vor suich worþ bold ȝif þu fliȝ*st*   405
Þat wle flo ȝif þu [n]isvicst ;
Ȝif he isiþ þat þu nart areȝ
He wile of bore wrchen bareȝ.
& forþi, þeȝ þe Niȝtingale

f. 236 r/a   Were aferd, ho spac bolde tale.   410
' *H*ule,' ho seide, ' wi dostu so ?
Þu singest a winter " wolawo " ;
Þu singest so doþ hen a snowe—
Al þat ho singeþ hit is for wowe.
A wintere þu singest wroþe & ȝomere,   415
An eure þu art dumb a sumere.
Hit is for þine fule niþe
Þat þu ne miȝt mid us bo bliþe,
Vor þu forbernest wel neȝ for onde
Wane ure blisse cumeþ to londe.   420
Þu farest so doþ þe ille :
Evrich blisse him is unwille ;
Grucching & luring him boþ rade
Ȝif he isoþ þat men boþ glade ;
He wolde þat he iseȝe   425
Teres in evrich monnes eȝe.
Ne roȝte he þeȝ flockes were
Imeind bi toppes & bi here :
Also þu dost on þire side,

405 fliȝst] *C* fliȝste; *J* flyhst: [*Str*], *Ga*
406 nisvicst] *C* isvicst *with* is *expuncted in lighter ink*; *J* swykst:
      [*Str*], *A*
411 Hule] *C* ule *preceded by directing letter* H, *for which the rubricator
      wrote an initial* Þ, *giving the reading* Þule; *J similarly* Þule, *but
      here the directing letter is also wrong, i.e.* Þ: *We*
416–619 An, an] *C: In these lines* An *or* an *has on twelve occasions been
      altered to* And *or* and *by a later hand*

Vor wanne snov liþ þicke & wide   430
An alle wiʒtes habbeþ sorʒe,
Þu singest from eue fort a morʒe.
Ac ich alle blisse mid me bringe,
Ech wiʒt is glad for mine þinge
& blisseþ hit wanne ich cume,   435
& hiʒteþ aʒen mine kume.
Þe blostme ginneþ springe & sprede,
Boþe ine tro & ek on mede.
Þe lilie mid hire faire wlite
Wolcumeþ me—þat þu hit w[i]te !—   440
Bid me mid hire faire blo
Þat ich shulle to hire flo.
Þe rose also, mid hire rude

f. 236 r/b   Þat cumeþ ut of þe þornevvode,
Bit me þat ich shulle singe   445
Vor hire luue one skentinge.
& ich so do þurʒ niʒt & dai—
Þe more ich singe þe more i mai—
An skente hi mid mine songe,
Ac noþeles noʒt ouerlonge :   450
Wane ich iso þat men boþ glade
Ich nelle þat hi bon to sade;
Wan is ido vor wan ich com
Ich fare aʒen, & do wisdom.
Wane mon hoʒeþ of his sheue,   455
An falevv icumeþ on grene leue,
Ich fare hom & nime leue.
Ne recche ich noʒt of winteres reue ;
Wan ich iso þat cumeþ þat harde
Ich fare hom to min erde,   460
& habbe boþe luue & þonc
Þat ich her com & hider swonk.
Þan min erende is ido
Sholde ich bileue ? Nai ! Warto ?

431 An] *see* 416 *footnote*   440 wite] *C* wte; *J* wite: *Mo*
441 Bid] *altered from* Bit; *J* Bid   449 An] *see* 416 *footnote*
458 reue] *C* rene; *J* teone: *GS*

Vor he nis noþer ȝep ne wis   465
Þat longe abid þar him nod nis.'
   Þos Hule luste & leide an hord
Al þis mot, word after word,
An after þoȝte hu he miȝte
Ansvere uinde best mid riȝte :   470
Vor he mot hine ful wel biþenche
Þat is aferd of plaites wrenche.
   ' Þv aishest me,' þe Hule sede,
' Wi ich a winter singe & grede.
Hit is gode monne iwone—   475
An was from þe worlde frome—
Þat ech god man his frond icnowe

f. 236 v/a   An blisse mid hom sume þrowe
In his huse, at his borde,
Mid faire speche & faire worde.   480
& hure & hure to Cristes masse,
Þane riche & poure, more & lasse,
Singeþ cundut niȝt & dai,
Ich hom helpe what ich mai.
& ek ich þenche of oþer þinge   485
Þane to pleicn oþer to singe.
Ich habbe herto gode ansuare
Anon iredi & al ȝare ;
Vor sumeres tide is al to wlonc
An doþ misreken monnes þonk ;   490
Vor he ne recþ noȝt of clennesse,
Al his þoȝt is of golnesse ;
Vor none dor no leng nabideþ,
Ac eurich upon oþer rideþ.
Þe sulue stottes ine þe stode   495
Boþ boþe wilde & merewode ;
& þu sulf art þaramong,
For of golnesse is al þi song,
An aȝen þet þu vvlt teme
Þu art wel modi & wel breme.   500

      469 An] *see* 416 *footnote*
      499 An] *see* 416 *footnote*

Sone so þu hauest itrede
Ne miȝtu leng a word iqueþe,
Ac pipest also doþ a mose
Mid chokeringe mid steune hose.
ȝet þu singst worse þon þe heisugge   505
Þat fliȝþ bi grunde among þe stubbe :
Wane þi lust is ago
Þanne is þi song ago also.
A sumere chorles awedeþ
& uorcrempeþ & uorbredeþ.   510
Hit nis for luue noþeles,

f. 236 v/b   Ac is þe chorles wode res ;
Vor wane he haueþ ido his dede
Ifallen is al his boldhede ;
Habbe he istunge under gore   515
Ne last his luue no leng more.
Also hit is on þine mode :
So sone so þu sittest a brode
Þu forlost al þine wise.
Also þu farest on þine rise :   520
Wane þu hauest ido þi gome
Þi steune goþ anon to shome.
Ac wane niȝtes cumeþ longe
& b[r]ingeþ forstes starke an stronge,
Þanne erest hit is isene   525
War is þe snelle, war is þe kene :
At þan harde me mai auinde
Wo geþ forþ, wo liþ bihinde.
Me mai ison at þare node
Wan me shal harde wike bode ;   530
Þanne ich am snel & pleie & singe,
& hiȝte me mid mi skentinge.

---

501 hauest] *altered from* haust *probably by the same hand; J* hauest
502 iqueþe] *altered to* iquede *by a later hand; J* iqueþe
506 Þat] *C* ȝat; *J* Þat: *Str*
515 istunge] *altered to* isstunge *by a different hand; J* istunge
516 leng] *altered to* lenger *by a different hand; J* leng
524 bringeþ] *C* bingeþ *corrected to* bringeþ *by a different hand; J*
      bryngeþ: *We*

Of none wintere ich ne recche,
Vor ich nam non asvnde wrecche.
& ek ich frouri uele wiȝte 535
Þat mid hom nabbed none miȝtte.
Hi boþ hoȝfule & uel arme,
An secheþ ȝorne to þe warme.
Oft ich singe uor hom þe more
For lutli sum of hore sore. 540
Hu þincþ þe ? Artu ȝut inume,
Artu mid riȝte ouercume ? '
        ' Nay, nay,' sede þe Niȝtingale,
' Þu shalt ihere an oþer tale.
ȝet nis þos speche ibroȝt to dome. 545

f. 237 r/a Ac bo wel stille & lust nu to me !
Ich shal mid one bare worde
Do þat þi speche wrþ forworþe.'
        ' Þat nere noht riȝt,' þe Hule sede,
' Þu hauest bicloped also þu bede, 550
An ich þe habbe iȝiue ansuare.
Ac ar we to unker dome fare
Ich wille speke toward þe
Also þu speke toward me,
An þu me ansuare ȝif þu miȝt. 555
Seie me nu, þu wrecche wiȝt,
Is in þe eni oþer note
Bute þu hauest schille þrote ?
Þu nart noȝt to non oþer þinge
Bute þu canst of chateringe ; 560
Vor þu art lutel an unstrong,
An nis þi reȝel no þing long.
Wat dostu godes among monne ?
Na mo þe deþ a wercche wranne !
Of þe ne cumeþ non oþer god 565
Bute þu gredest suich þu bo wod ;

538 An] *see 416 footnote*
548 wrþ] *C* wrht (*? for* wrth)*; J* wrþ *: Str*
555 ansuare] *altered to* ansuere *by a different hand; J* onswere
561 an] *see 416 footnote*   562 An] *see 416 footnote*
564 mo] *altered to* more *by a later hand; J* mo

An bo þi piping ouergo
Ne boþ on þe craftes na mo.
Alured sede, þat was wis—
He miȝte wel, for soþ hit is :   570
" Nis no man for is bare songe
Lof ne wrþ noȝt suþe longe ; "
Vor þat is a forworþe man
Þat bute singe noȝt ne can.
Þu nart bute on forworþe þing :   575
On þe nis bute chatering.
Þu art dim an of fule howe,
An þinchest a lutel soti clowe.
Þu nart fair, no þu nart strong,

f. 237 r/b   Ne þu nart þicke, ne þu nart long.   580
Þu hauest imist al of fairhede,
An lutel is al þi godede.
An oþer þing of þe ich mene :
Þu nart vair, ne þu nart clene
Wane þu comest to manne haȝe,   585
Þar þornes boþ & ris idraȝe
Bi hegge & bi þicke wode.
Þar men goþ oft to hore node
Þarto þu draȝst, þarto þu wnest,
An oþer clene stede þu schunest.   590
Wan ich flo niȝtes after muse
I mai þe uinde ate rumhuse ;
Among þe wode, among þe netle
Þu sittest & singst bihinde þe setle.
Þar me mai þe ilomest finde   595
Þar men worpeþ hore bihinde.
Ȝet þu atuitest me mine mete
An seist þat ich fule wiȝtes ete ;
Ac wat etestu—þat þu ne liȝe !—
Bute attercoppe & fule uliȝe   600
& wormes, ȝif þu miȝte finde

574 can] *altered from* gan *by the same hand;* **J** can
577 an] *see* 416 *footnote*   582 An] *see* 416 *footnote*
594 setle] **C** secle ; **J** seotle: *GS*

Among þe uolde of harde rinde ?
ʒet ich can do wel gode wike,
Vor ich can loki manne wike ;
An mine wike boþ wel gode,   605
Vor ich helpe to manne uode.
Ich can nimen mus at berne
An ek at chirche ine þe derne :
Vor me is lof to Cristes huse,
To clansi hit wiþ fule muse ;   610
Ne schal þar neure come to
Ful wiʒt, ʒif ich hit mai iuo.
An ʒif me lust, one mi skentinge,
f. 237 v/a   To wernen oþer wnienge,
Ich habbe at wude trou wel grete   615
Mit þicke boʒe no þing blete,
Mid iui grene al bigrowe,
Þat eure stont iliche iblowe
An his hou neuer ne uorlost,
Wan hit sniuþ, ne wan hit frost.   620
Þarin ich habbe god ihold,
A winter warm, a sumere cold :
Wane min hus stont briʒt & grene
Of þine nis no þing isene.

ʒet þu me telst of oþer þinge,   625
Of mine briddes seist gabbinge,
Þat hore nest nis noʒt clene :
Hit is fale oþer wiʒte imene,
Vor hors a stable & oxe a stalle
Doþ al þat hom wule þar falle,   630
An lutle children in þe cradele—
Boþe chorles an ek aþele—
Doþ al þat in hore ʒoeþe
Þat hi uorleteþ in hore duʒeþe.
Wat can þat ʒongling hit bihede ?   635
ʒif hit misdeþ, hit mod nede.
A uorbisne is of olde ivvrne,

608 An] *see* 416 *footnote*   619 An] *see* 416 *footnote*
630, 633 Doþ] C Boþ ; J Doþ : *Str*

Þat node makeþ old wif urne.
An ȝet ich habbe an oþer andsware :
Wiltu to mine neste uare   640
An loki hu hit is idiȝt ?
Ȝif þu art wis, lorni þu miȝst :
Mi nest is holȝ & rum a midde,
So hit is softest mine bridde ;
Hit is broiden al abute   645
Vrom þe neste uor wiþute.
Þarto hi god to hore node ;

f. 237 v/b

Ac þat þu menest ich hom forbode.
We nimeþ ȝeme of manne bure
An after þan we makeþ ure :   650
Men habbet, among oþer iwende,
A rumhus at hore bures ende,
Vorþat hi nelleþ to uor go ;
An mine briddes doþ also.
Site nu stille, chaterestre !   655
Nere þu neuer ibunde uastre ;
Herto ne uindestu neuer andsware.
Hong up þin ax ! Nu þu miȝt fare ! '
    Þe Niȝtingale at þisse worde
Was wel neȝ ut of rede iworþe,   660
An þoȝte ȝorne on hire mode
Ȝif ho oȝt elles understode,
Ȝif ho kuþe oȝt bute singe
Þat miȝte helpe to oþer þinge.
Herto ho moste andswere uinde,   665
Oþer mid alle bon bihinde :
An hit is suþe strong to fiȝte
Aȝen soþ & aȝen riȝte.
He mot gon to al mid ginne,
Wan þe horte boþ on winne ;   670
An þe man mot on oþer segge :
He mot bihemmen & bilegge,
Ȝif muþ wiþute mai biwro
Þat me þe horte noȝt niso.

670 winne] C þinne *or* winne; J þinne

An sone mai a word misreke   675
Þar muþ shal aзen horte speke,
An sone mai a word misstorte
Þar muþ shal speken aзen horte.
Ac noþeles, зut upe þon,
Her is to red wo hine kon,   680
Vor neuer nis wit so kene

f. 238 r/a So þane red him is a wene ;
Þanne erest kumed his зephede
Þone hit is alre mest on drede.
For Aluered seide of olde quide—   685
An зut hit nis of horte islide :
' Wone þe bale is alre hecst
Þonne is þe bote alre necst ; '
Vor wit west among his sore,
An for his sore hit is þe more.   690
Vorþi nis neuere mon redles
Ar his horte bo witles,
Ac зif þat he forlost his wit
Þonne is his redpurs al toslit :
Зif he ne kon his wit atholde   695
Ne uint he red in one uolde.
Vor Alu[er]id seide, þat wel kuþe—
Eure he spac mid soþe muþe :
' Wone þe bale is alre hecst
Þanne is þe bote alre nest.'   700
      Þe Niзtingale al hire hoзe
Mid rede hadde wel bitoзe ;
Among þe harde, among þe toзte,
Ful wel mid rede hire biþoзte,
An hadde andsuere gode ifunde   705
Among al hire harde stunde.
    ' Hule, þu axest me,' ho seide,
' Зif ich kon eni oþer dede
Bute singen in sum[er]e tide,

697 Aluerid] *C* aluid ; *J* alured: [*Str, Ga*]
707 Hule] *C* Nule, *in which rubric* N *is written over a badly-drawn
    directing letter* H; *J* [ ]le *without initial, presumably* [V]le: [*Ste*], We
709 sumere] *C and J* sume: [*Mä footnote*]

An bringe blisse for & wide.   710
Wi axestu of craftes mine ?
Betere is min on þan alle þine :
Betere is o song of mine muþe
Þan al þat eure þi kun kuþe.
An lust ! Ich telle þe wareuore :   715

f. 238 r/b

Wostu to wan man was ibore ?—
To þare blisse of houene riche,
Þar euer is song & murзþe iliche ;
Þider fundeþ eurich man
Þat eni þing of gode kan.   720
Vorþi me singþ in holi chirche
An clerkes ginneþ songes wirche,
Þat man iþenche bi þe songe
Wider he shal, & þar bon longe ;
Þat he þe murзþe ne uorзete,   725
Ac þarof þenche & biзete,
An nime зeme of chirche steuene
Hu murie is þe blisse of houene.
Clerkes, munekes & kanunes,
Þar boþ þos gode wicketunes,   730
Ariseþ up to midelniзte
An singeþ of þe houene liзte,
An prostes upe londe singeþ
Wane þe liзt of daie springeþ.
An ich hom helpe wat i mai :   735
Ich singe mid hom niзt & dai ;
An ho boþ alle for me þe gladdere
An to þe songe boþ þe raddere.
Ich warni men to here gode
Þat hi bon bliþe on hore mode,   740
An bidde þat hi moten iseche
Þan ilke song þat euer is eche.
Nu þu miзt, Hule, sitte & clinge ;
Heramong nis no chateringe :
Ich graunti þat we go to dome   745

713 of] *C* os; *J* of
745 we] *C* þe *or* we; *J* þu

Tofore þe sulfe þe Pope of Rome.
Ac abid, ȝete noþeles
Þu shalt ihere an oþer þes.
Ne shaltu, for Engelonde,

f. 238 v/a

At þisse worde me atstonde.   750
Wi atuitestu me mine unstrengþe
An mine ungrete & mine unlengþe,
An seist þat ich nam noȝt strong
Vor ich nam noþer gret ne long ?
Ac þu nost neuer wat þu menst,   755
Bute lese wordes þu me lenst :
For ich kan craft, & ich kan liste,
An þareuore ich am þus þriste.
Ich kan wit & song mani eine,
Ne triste ich to non oþer maine ;   760
Vor soþ hit is þat seide Alured :
" Ne mai no strengþe aȝen red."
Oft spet wel a lute liste
Þar muche strengþe sholde miste :
Mid lutle strengþe þurȝ ginne   765
Castel & burȝ me mai iwinne ;
Mid liste me mai walle[s] felle
An worpe of horsse kniȝtes snelle.
Vuel strengþe is lutel wurþ,
Ac wisdom [ne wrþ neuer vnwrþ.   770
Þu myht iseo þurh alle þing
Þat wisdom] naueþ non euening.
An hors is strengur þan a mon,
Ac, for hit non iwit ne kon,
Hit berþ on rugge grete semes,   775
An draȝþ biuore grete temes,
An þoleþ boþe ȝerd & spure,
An stont iteid at mulne dure :

746 þe sulfe þe Pope] J þe sulve pope
748 ihere an oþer þes] C wes (? or þes): J abyde on oþer bles, *with bles added by a different hand*
757 craft] C crast ; J craft   767 walles] C walle; J walles: *Str*
770-2 *Omission in C due to haplography; missing words supplied from* J: *Str*

An hit deþ þat mon hit hot,
An, forþan þat hit no wit not,   780
Ne mai his strenþe hit ishilde
Þat hit nabuзþ þe lutle childe.
Mon deþ mid strengþe & mid witte
Þat oþer þing nis non his fitte :
Þeз alle strengþe at one were   785
Monnes wit зet more were ;
Vorþe mon mid his crafte
Ouerkumeþ al orþliche shafte.
Also ich do mid mine one songe
Bet þan þu al þe зer longe :   790
Vor mine crafte men me luuieþ,
Vor þine strengþe men þe shunieþ.
Telstu bi me þe wurs forþan
Þat ich bute anne craft ne kan ?
Зif tueie men goþ to wraslinge   795
An eiþer oþer faste þringe,
An þe on can swenges suþe fele,
An kan his wrenches wel forhele,
An þe oþer ne can sweng but anne,
An þc is god wiþ eche manne,   800
An mid þon one leiþ to grunde
Anne after oþer a lutle stunde,
Wat þarf he recche of a mo swenge
Þone þe on him is swo genge ?
Þu seist þat þu canst fele wike.   805
Ac euer ich am þin unilike :
Do þine craftes alle togadere,
Зet is min on [on] horte betere.
Oft þan hundes foxes driueþ
Þe kat ful wei him sulue liueþ,   810
Þeз he ne kunne wrench bute anne ;
Þe fox so godne ne can nanne,
Þe[з] he kunne so uele wrenche

f. 238 v/b

805 Þu] *C and J* þe : *Mä*
808 min on on horte] *C* min on horte ; *J* myn on heorte
812 fox] *C and J* for : [*Ste*], *We*   813 Þeз] *C* þe ; *J* þey : *Mä*

Þat he wenþ eche hunde atprenche ;
Vor he can paþes riȝte & woȝe,   815
An he kan hongi bi þe boȝe,
An so forlost þe hund his fore,
An turnþ aȝen eft to þan more.
Þe uox kan crope bi þe heie,

f. 239 r/a   An turne ut from his forme weie,   820
An eft sone kume þarto.
Þonne is þe hundes smel fordo :
He not þurȝ þe imeinde smak
Weþer he shal auorþ þe abak.
Ȝif þe uox mist of al þis dwole,   825
At þan ende he cropþ to hole ;
Ac naþeles mid alle his wrenche
Ne kan he hine so biþenche—
Þeȝ he bo ȝep an suþe snel—
Þat he ne lost his rede uel.   830
Þe cat ne kan wrench bute anne,
Noþer bi dune ne bi uenne,
Bute he kan climbe suþe wel ;
Þarmid he wereþ his greie uel.
Also ich segge bi mi solue :   835
Betere is min on þan þine twelue.'
    ' Abid ! Abid ! ' þe Ule seide,
' Þu gest al to mid swikelede.
Alle þine wordes þu bileist
Þat hit þincþ soþ, al þat þu seist,   840
Alle þine wordes boþ isliked,
An so bisemed an biliked,
Þat alle þo þat hi auoþ,
Hi weneþ þat þu segge soþ.
Abid ! Abid ! me shal þe ȝene ;   845
Nu hit shal wrþe wel isene
Þat þu hauest muchel iloȝe,
Wone þi lesing boþ unwroȝe.
Þu seist þat þu singist mankunne,
& techest hom þat hi fundieþ honne   850

Vp to þe songe þat eure ilest.
Ac hit is alre wnder mest
Þat þu darst liȝe so opeliche.

f. 239 r/b
Wenest þu hi bringe so liȝtliche
To Godes riche al singinge ?   855
Nai, nai, hi shulle wel auinde
Þat hi mid longe wope mote
Of hore sunnen bidde bote,
Ar hi mote euer kume þare.
Ich rede þi þat men bo ȝare   860
An more wepe þane singe,
Þat fundeþ to þan houenkinge :
Vor nis no man witute sunne.
Vorþi he mot, ar he wende honne,
Mid teres an mid wope bete,   865
Þat him bo sur þat er was swete.
Þarto ich helpe—God hit wot !
Ne singe ih hom no foliot,
For al mi song is of longinge
An imend sumdel mid woninge,   870
Þat mon bi me hine biþenche,
Þat he groni for his unwrenche.
Mid mine songe ich hine pulte,
Þat he groni for his gulte.
Ȝif þu gest herof to disputinge,   875
Ich wepe bet þane þu singe :
Ȝif riȝt goþ forþ, & abak wrong,
Betere is mi wop þane þi song.
Þeȝ sume men bo þurȝut gode
An þurȝut clene on hore mode,   880
Hon longeþ honne noþeles :
Þat boþ her, wo is hom þes,
Vor, þeȝ hi bon hom solue iborȝe,
Hi ne soþ her nowiȝt bote sorwe ;
Vor oþer men hi wepeþ sore   885
An for hom biddeþ Cristes ore.
Ich helpe monne on eiþer halue,

855 singinge] J singinde   869 mi] C me ; J my: Mä

f. 239 v/a

Mi muþ haueþ tweire kunne salue :
Þan gode ich fulste to longinge,
Vor þan hin longeþ ich him singe ;   890
An þan sunfulle ich helpe alswo,
Vor ich him teche ware is wo.
ʒet ich þe ʒene in oþer wise :
Vor þane þu sittest on þine rise
Þu draʒst men to fleses luste,   895
Þat wlleþ þine songes luste ;
Al þu forlost þe murʒþe of houene,
For þarto neuestu none steuene.
Al þat þu singst is of golnesse,
For nis on þe non holinesse ;   900
Ne wened na man for þi pipinge
Þat eni preost in chircce singe.
ʒet i þe wulle an oder segge,
ʒif þu hit const ariht bilegge :
Wi nultu singe an oder þeode   905
Þar hit is muchele more neode ?
Þu neauer ne singst in Irlonde,
Ne þu ne cumest noʒt in Scotlonde.
Hwi nultu fare to Noreweie,
An singin men of Galeweie,   910
Þar beoð men þat lutel kunne
Of songe þat is bineoðe þe sunne ?
Wi nultu þare preoste singe
An teche of þire writelinge,
An wisi hom mid-þire steune   915
Hu engeles singeð ine heouene ?
Þu farest so doð an ydel wel
Þat springeþ bi burne þat is snel,
An let fordrue þe dune,
& floþ on idel þar adune.   920
Ac ich fare boþe norþ & soþ,

f. 239 v/b

In eauereuch londe ich am cuuþ :
East & west, feor & neor,

918 Þat . . . þat] *C* Þar . . . þar; *J* Þ' . . . þat; *Ga*
920 floþ] *C* floh; *J* flohþ; [*Mä, GS*]

F

I do wel faire mi meoster
An warni men mid mine bere,   925
Þat þi dweole song heo ne forlere.
Ich wisse men mid mine songe,
Þat hi ne sunegi nowiht longe ;
I bidde hom þat heo iswike,
Þat heom seolue ne biswike :   930
For betere is þat heo wepen here
Þan elleshwar to beon deoulene fere.'

   Þe Niȝtingale was igremet,
An ek heo was sumdel ofchamed,
For þe Hule hire atwiten hadde   935
In hwucche stude he sat an gradde,
Bihinde þe bure, among þe vvede,
Þar men goð to here neode ;
An sat sumdel & heo biþohte,
An wiste wel on hire þohte   940
Þe wraþþe binimeþ monnes red.
For hit seide þe King Alfred :
' Sel[d]e e[re]ndeð wel þe loþe,
An selde plaideð wel þe wroþe ; '
For wraþþe meinþ þe horte blod   945
Þat hit floweþ so wilde flod
An al þe heorte ouergeþ,
Þat heo naueþ no þing bute breþ,
An so forleost al hire liht
Þat heo ne siþ soð ne riht.   950
Þe Niȝtingale hi understod,
An ouergan lette hire mod.
He mihte bet speken a sele
Þan mid wraþþe wordes deale.
   ' Hule,' heo seide, ' lust nu hider !   955

f. 240 r/a
Þu schalt falle, þe wei is slider.
Þu seist ich fleo bihinde bure :
Hit is right, þe bur is ure.

---

927 mine] *altered from* min *by the same hand;* J myne
933 igremet] J agromed
943 Selde] C Sele; J Selde: [*Mä*]. erendeð] C endeð; J endeþ
955 Hule heo seide] C Þule heo seide; J Þe vle seyde

Þar lauerd liggeþ & lauedi
Ich schal heom singe & sitte bi. 960
Wenstu þat uise men forlete
For fule venne þe riȝtte strete,
Ne sunne þe later shine
Þeȝ hit bo ful ine nest þine ?
Sholde ich for one hole brede 965
Forlete mine riȝte stede,
Þat ich ne singe bi þe bedde
Þar louerd haueþ his loue ibedde ?
Hit is mi riȝt, hit is mi laȝe
Þat to þe hexst ich me draȝe. 970
Ac ȝet þu ȝelpst of þine songe
Þat þu canst ȝolle wroþe & stronge,
An seist þu uisest mankunne
Þat hi biwepen hore sunne.
Solde euch mon vvonie & grede 975
Riȝt suich hi weren unlede,
Solde hi ȝollen also þu dest,
Hi miȝte oferen here prost.
Man schal bo stille & noȝt grede ;
He mot biwepe his misdede, 980
Ac þar is Cristes heriinge,
Þar me shal grede & lude singe :
Nis noþer to lud ne to long
At riȝte time chirche song.
Þu ȝolst & wones, & ich singe, 985
Þi steuene is wop, & min skentinge.
Euer mote þu ȝolle & wepen
Þat þu þi lif mote forleten,
An ȝollen mote þu so heȝe
Þat ut berste bo þin eȝe ! 990
Weþer is betere of twere twom,
Þat mon bo bliþe oþer grom ?

f. 240 r/b

964 ine nest] *J* in neste
966 stede] *altered from* stude *by the same hand; J* stede
970 Þat . . . hexst] *C* Þar . . . herst; *J* Þat . . . hexste: *A*
978 prost] *C* brost; *J* preost: [*Mä*]
991 twere] *J* tweyre

So bo hit euer in unker siþe
Þat þu bo sori, & ich bliþe !
3ut þu aisheist wi ich ne fare   995
Into oþer londe & singe þare.
No !   Wat sholde ich among hom do,
Þar neuer blisse ne com to ?
Þat lond nis god, ne hit nis este,
Ac wildernisse hit is & weste :   1000
Knarres & cludes houentinge,
Snou & ha3el hom is genge ;
Þat lond is grislich & unuele.
Þe men boþ wilde & unisele,
Hi nabbeþ noþer griþ ne sibbe.   1005
Hi ne reccheþ hu hi libbe :
Hi eteþ fihs an flehs unsode
Suich wulues hit hadde tobrode,
Hi drinkeþ milc & wei þarto—
Hi nute elles wat hi do ;   1010
Hi nabbeþ noþ[er] win ne bor,
Ac libbeþ also wilde dor ;
Hi goþ biti3t mid ru3e uelle,
Ri3t suich hi comen ut of helle.
Þe3 eni god man to hom come—   1015
So wile dude sum from Rome—
For hom to lere gode þewes,
An for to leten hore unþewes,
He mi3te bet sitte stille,
Vor al his wile he sholde spille :   1020
He mi3te bet teche ane bore
To we3e boþe sheld & spere,
Þan me þat wilde folc ibringe
f. 240 v/a   Þat hi *me wolde* ihere singe.
Wat sol[d]ich þar mid mine songe ?   1025
Ne sunge ich hom neuer so longe
Mi song were ispild ech del ;
For hom ne mai halter ne bridel

1011 noþer] *C* noþ; *J* noht: *Mä*
1024 me wolde] *C* me segge wolde; *J* me wolde: *Str*
1025 soldich] *C* sol ich; *J* scholdich: *A*

Bringe vrom hore wode wise,
Ne mon mid stele ne mid ire.   1030
Ac war lond is boþe este & god,
An þar men habbeþ milde mod,
Ich noti mid hom mine þrote ;
Vor ich mai do þar gode note
An bringe hom loue tiþinge,   1035
Vor ich of chirche songe singe.
Hit was iseid in olde laȝe—
An ȝet ilast þilke soþsaȝe—
Þat man shal erien an sowe
Þar he wenþ after sum god mowe,   1040
For he is wod þat soweþ his sed
Þar neuer gras ne sprinþ ne bled.'
    Þe Hule was wroþ, to cheste rad
Mid þisse worde, hire eȝen abrad :
' Þu seist þu witest manne bures,   1045
Þar leues boþ & faire flores,
Þar two iloue in one bedde
Liggeþ biclop[t] & wel bihedde.
Enes þu sunge—ic wod wel ware—
Bi one bure, & woldest lere   1050
Þe lefdi to an uuel luue ;
An sunge boþe loȝe & buue,
An lerdest hi to don shome
An vnriȝt of hire licome.
Þe louerd þat sone underȝat ;   1055
Liim & grine & wel eiwat
Sette & lede þe for to lacche.
Þu come sone to þan hacche,
Þu were inume in one grine ;
Al hit aboȝte þine shine ;   1060
Þu naddest non oþer dom ne laȝe
Bute mid wilde horse were todraȝe.

f. 240 v/b

1029 wode] *C* wude; *J* wode: *Str*
1031 lond] *C* long; *J* lond: *Wr*
1048 biclopt] *C* biclop; *J* iclupt: *A*
1056 grine &] *C* grineþ; *J* grune &: *A*
1057 lede] *C* ledde; *J* leyde

Vonde ʒif þu miʒt eft misrede
Waþer þu wult, wif þe maide :
Þi song mai bo so longe genge   1065
Þat þu shalt wippen on a sprenge.'
    Þe Niʒtingale at þisse worde
Mid sworde an mid speres orde,
Ʒif ho mon were, wolde fiʒte ;
Ac þo ho, bet do ne miʒte   1070
Ho uaʒt mid hire wise tunge.
' Wel fiʒt þat wel specþ,' seiþ in þe songe.
Of hire tunge ho nom red ;
' Wel fiʒt þat wel specþ,' seide Alured.
    ' Wat ! seistu þis for mine shome ?   1075
Þe louerd hadde herof grame.
He was so gelus of his wiue
Þat he ne miʒte, for his liue,
Iso þat man wiþ hire speke,
Þat his horte nolde breke.   1080
He hire bileck in one bure,
Þat hire was boþe stronge & sure.
Ich hadde of hire milse an ore,
An sori was for hire sore,
An skente hi mid mine songe   1085
Al þat ich miʒte, raþe an longe.
Vorþan þe kniʒt was wiþ me wroþ,
Vor riʒte niþe ich was him loþ.
He dude me his oʒene shome,
Ac al him turnde it to grome.   1090
Þat underyat þe king Henri—
f. 241 r/a   Iesus his soule do merci !—
He let forbonne þene kniʒt,
Þat hadde idon so muchel unriʒt
Ine so gode kinges londe :   1095
Vor riʒte niþe & for fule onde
Let þane lutle fuʒel nime
An him fordeme lif an lime.
Hit was wrþsipe al mine kunne,

1070 miʒte] *altered from* micte *by the same hand;* J mihte

Forþon þe kniȝt forles his wunne   1100
An ȝaf for me an hundred punde ;
An mine briddes seten isunde,
An hadde soþþe blisse & hiȝte,
An were bliþe, & wel miȝte.
Vorþon ich was so wel awreke   1105
Euer eft ich darr þe bet speke :
Vor hit bitidde ene swo
Ich am þe bliþur euer mo.
Nu ich mai singe war ich wulle,
Ne dar me neuer eft mon agrulle.   1110
Ac þu eremi[n]g ! þu wrecche gost !
Þu ne canst finde, ne þu nost,
An holȝ stok þar þu þe miȝt hude,
Þat me ne twengeþ þine hude.
Vor children, gromes, heme & hine,   1115
Hi þencheþ alle of þire pine :
Ȝif hi muȝe iso þe sitte
Stones hi doþ in hore slitte,
An þe totorued & toheneþ,
An þine fule bon tosheneþ.   1120
Ȝif þu art iworpe oþer ishote
Þanne þu miȝt erest to note ;
Vor me þe hoþ in one rodde,
An þu, mid þine fule codde
An mid þine ateliche swore,   1125
Biwerest manne corn urom dore.
Nis noþer noȝt, þi lif ne þi blod,
Ac þu art shueles suþe god.
Þar nowe sedes boþ isowe,
Pinnuc, golfinc, rok, ne crowe   1130
Ne dar þar neuer cumen ihende
Ȝif þi buc hongeþ at þan ende ;
Þar tron shulle a ȝere blowe,
An ȝunge sedes springe & growe,

f. 241 r/b

1106 darr] C dart; J dar: A
1111 ereming] C eremig; J ermyng: We
1125 swore] C spore; J sweore: Ga

Ne dar no fuȝel parto uonge   1135
Ȝif þu art þarouer ihonge.
Þi lif is eure luþer & qued :
Þu nard noȝt bute ded.
Nu þu miȝt wite sikerliche
Þat þine leches boþ grisliche   1140
Þe wile þu art on lifdaȝe,
Vor wane þu hongest islaȝe
Ȝut hi boþ of þe ofdradde,
Þe fuȝeles þat þe er bigradde.
Mid riȝte men boþ wiþ þe wroþe,   1145
For þu singist euer of hore loþe :
Al þat þu singst, raþe oþer late,
Hit is euer of manne unwate ;
Wane þu hauest a niȝt igrad
Men boþ of þe wel sore ofdrad.   1150
Þu singst þar sum man shal be ded ;
Euer þu bodest sumne qued :
Þu singst aȝen eiȝte lure,
Oþer of summe frondes rure,
Oþer þu bodes huses brune,   1155
Oþer ferde of manne, oþer þoues rune,
Oþer þu bodest cualm of oreue,
Oþer þat londfolc wurþ idorue,
Oþer þat wif lost hire make,
f. 241 v/a   Oþer þu bodest cheste an sake.   1160
Euer þu singist of manne hareme,
Þurȝ þe hi boþ sori & areme ;
Þu ne singst neuer one siþe
Þat hit nis for sum unsiþe.
Heruore hit is þat me þe shuneþ   1165
An þe totorueþ & tobuneþ
Mid staue & stoone & turf & clute,
Þat þu ne miȝt no war atrute.
Dahet euer suich budel in tune
Þat euer bodeþ unwreste rune,   1170
An euer bringeþ vuele tiþinge,
An þat euer specþ of vuele þinge !

God Almiȝti wrþe him wroþ,
An al þat werieþ linnene cloþ ! '
   Þe Hule ne abot noȝt swiþ longe,   1175
Ah ȝef ondsware starke & stronge.
' Wat !' quaþ ho, ' hartu ihoded,
Oþer þu kursest al unihoded ?
For prestes wike, ich wat, þu dest ;
Ich not ȝef þu were ȝaure prest,   1180
Ich not ȝef þu canst masse singe :
Inoh þu canst of mansinge.
Ah hit is for þine alde niþe
Þat þu me akursedest oðer siðe.
Ah þarto is lihtlich ondsware :   1185
" Drah to þe ! " cwað þe cartare.
Wi attwitestu me mine insihte,
An min iwit, & mine miȝte ?
For ich am witi, ful iwis,
An wod al þat to kumen is :   1190
Ich wot of hunger, of hergonge,
Ich wot ȝef men schule libbe longe,
Ich wat ȝef wif luste hire make,
Ich wat þar schal beo niþ & wrake,
Ich wot hwo schal beon *an*honge   1195
Oþer elles fulne deþ afonge.
Ȝef men habbeþ bataile inume
Ich wat hwaþer schal beon ouerkume.
Ich wat ȝif cwalm scal comen on orfe,
An ȝif dor schul ligge *a*storue ;   1200
Ich wot ȝef treon schule blowe,
Ich wat ȝef cornes schule growe,
Ich wot ȝef huses schule berne,
Ich wot ȝef men schule eorne oþer erne,
Ich wot ȝef sea schal schipes drenche,   1205
Ich wot ȝef smiþes schal uuele clenche.
An ȝet ich con muchel more :
Ich con inoh in bokes lore,

f. 241 v/b

1175 swiþ] J swiþe
1195 anhonge] C & honge; J anhonge: [Ste], Wr
1200 astorue] C & storue; J astorue: Str

An eke ich can of þe goddspelle
More þan ich nule þe telle ;   1210
For ich at chirche come ilome
An muche leorni of wisdome.
Ich wat al of þe tacninge
An of oþer feole þinge.
Ʒef eni mon schal rem abide   1215
Al ich hit wot ear hit itide.
Ofte for mine muchele iwitte
Wel sorimod & worþ ich sitte.
Wan ich iseo þat sum wrechede
Is manne neh, innoh ich grede :   1220
Ich bidde þat men beon iwarre
An habbe gode reades ʒarre.
For Alfred seide a wis word—
Euch mon hit schulde legge on hord :
" Ʒef þu isihst [her] he beo icume   1225
His str[e]ncþe is him wel neh binume."
An grete duntes beoþ þe lasse

f. 242 r/a

Ʒef me ikepþ mid iwarnesse :
An flo schal toward misʒenge
Ʒef þu isihst hu fleo of strenge,   1230
For þu miʒt blenche vvel & fleo
Ʒif þu isihst heo to þe teo.
Þat eni man beo falle in odwite,
Wi schal he me his sor atwite ?
Þah ich iseo his harm biuore   1235
Ne comeþ hit noʒt of me þaruore.
Þah þu iseo þat sum blind mon,
Þat nanne rihtne wei ne con,

1218 worþ] J wroþ   1221 iwarre] C iwarte ; J warre : Ga
1222 ʒarre] C ʒarte ; J yare : Ga
1225 Between isihst and he a space of up to about ten letters has been left
     blank in C; J isyst . her . heo (i.e. with stops before and after her) :
     [Wr, We]
1226 strencþe] C strncþe ; J strengþe : Ga
1229 an flo] C an fleo ; J & fleo : [Ga], A
1233 Þat . . . odwite] J þauh . . . edwite
1235 Þah] altered from þat by the same hand ; J þauh
1236 þaruore] C þaruare ; J þarfore : Ga

To þare diche his dweole fulied,
An falleþ, and þarone sulied,   1240
Wenest þu, þah ich al iseo,
Þat hit for me þe raþere beo ?
Alswo hit fareþ bi mine witte :
Hwanne ich on mine bowe sitte
Ich wot & iseo swiþe brihte   1245
An summe men kumed harm þarrihte,
Schal he, þat þerof no þing not,
Hit wite me, for ich hit wot ?
Schal he his mishap wite me
For ich am wisure þane he ?   1250
Hwanne ich iseo þat sum wrechede
Is manne neh, inoh ich grede,
An bidde inoh þat hi heom schilde,
For toward heom is [harm vnmylde].
Ah þah ich grede lude an stille   1255
Al hit itid þurþ Godes wille.
Hwi wulleþ men of me hi mene,
Þah ich mid soþe heo awene ?
Þah ich hi warni al þat ȝer,
Nis heom þerfore harem no þe ner.   1260

f. 242 r/b

Ah ich heom singe, for ich wolde
Þat hi wel understonde schulde
Þat sum unselþe heom is ihende
Hwan ich min huing to heom sende.
Naueþ no man none sikerhede,   1265
Þat he ne mai wene & adrede
Þat sum unhwate neþ him beo,
Þah he ne conne hit iseo.
Forþi seide Alfred swiþe wel—
And his worde was goddspel—   1270
Þat euereuch man, þe bet him beo,
Eauer þe bet he hine beseo ;
Ne truste no mon to his weole

1254 harm vnmylde] *supplied from J; C has a blank after* is, *and a
later hand has added a cross in the margin:* Ste
1264 huing] *altered to* song *by a later hand; J* huyng

To swiþe, þah he habbe ueole :
" Nis nout so hot þat hit nacoleþ,   1275
Ne noȝt so hwit þat hit ne soleþ,
Ne noȝt so leof þat hit ne aloþeþ,
Ne noȝt so glad þat hit ne awroþeþ :
Ah eauere euh þing þat eche nis
Agon schal, & al þis worldes blis."   1280
Nu þu miȝt wite readliche
Þat eauere þu spekest gideliche,
For al þat þu me seist for schame,
Euer þe seolue hit turneþ to grome.
Go so hit go, at eche fenge   1285
Þu fallest mid þine ahene swenge :
Al þat þu seist for me to schende,
Hit is mi wurschipe at þan ende.
Bute þu wille bet aginne
Ne schaltu bute schame iwinne.'   1290
    Þe Niȝtingale sat & siȝte,
& hohful was, & ful wel miȝte,
For þe Hule swo ispeke hadde

f. 242 v/a An hire speche swo iladde,
Heo was hoþful & erede   1295
Hwat heo þarafter hire sede.
An neoþeles heo hire understod.
' Wat ! ' heo seide, ' Hule, artu wod ?
Þu ȝeolpest of seolliche wisdome ;
Þu nustest wanene he þe come,   1300
Bute hit of wicche crefte were.
Þarof þu, wrecche, moste þe skere,
Ȝif þu wult among manne boe,
Oþer þu most of londe fleo ;
For alle þeo þat þerof cuþe,   1305
Heo uere ifurn of prestes muþe
Amanset : swuch þu art ȝette,
Þu wiecche crafte neauer ne lete.
Ich þe seide nu lutel ere,

1275 nout] *with* t *added by the same hand;* J noht
1300 nustest] *altered from* miȝtest *by the same hand;* J nustest
1306 uere] *with* u *expuncted and* vv *in the margin in a later hand:* J weren

An þu askedest ȝef ich were,   1310
A bisemere, to preost ihoded :
Ah þe mansing is so ibroded,
Þah no preost a londe nere,
A wrecche neoþeles þu were,
For eauereuch chil þe cleopeþ fule,   1315
An euereuch man a wrecche hule.
Ich habbe iherd, & soþ hit is,
Þe mon mot beo wel storrewis
Þat wite innoþ of wucche þinge kume,
So þu seist þe is iwune :   1320
Hwat canstu, wrecche þing, of storre,
Bute þat þu bihaltst hi feorre ?
Alswo deþ mani dor & man
Þeo of swucche nawiht ne con.
On ape mai a boc bihalde,   1325
An leues wenden & eft folde,
Ah he ne con þe bet þaruore
Of clerkes lore, top ne more :
Þah þu iseo þe steorre alswa
Nartu þe wisure neauer þe mo.   1330
Ah ȝet þu, fule þing, me chist,
An wel grimliche me atwist
Þat ich singe bi manne huse
An teache wif breke spuse.
Þu liest iwis, þu fule þing,   1335
Þ[urh] me nas neauer ischend spusing.
Ah soþ hit is, ich singe & grede
Þar lauedies beoþ & faire maide,
& soþ hit is, of luue ich singe :
For god wif mai i spusing   1340

f. 242 v/b

1315 chil] *altered to* child *by a later hand; J* chid
1319 Þat wite innoþ] *C* An wite innoþ; *J* & wite inoh: *A.* kume]
      cancelled and rewritten in the margin in a later hand; J cume
1320 þe] *C* þ' (*i.e.* þat *or* þer); *J* þ': *A*
1321 Hwat] *with* w *formed out of a partially written* a; *J* Hwat
1322 bihaltst] *C and J* bihaitest: [*Mä 852 footnote, GS p. 91*]
1324 swucche] *C* hswucche; *J* suyche: *We*
1325 boc] *altered from* boe (? *by the same hand*); *J* bok
1336 Þurh] *C* Þ (*for* Þ'); *J* Þurh: *Str*

Bet luuien hire oӡene were
Þane awer hire copenere,
An maide mai luue cheose
Þat hire wurþschipe ne forleose,
An luuie mid rihte luue   1345
Þane þe schal beon hire buue.
Swiche luue ich itache & lere,
Þerof beoþ al mine ibere.
Þah sum wif beo of nesche mode—
For wummon beoþ of softe blode—   1350
Þat heo, *for* sume sottes lore
Þe ӡeorne bit & sikeþ sore,
Misrempe & misdo summe stunde,
Schal ich þaruore beon ibunde ?
Ӡif wimmen luuieþ unrede,   1355
Hwi [wi]tistu me hore misdede ?
Ӡef wimmon þencheþ luuie derne
Ne ne mai ich mine songes werne.
Wummon mai pleie under cloþe
Weþer heo wile, wel þe wroþe,   1360
& heo mai do bi mine songe

f. 243 r/a   Hwaþer heo wule, wel þe wronge ;
For nis a worlde þing so god
Þat ne mai do sum ungod
Ӡif me hit wule turne amis :   1365
*F*or gold & seoluer, god hit is,
An noþeles þarmid þu miӡt
Spusbruche buggen & unriӡt ;
Wepne beoþ gode griþ to halde,

1341 hire] *altered from* hite (*? by a contemporary hand*); *J* hire: [*Ste*].
    We
1342 Þane awer hire] *C* Þane awet hire; *J* þan on oþer hire: *We*
1351 for] *C* p' (*i.e.* par) *expuncted by a later hand which has added* for
    in the margin; *J* vor: *GS*
1353 Misrempe . . . summe] *C* Mistempe . . . sumne, *in the margin*
    steppe *in a later hand*; *J* Misnyme . . . sume: *Ga*
1356 Hwi witistu] *C* Hwitistu; *J* Witestu: *GS*
1360 Weþer] *corrected from* Weþet *in a contemporary hand*; *J* Hweþer:
    We
1366 For] *C* Eor *expuncted, and* euere *in the margin in a later hand*; *J*
    Vor: *Ga*

Ah neoþeles þarmide beoþ men acwalde   1370
Aȝeines riht *an* fale londe
Þar þeoues hi bereð an honde.

Alswa hit is bi mine songe :
Þah h*e* beo god, me hine mai misfonge
An drahe hine to sothede   1375
An to oþre uuele dede.

Ah schaltu, wrecch, luue tele ?
Bo wuch ho bo, vich luue is fele
Bitweone wepmon & wimmane ;
Ah ȝef heo is atbroide, þenne   1380
He is unfele & forbrode.

Wroþ wurþe heom þe holi rode,
Þe rihte ikunde swo forbreideþ !
W*u*nder hit is þat heo nawedeþ—
An swo heo doþ, for heo beoþ wode   1385
Þe bute nest goþ to brode.

Wummon is of nesche flesche,
An flesches lustes is strong to cwesse ;
Nis wunder nan þah he abide,
For flesches lustes hi makeþ slide :   1390
Ne beoþ heo noþt alle forlore
Þat stumpeþ at þe flesches more,
For moni wummon haueþ misdo
Þat aris[t] op of þe slo.

Ne beoþ noþt ones alle sunne,   1395
Forþan hi beoþ tweire kunne :
Sun arist of þe flesches luste,
An sum of þe gostes custe.

Þar flesch draheþ men to drunnesse
& to wrouehede & to golnesse,   1400
Þe gost misdeþ þurch niþe an onde,
& seoþþe mid murhþe of monne shonde,

f. 243 r/b

1371 an fale] *C* & fale; *J* of alle: [*Wr*], *We*
1374 he] *C and J* heo: *Str*
1384 Wunder] *C* Winder; *J* Wunder: *We*
1389 Nis] *corrected from* His; *J* Nis
1394 arist] *C* aris; *J* aryst: *We*
1400 wrouehede] *the reading* wronchede *is impossible, since the fifth
    letter is clearly* e (*with a hairline*), *not* c; *J* wlonkhede

An ȝeoneþ after more & more
An lutel rehþ of milce & ore,
An stiȝþ on heþ þurþ modinesse   1405
An ouerhoheð þanne lasse.
Sei me sooþ, ȝef þu hit wost,
Hweþer deþ vvurse, flesch þe gost ?
Þu miȝt segge, ȝef þu wult,
Þat lasse is þe flesches gult :   1410
Moni man is of his flesche clene
Þat is mid mode deouel imene.
Ne schal non mon vvimman bigrede,
An flesches lustes hire upbreide ;
Swuch he may telen of golnesse   1415
Þat sunegeþ wurse i modinesse.
Ȝet ȝif ich schulde a luue bringe
Wif oþer maide hwanne ich singe,
Ich wolde wiþ þe maide holde,
Ȝif þu hit const ariht atholde.   1420
Lust *nu* ! Ich segge þe hwaruore
Vp to þe toppe from þe more :
Ȝef maide luueþ dernliche
Heo stumpeþ & falþ icundeliche ;
For þah heo sum hwile pleie   1425
Heo nis nout feor ut of þe weie ;
Heo mai hire guld atwende
A rihte weie þurþ chirche bende,
An mai eft habbe to make

f. 243 v/a   Hire leofmon wiþute sake,   1430
An go to him bi daies lihte
Þat er stal to bi þeostre nihte.
An ȝunling not hwat swuch þing is,
His ȝunge blod hit draȝeþ amis,
An sum sot mon hit tihþ þarto   1435
Mid alle þan þat he mai do :

1407 me sooþ] C messoþ *altered from* mesooþ *by the same hand; J*
me soþ*: Wr*
1415 he may telen] C he may tellen, *with* y *and first* l *on erasures; J*
heo mahte beo*: [Str], A*
1417 Ȝet] C Bet; J Hwet*: A*   1421 nu] C un; J nv: GS

He comeþ & fareþ, & beod & bid,
An heo bistant & ouersid,
An hi sehþ ilome & longe.
Hwat mai þat chil þah hit misfonge ?　　　1440
Hit nuste neauer hwat hit was,
Forþi hit þohte fondi þas,
An wite iwis hwuch beo þe gome
Þat of so wilde makeþ tame.
Ne mai ich for reoþe lete,　　　　　　1445
Wanne ich iseo þe tohte ilete
Þe luue bring[þ] on þe ʒunglinge,
Þat ich of murʒþe him ne singe.
Ich teache heom bi mine songe
Þat swucch luue ne lest noʒt longe ;　　1450
For mi song lutle hwile ilest,
An luue ne deþ noʒt bute rest
On swuch childre, & sone ageþ,
An falþ adun þe hote breþ.
Ich singe mid heom one þroʒe,　　　　1455
Biginne on heh & endi laʒe,
An lete mine songes falle
An lutle wile adun mid alle.
Þat maide wot, hwanne ich swike,
Þat luue is mine songes iliche :　　　　1460
For hit nis bute a lutel breþ
Þat sone kumeþ & sone geþ.
Þat child bi me hit understond,
f. 243 v/b　　An his unred to red vvend,
An iseʒþ wel bi mine songe　　　　　1465
Þat dusi luue ne last noʒt longe.
Ah wel ich wule þat þu hit wite :
Loþ me beoþ wiues utschute ;
Ah wif mai of me nime ʒeme,

1437 & beod & bid] J and beod abid
1438 J & he bistarte an oþer sid
1439 An hi sehþ] C An bi sehþ; J & bi sekþ
1447 bringþ] C and J bring: Str　　1448 of] C os; J of
1449 teache] C reache altered from dreache altered from treache; J
　　theche: [Str], A　　1457 mine] C mines; J mine: Str
1469 wif mai of me] C ʒif mai of of me; J wif may of me: We

G

Ich ne singe naþt hwan ich teme.   1470
An wif ah lete soƚtes lore,
Þah spusingbendes þuncheþ sore.
Wundere me þungþ wel starc & stor,
Hu eni mon so eauar for,
Þat e his heorte miȝte driue   1475
[T]o do hit to oþers mannes wiue.
For oþer hit is of twam þinge,
Ne mai þat þridde no man bringe :
Oþar þe lauerd is wel aht,
Oþer aswunde & nis naht.   1480
Ȝef he is wurþful & aht man,
Nele no man þat wisdon can
Hure of is wiue do him schame,
For he mai him adrede grame,
An þat he forleose þat þer hongeþ,   1485
Þat him eft þarto noȝt ne longeþ ;
An þah he þat noȝt ne adrede,
Hit is unriȝt & gret sothede
[T]o misdon one gode manne,
An his ibedde from him spanne.   1490
Ȝef hire lauerd is forwurde,
An unorne at bedde & at borde,
Hu miȝte þar beo eni luue
Wanne a swuch cheorles buc hire ley buue?
Hu mai þar eni luue beo   1495
Þar swuch man gropeþ hire þeo ?
Herbi þu miȝt wel understonde
f. 244 r/a   Þat on his aren, þat oþer schonde,
To stele to oþres mannes bedde.
For ȝif aht man is hire bedde   1500
Þu miȝt wene þat þe mistide,
Wanne þu list bi hire side,
An ȝef þe lauerd is a wercche,
Hwuch este miȝtistu þar *uecche* ?

1471 soƚtes] *C* sortes; *J* sottes: *We*   1476 To] *C* An *o*; *J* To: *Str*
1489 To] *C* An *o*; *J* To: *Str*   1494 ley] *C* ley *or* leþ; *J* lay
1498 *J* Þat on is at þen oþres schonde
1504 uecche] *C* necche; *J* vecche: *GS*

3if þu biþenchest hwo hire ofligge   1505
Þu mi3t mid wlate þe este bugge.
Ich not hu mai eni freoman
For hire sechen after þan ;
3ef he biþencþ bi hwan he lai
Al mai þe luue gan awai.'   1510
   Þe Hule was glad of swuche tale ;
Heo þo3te þatte Nihtegale,
Þah heo wel speke atte frume,
Hadde at þen ende misnume,
An seide, ' *Nu* ich habbe ifunde   1515
Þat maidenes beoþ of þine imunde :
Mid heom þu holdest, & heom biwerest,
An ouerswiþe þu hi herest.
Þe lauedies beoþ to me iwend,
To me heo hire mode send.   1520
For hit itit ofte & ilome
Þat wif & were beoþ unisome,
& þerfore þe were gulte,
Þat leof is over wummon to pulte,
An speneþ on þare al þat he haueþ,   1525
An siueþ þare þat no riht naueþ,
An haueþ attom his ri3te spuse,
Wowes weste & lere huse,
Wel þunne isch[r]ud & iued wroþe,
An let heo bute mete & cloþe.   1530
Wan he comeþ ham eft to his wiue
Ne dar heo no3t a word ischire ;
He chid & gred swuch he beo wod,
An ne bringþ hom non oþer god.
Al þat heo deþ him is unwille,   1535
Al þat heo spekeþ, hit is him ille,
An oft, hwan heo no3t ne misdeþ,
Heo haueþ þe fust in hire teþ.

f. 244 r/b

1509 biþencþ] *C* biþeneþ ; *J* biþenkþ : [*We*], *GS*
1515 Nu] *C* un ; *J* nv   1524 over] *J* oþer
1528 &] *C* l' ; *J* and : [*We*], *GS*
1529 ischrud] *C* ischud ; *J* isrud : *Ga*
1534 hom] *C* heom ; *J* hom : *Str*

Nis nan mon þat ne mai ibringe
His wif amis mid swucche þinge ;   1540
Me hire mai so ofte misbeode
Þat heo do wule hire ahene neode.
La, Godd hit wot ! heo nah iweld,
Þa[h] heo hine makie kukeweld.
For hit itit lome & ofte   1545
Þat his wif is wel nesche & softe,
Of faire bleo & wel idiht :
Wi ! hit is þe more unriht
Þat he his luue spene on þare
Þat nis wurþ one of hire heare.   1550
An swucche men beoþ wel manifolde
Þat wif ne kunne noþt ariȝt holde :
Ne mot non mon wiþ hire speke ;
He ueneð heo wule anon tobreke
Hure spusing, ȝef heo lokeþ   1555
Oþer wiþ manne faire spekeþ.
He hire biluþ mid keie & loke :
Þarþurh is spusing ofte tobroke,
For ȝef heo is þarto ibroht
He deþ þat heo nadde ear iþoht.   1560
Dahet þat to swuþe hit bispeke,
Þah swucche wiues *hi* awreke !
Herof þe lauedies to me meneþ
An wel sore me ahweneþ ;
Wel neh min heorte wule tochine   1565

f. 244 v/a   Hwon ich biholde hire pine.
Mid heom ich wepe swiþe sore,
An for heom bidde Cristis ore,
Þat þe lauedi sone aredde
An hire sende betere ibedde.   1570
An oþer þing ich mai þe telle
Þat þu ne schald, for þine felle,
Ondswere none þarto finde ;
Al þi sputing schal aswinde :

1539 Nis] *C* Wis; *J* Nis: *Ga*   1544 Þah] *C* Þa; *J* Þah: *Str*
1562 hi] *C* hire; *J* heom: *GS*   1567 swiþe] *C* swise; *J* swiþe: *Str*

Moni chapmon & moni cniht   1575
Luueþ & hald his wif ariht,
An swa deþ moni bondeman.
Þat gode wif deþ after þan,
An serueþ him to bedde & to borde
Mid faire dede & faire worde,   1580
An ӡeorne fondeþ hu heo muhe
Do þing þat him beo iduӡe.
Þe lauerd into þare þeode
Fareþ ut, on þare beire nede,
An is þat gode wif unbliþe   1585
For hire lauerdes houdsiþe,
An sit & sihð wel sore oflonged,
An hire sore an horte ongred
Al for hire louerdes sake
Haueþ daies kare & niӡtes wake,   1590
An swuþe longe hire is þe hwile,
An e[c]h steape hire þunþ a mile.
Hwanne oþre slepeþ hire abute
Ich one lust þar wiðþute,
An wot of hire sore mode,   1595
An singe a niӡt for hire gode :
An mine gode song, for hire þinge,
Ich turne sundel to murni[n]ge.
Of hure seorhe ich bere sume,
f. 244 v/b   Forþan ich am hire wel welcume : 1600
Ich hire helpe hwat i mai,
For hoӡeþ þane rehte wai.
Ah þu me hauest sore igramed
Þat min heorte is wel neh alamed,
Þat ich mai unneaþe speke ;   1605
Ah ӡet ich wule forþure reke.
Þu seist þat ich am manne loð,
An euereuch man is wið me wroð,
An me mid stone & lugge þreteþ,

1576 hald his] *C* hlad hif; *J* halt his: [*We*]
1586 houdsiþe] *J* houþsyþe   1592 ech] *C* ek; *J* vych: *Ga*
1598 murninge] *C* murnige; *J* murnynge: *Wr*   1602 hoӡeþ] *J* howeþ
1607 loð] *C* wrað *altered to* loð, *but* w *has not been cancelled; J* loþ: *A*

An me tobusteþ & tobeteþ ;   1610
An hwanne heo habeþ me ofslahe
Heo hongeþ me on heore hahe,
Þar ich aschewele pie an crowe
Fron þan þe þar is isowe.
Þah hit beo soþ, ich do heom god   1615
An for heom ich chadde mi blod.
Ich do heom god mid mine deaþe :
Waruore þe is wel unneaþe,
For þah þu ligge dead & clinge
Þi deþ nis naþt to none þinge.   1620
Ich not neauer to hwan. þu miȝt,
For þu nart bute a wrecche wiȝt ;
Ah þah mi lif me beo atschote,
Þe ȝet ich mai do gode note :
Me mai up one smale sticke   1625
Me sette a wude ine þe þicke,
An swa mai mon tolli him to
Lutle briddes & iuo,
An swa me mai mid me biȝete
Wel gode brede to his mete.   1630
Ah þu neure mon to gode
Liues ne deaþes stal ne stode :
Ich not to hwan þu bretst þi brod,
Liues ne deaþes ne deþ hit god.'
                Þe Nihtegale ih[e]rde þis,   1635
An hupte uppon on blowe ris,
An herre sat þan heo dude ear.
' Hule,' heo seide, ' beo nu wear !
Nulle ich wiþ þe plaidi na more,
For her þe mist þi rihte lore :   1640
Þu ȝulpest þat þu art manne loþ
An euereuch wiht is wið þe worþ ;
An mid ȝulinge & mid igrede
Þu wanst wel þat þu art unlede.

f. 245 r/a (at line 1634)

1618 Waruore] J þaruore. unneaþe] C inmeaþe ; J unmeþe : GS
1633 bretst þi brod] C breist þi brod ; J breist þi word : [Str, GS p. 93]
1635 iherde] C ihrde ; J iherde : Wr
1641 ȝulpest] first downstroke of u altered from e ; J yelpes

Þu seist þat gromes þe ifoð 1645
An heie on rodde þe anhoð,
An þe totwichet & toschakeð,
An summe of þu schawles makeð.
Me puncþ þat þu forleost þat game :
Þu ȝulpest of þire oȝe schame ; 1650
Me puncþ þat þu me gest an honde :
Þu ȝulpest of þire oȝene schonde.'
Þo heo hadde þeos word icwede
Heo sat in one faire stude,
An þarafter hire steuene dihte 1655
An song so schille & so brihte
Þat feor & ner me hit iherde.
Þaruore anan to hire cherde
Þrusche & þrostle & wudewale,
An fuheles boþe grete & smale ; 1660
Forþan heom þuhte þat heo hadde
Þe Houle ouercome, uorþan heo gradde
An sungen alswa uale wise ;
An blisse was among þe rise,
Riȝt swa me gred þe manne a schame 1665
Þat taueleþ & forleost þat gome.
    Þeos Hule, þo heo þis iherde,
f. 245 r/b ' Hauestu,' heo seide, ' ibanned ferde,
An wultu, wreche, wið me fiȝte ?
Nai, nai ! nauestu none miȝte ! 1670
Hwat gredeþ þeo þat hider come ?
Me puncþ þu ledest ferde to me.
Ȝe schule wite, ar ȝe fleo heonne,
Hwuch is þe strenþe of mine kunne,
For þeo þe haueþ bile ihoked 1675
An cliures charpe & wel icroked,
Alle heo beoþ of mine kunrede,
An walde come ȝif ich bede.

1649 puncþ] C þunch; J þinkþ: Str. þu] C þir; J þu: GS
1651 puncþ] C þunch; J þinkþ: Str
1652 schonde] C scho'me ; J schonde: Ga
1670 Nai nai] altered from Na nai by the same hand; J Na nay. none]
    altered from no by the same hand; J none
1672 puncþ] altered from punch by the same hand; J þinkþ

Þe seolfe coc, þat wel can fiȝte,
He mot mid me holde mid riȝte,   1680
For boþe we habbeþ steuene briȝte,
An sitteþ under weolkne bi niȝte.
Schille ich an utest uppen ow grede,
Ich schal swo stronge ferde lede
Þat ower prude schal aualle.   1685
A tort ne ȝiue ich for ow alle !
Ne schal, ar hit beo fulliche eue,
A wreche feþer on ow bileaue.
Ah hit was unker uoreward,
Þo we come hiderward,   1690
Þat we þarto holde scholde
Þar riht dom us ȝiue wolde.
Wultu nu breke foreward ?
Ich wene dom þe þing[þ] to hard ;
For þu ne darst domes abide,   1695
Þu wult nu, wreche, fiȝte & chide.
Ȝet ich ow alle wolde rede,
Ar ich utheste uppon ow grede,
Þat ower fihtlac leteþ beo,
An ginneþ raþe awei fleo ;   1700
For bi þe cliures þat ich bere,
f. 245 v/a   Ȝef ȝe abideþ mine here,
Ȝe schule an oþer wise singe
An acursi alle fiȝtinge ;
Vor nis of ow non so kene   1705
Þat durre abide mine onsene.'
Þeos Hule spac wel baldeliche,
For þah heo nadde swo hwatliche
Ifare after hire here,
Heo walde neoþeles ȝefe answere   1710
Þe Niȝtegale mid swucche worde.

1681 habbeþ] C hableþ; J habbe: GS
1682 weolkne] C weoline; J welkne: [GS]
1685 ower prude] C ower proude; J oure prude: A
1694 þingþ] C þing; J þinkþ: Ga   1697 Ȝet] C Ȝot; J Yet: Str
1698 Ar ich] C Ariht; J Ar ich: [We], GS
1711 C and J begin a new paragraph here, presumably in error for
     1717: GS

For moni man mid speres orde
Haueþ lutle strencþe, & mid his chelde,
Ah neoþeles in one felde
Þurh belde worde an mid ilete   1715
Deþ his iuo for arehþe swete.

　　Þe Wranne, for heo cuþe singe,
Þar com in þare moreȝen[i]nge
To helpe þare Niȝtegale ;
For þah heo hadde steuene smale   1720
Heo hadde gode þorte & schille,
An fale manne song a wille.
Þe Wranne was wel wis iholde,
For þeȝ heo nere ibred a wolde,
Ho was itoȝen among mankenne   1725
An hire wisdom brohte þenne.
Heo miȝte speke hwar heo walde,
Touore þe king þah heo scholde.
' Lusteþ,' heo cwaþ, ' lateþ me speke !
Hwat ! wulle ȝe þis pes tobreke,   1730
An do þan [kinge] swuch schame ?
Ȝe ! nis he nouþer ded ne lame.
Hunke schal itide harm & schonde
Ȝef ȝe doþ griþbruche on his londe.
Lateþ beo, & beoþ isome,   1735
An fareþ riht to ower dome,
An lateþ dom þis plaid tobreke,
Alswo hit was erur bispeke.'
　　' Ich an wel,' cwað þe Niȝtegale,
' Ah, Wranne, naþt for þire tale,   1740
Ah do for mire lahfulnesse :
Ich nolde þat unrihtfulnesse
Me at þen ende ouerkome.
Ich nam ofdrad of none dome.

f. 245 v/b (left margin, beside line 1736)

1717 *See* 1711 *footnote*
1718 moreȝeninge] *C* moreȝennge ; *J* moreweninge: *Str*
1724 *In C this line is displaced and follows line* 1735 *at the foot of fol.*
　　245 v/a; *in J the arrangement of the lines is correct.* þeȝ] *C* þeg ;
　　J þeih
1725 mankenne] *C* mannenne ; *J* mankunne: *Mo*
1731 do þan kinge swuch] *C* do þanne swuch ; *J* do þanne such: *Str*

Bihote ich habbe, soþ hit is,   1745
Þat Maister Nichole, þat is wis,
Bituxen vs deme schulde,
An ȝet ich wene þat he wule.
Ah war mihte we hine finde ? '
Þe Wranne sat in ore linde ;   1750
' Hwat ! nuste ȝe,' cwaþ heo, ' his hom ?
He wuneþ at Porteshom,
At one tune ine Dorsete,
Bi þare see in ore utlete.
Þar he demeþ manie riȝte dom,   1755
An diht & writ mani wisdom,
An þurh his muþe & þurh his honde
Hit is þe betere into Scotlonde.
To seche hine is lihtlich þing,
He naueþ bute one woning.   1760
Þat his bischopen muchel schame,
An alle þan þat of his nome
Habbeþ ihert, & of his dede.
Hwi nulleþ hi nimen heom to rede
Þat he were mid heom ilome,   1765
For teche heom of his wisdome,
An ȝiue him rente a uale stude
Þat he miȝte heom ilome be mide ? '
    ' Certes,' cwaþ þe Hule, ' þat is soð,

f. 246 r/a   Þeos riche men wel muche misdoð   1770
Þat leteþ þane gode mon,
Þat of so feole þinge con,
An ȝiueþ rente wel misliche,
An of him leteþ wel lihtliche ;
Wið heore cunne heo beoþ mildre   1775
An ȝeueþ rente litle childre :
Swo heore wit hi demþ a dwole,
Þat euer abid Maistre Nichole.
Ah ute we þah to him fare,

1748 ȝet] C ȝef; J yet: [Str], We
1751 nuste ȝe] C miȝte ȝe or nuȝte ȝe; J mihte yet (with y altered from h): Ga
1754 þare] C þar' (i.e. þarer); J þare: GS

For þar is unker dom al ȝare.'   1780
   ' Do we,' þe Niȝtegale seide ;
' Ah wa schal unker speche rede,
An telle touore unker deme ? '
   ' Þarof ich schal þe wel icweme,'
Cwaþ þe Houle, ' for al, ende of orde,   1785
Telle ich con, word after worde.
An ȝef þe þincþ þat ich misrempe
Þu stond aȝein & do me crempe.'
Mid þisse worde forþ hi ferden,
Al bute here & bute uerde,   1790
To Portesham þat heo bicome.
Ah hu heo spedde of heore dome
Ne can ich eu na more telle.
Her nis na more of þis spelle.

Explicit

1793 can] *C* chan; *J* can: *Ga*
Explicit *is supplied from J*

NOTES

NOTES

(A list of abbreviations is given on p. 1)

In compiling these Notes it has been assumed that the reader will use them in conjunction with the Glossary.

1. **sumere dale,** a summer-valley, i.e. perhaps ' a valley with a sunny or southerly aspect ', or simply ' a valley in summer ', providing the kind of seasonal reference common at the beginning of poems [cf. Helen E. Sandison, *The ' Chanson d'aventure ' in Middle English*, Bryn Mawr College Monographs No. 12 (1913), pp. 26f].

An attempt has been made to derive *sumere* from OE *sum* ' a certain '. This involves three difficulties: (*a*) the word is not found together with *one* (i.e. OE *ān* and its derivatives); (*b*) *dale* is historically neuter (<OE *dæl, dalu*), whereas *sumere* is dat. and prepos. fem.; (*c*) granted a fem. *dale* (there are rare cases of ME words with gender other than that of their OE etymons) we should expect the termination *-re* with *one* (i.e. *ore*) rather than with *sum*. [Cf. C. L. Wrenn, Bib. 41.]

2. **hale.** The meaning is discussed by A. H. Smith, s. *halh*, who cites the OE gloss (Wright-Wülcker 326, 9), which has *heal*, with *hyrne* (cf. *hurne*, O&N, 14) as an alternative, glossing Latin *angulus* 'angle, corner '.

9f. On the rhyme see 1467f, note. The *u* of **custe** is from OE *y*, that of **wuste** is an OE *u* [cf. A. Gabrielson, *The Influence of* W- *in OE as seen in the ME Dialects* (1912), p. 114 (§ 203)]. **hi.** Probably the SE fem. sg. [see S. T. R. O. d'Ardenne, Bib. 50]; cf. 185 where the construction is the same, and where *hi* must be nom. sg. fem. (and cf. 304–8, note, and the emendation at 1439). The use of grammatical gender may offer some difficulty in translation. The words *owl* and *nightingale* are historically fem., but the word *falcon* is masc. historically. Grammatical gender is used without regard to sex, so that at times (e.g. 101ff) there is incongruity in translation if the gender is kept.

13f. **speche.** For the meaning see Introduction, p. 28. J's *þo speke* (' then to speak ') does not provide a satisfactory rhyme, either with C's **breche** or J's *beche*. C. T. Onions [in *A grammatical miscellany offered to Otto Jespersen*, edited by N. Bøgholm, Aage Brusendorff and C. A. Bodelsen (1930), pp. 105–8] has adduced the name *Brechyn-hurne* (probably an error for *Brecheshurne*) in the *Cartulary of Eynsham*. The C reading is thus confirmed in collocation with *hurne*. The word is to be derived from OE *brēc* [q.v. in A .H. Smith], *brǣc* ' land broken up for cultivation ', as had been suggested by some of the earlier editors.

Others had sought to defend J's *beche* as the original reading, deriving it from, either OE *bece* [q.v. in A. H. Smith] ' a valley ', or OE *bēce* ' a beech-tree '. The former is preferable in meaning, the latter would provide a more satisfactory rhyme.

17. **uaste.** As a description of the Nightingale's hedge J's *vaste* ' impenetrable ' is preferable in meaning to C's *waste* ' solitary, deserted '.

20. a uele cunne wise. *uele* may be regarded, either as an adjective qualifying *cunne* (pl. prepos. case after the prep. *a*), 'many kinds'; or (like *fela* in OE) *uele* may be regarded as governing *cunne*, which would then be gen. pl., 'many of kinds '. In either case *wise* is gen. dependent on *cunne*. Translate, ' in many kinds of song '.

21f. þe dreim . . . he. The pronoun repeats the subject. Translate, ' The sound seemed rather to be that of a harp or fife '. **þan he nere,** 'than otherwise'.

26. tide. For the canonical hours cf. 323–8.

31. Translate, ' It seemed to her [quite] foul regarding the Owl ' [Kenyon, Bib. 29] ; or, less literally, ' To her everything about the Owl seemed nasty.'

37. falt mi tonge. The subject here follows the verb for the sake of the rhyme. The phrase is well established in ME (and early MnE) [cf. *MED*, s. *folden*, v. (2), 2(b), where it is given the meaning ' speech fails '].

52. Literally, ' May it so befall that I might ! ' or, more freely, ' If only I had a chance to do so ! '

54. wise. *w* often stands for *wu*, e.g. in *wnder* 852, *wnest* 589, *wrste* 121, and the common *wrþ(e*, but *w* cannot properly stand for *wi*. Cf. *w[i]te* 440. Both meanings, ' manner ' and ' tune ', fit the context, but the latter is perhaps to be preferred.

63f. tukest . . . ouer smale fuȝele. (1) The v. *tuke* normally takes a direct object [see *NED*, s.v. *tuck*, v.¹]. If it is transitive two readings are possible: either, (*a*) *ouer-smale*, a compound adj., ' exceedingly small ' (thus Grattan), or, (*b*) in both MSS *ouer* is emended to *oþer*, ' you maltreat other little birds ' (thus Hall). (2) If the normal construction is ignored, it might be possible to take *ouer* to be a prep.; a unique intr. use of the v. *tuck* is assumed here by *NED*. The meaning would be, ' you tousle over little birds ', or, more freely, avoiding the construction, ' you tousle little birds all over.' This is the interpretation of the earlier editions, adopted in the present edition as perhaps the least objectionable. Cf. 83 note. (3) By taking **miȝt ouer** to mean ' you have power over ' [a suggestion made to me by Mr R. W. Burchfield of Oxford with reference to *Ormulum* 8043f, for which see *NED*, s. *may*, v., B. I. 1], we may read : *& þu tukest vvroþe & vuele, vvhar þu miȝt over smale fuȝele*, ' And you torment angrily and cruelly wherever you have power over little birds.' The objection to this reading is that here, once again, we should expect an object for *tukest* [but cf. 274, note]. **vuele/fuȝele.** For the rhyme see 277f note.

65–8. Cf. 279f. See Introduction, p. 33. Bruce Dickins [Bib. 37] refers to a Norwich misericord [reproduced in F. Bond, *Woodcarvings in English Churches* (1910), p. 47] as an illustration of the mobbing of owls as a theme in medieval English art. A number of representations are to be found also on roof-bosses. [For an illustration of one of them, in Sherborne Abbey, see C. J. P. Cave, *Roof Bosses in Medieval Churches*, 1948, No. 206 (and cf. p. 73).] **kunne/honne.** On the rhyme see 1725f, note.

72. in monie volde. Grattan (p. 85) translates, ' to a high degree ', or ' a thousand times ', saying, ' There seems to be no evidence for the translation " in many respects " ' adopted by the editors. But cf. *MED, s. felefold*, adv.

73. Hinckley [Bib. 42] suggests that better sense is obtained by transposing **bodi** and **swore**.

78. **mist.** This may be a genuine form derived, with loss of ʒ, from *miʒst* (cf. 642 and note). The form *miʒst* itself is, however, so exceptional that it seems more plausible to account for *mist* by assuming substitution of *s* for ʒ [cf. 242, note and 1751, note]. *miʒt* is the regular form in this part of the MS.

82. **on of.** Dickins and Wilson take this to mean ' all there is to ', and so translate attractively, ' And that is all there is in your song.' No parallel is adduced by them for this idiom, and the more literal ' one of ' also gives sense.

83. **þretest to.** The construction is unusual ; *þrete* is normally transitive. (For a similarly unusual construction cf. 63f, note.)

85. ' " It would be more natural to you in respect of a frog," i.e. " A frog would suit you better." *to one frogge* is the virtual object of *were*. The same construction is implied in *Ov nas neuer icunde parto*, (114) ' (Hall).

86. **cogge.** For the meaning ' a cog wheel ' see A. H. Smith, s.v. Under the wheel of a mill appears to have been traditionally regarded as the habitation of a frog. It is so in a fable of Marie de France (Warnke, No. III). [Cf. Hinckley, Bib. 39, and Introduction, p. 32.]

94. Literally, ' You nurture in them a very foul progeny ', i.e. ' When you feed them you feed very foul offspring.'

99f. A proverb common in Latin, English, French, and many other languages. It occurs in the context of the fable of The Owl and the Falcon in the Latin translation of Nicholas Bozon's version of the fable. See Atkins, p. 199; and Appendix, pp. 160–2, 164.

101–38. See Appendix, pp. 159–64 for other versions of this fable.

102, 107. **his . . . he, ho . . . his.** Cf. 10, note. In 107 both MSS combine the fem. pron. *h(e)o* with the masc. *his*, the former according with the sex of the Falcon, the latter with the grammatical gender of the word *faukun*.

114. For the construction cf. 85 and note. Translate, ' It never was your nature to do that.'

121f. **mid þe alre wrste.** Contextually, ' with the worst muck of all '. *mid þe vyrste* J's ' with the first ' seems weaker. On the rhyme **wrste/toberste** see 1725f, note.

128. **fuliche spel**, full-length narrative. It is only a short saying, not a long tale, though indeed the poet has turned it into a suitable *exemplum*. Eggers renders the line happily, ' And longer fables oft say less.' [Cf. Stanley.]

135 and 138. The proverb is expressed in these two lines. It exists in Latin, French, and many other languages beside English. The application to the fable of The Owl and the Falcon is found also in Marie de France's version of the fable. See Appendix, pp. 159–64, and Atkins's note. The meaning of lines 135–8 is, ' Though an apple may roll from the tree where it and others with it grew up, though it may have got away from there, it clearly reveals from where it has come ', i.e. an apple from a poor tree will always reveal itself to be poor in taste, however far it may have left its origins behind.

141. For **he** = ' she ' see Glossary.

145f. For the rhyme see 277, note.

154. Ne kep ich noȝt. How this phrase came to mean ' I have no wish ' is discussed by G. V. Smithers in *E&GS*, 1 (1948), 101–13.

163-6. The Nightingale's advice, that the Owl should keep her wickedness concealed, is of course ironical.

174f. Translate, ' I have a stout castle throughout the length and breadth of my bough ', or, better perhaps, ' I have on my bough a castle, good in every respect ', for, as Hall suggests, it seems likely that **on brede & eck on lengþe** goes with **god.**

176. Wel fiȝt þat wel fliȝt. The distribution of this proverb is very wide. See Appendix, pp. 160–3. **seiþ þe wise,** ' says the wise man '. This kind of phrase introducing a proverb is very common in OFr and ME literature, e.g. Chaucer's *Troilus and Criseyde*, i, 694 [some survey of the distribution of this and related phrases is provided by E. Kölbing in his edition of *Ipomedon*, pp. 368f, note on line 220].

178. unwerste. The rhyme requires *unwreste*, the normal form supported by the J reading *vnwreste* ; but see 249, note.

180. ysome (adj.), like **faire**, qualifies **worde.** In OE it was usual, where two or more adjectives qualify a noun, to allow only one adj. to precede the n., the rest to follow it. [Cf. Ohthere's *Hy habbað swyðe lytle scypa & swyðe leohte*, King Alfred's *Orosius*, EETS (O.S.) 79, p. 19, 7f.] This order has been retained here [Cf. Kenyon, Bib. 29]. Translate, ' with civil and peaceable words '.

184. foȝe. C has *soȝe* [thus Grattan ; the other editors, except Stevenson, give *foȝe* as the MS reading]. The form *soȝe* is impossible, and must be emended, either to the familiar *soþe*, or to the rare *foȝe*.

If we emend to *soþe* we obtain an example of the very common collocation of *soþ* and *riȝt*, with which lines 668 and 950 may be compared. Instances of *ȝ* for *þ* are uncommon in the MS (the only clear example being *ȝat*, 506). The reading *soþe* would agree with J, and J is not as unreliable as has been made out [by Wells, pp. xiii–xvii, Gadow, p. 5, Atkins, pp. xxvii–xxix; but cf. Grattan, p. viii, and especially Dorothy Everett, *MÆ* 7 (1938), 141, who notes that there are times when J is better than C, e.g. line 123 (where J's *ibridde* is preferable to C's *bridde*), or 308 (where J has *hi*, C *him*)]. Even so, J does quite often ' emend ' his text to rid it of words or phrases he had difficulty with. If his exemplar had *foȝe* he might well alter it to *soþe* ; just as in line 14 he altered *breche* to *beche*. And if his exemplar, like C, actually had the incomprehensible *soȝe* (with confusion of long *s* and *f*, as in *ȝas* 149, or *os* 1448), he had every reason for his ' emendation '. Grattan, who rejects the reading *foȝe*, says, ' If a phrase parallel to the German *mit Fug und Recht* [a phrase that would correspond exactly to *mid foȝe & mid riȝte* (cf. Wells, and E. A. Kock, Bib. 27)] had ever existed in English, it is surely unlikely that it would have disappeared with such scanty traces.' This is a dangerous argument; for there are many words and phrases that survive in only one ME text. Besides, the traces are not so scanty; B. T. *Suppl.* quotes OE *mid gefoge* from the *Læceboc*, where the phrase means something like ' fittingly '. Palaeographically *foȝe* is perhaps a somewhat slighter emendation that *soþe*; and it leads to a less hackneyed phrase, which it would be a pity to lose.

185. hi. Cf. 10, note, and 1439, note.

191. Maister Nichole of Guldeforde. See Introduction, pp. 20–2.

204. gente & smale. Epithets characteristic of the ideal lady in medieval literature. Salome is so described in *Cursor Mundi* (13138), and Alison, the old carpenter's young wife, appears so to Nicholas in the Miller's Tale [*Canterbury Tales*, 1 (A), 3234; cf. D. S. Brewer, *MLR* 50 (1955), 267f].

208. ' **legge** goes better with *adun* than with *buue* ' (Hall).

211. him. ' The dat. pron. mostly in the 3rd person is used with intransitive verbs to reinforce the subject ' (Hall, p. 279, 34, quoted by Atkins). J's *nv* also makes sense.

223. schirchest. See 249, note.

225. Hit þincheþ. Impersonal construction taking the dat., here of two adjectives used as nouns, **wise & snepe.** Such pairs of opposites (cf. 482, 1668–78, note), which mean no more than ' all the world ', are common in ME [cf. K. Sisam's note on *Havelok*, 1008, in his revision of Skeat's edition].

231. þat is lof misdede, ' to whom wrong-doing is dear ', or, less literally, ' who delights in wrong-doing '. The indeclinable relative pron. *þat* is here the indirect obj. of *is lof.*

233. þeȝ hit bo unclene. The meaning appears to be that, though the proverb is on the subject of filth, many people quote it, because its association with King Alfred makes it respectable enough.

234. Literally, ' is common to the mouths of many men ', or, more freely, ' is on the lips of many people in common '.

235. Alured King. See Introduction, p. 34.

236. The meaning is probably, ' Anyone who knows himself to be foul shrinks away [from everybody].' It is the nursery situation of the child that keeps out of the way, knowing what state its pants are in, and not wanting anyone else to know.
  NED, s. *shun*, 5, quotes a similar intrans. use of the verb from Horstmann's *Altenglische Legenden*, 1878, p. 163, *For euer he schoneþ þat haþ misgilt,* ' He who has done wrong shrinks away.' [The rendering adopted here seems more satisfactory than the very forced translation of Wells, ' He (a person) shuns that which knows him—to be—foul.']

240. sene, ' vision, power of sight '. According to *NED* this is the last occurrence of the word, which is common in OE. (The only other occurrence in ME that is quoted by *NED* is from the *Ormulum*.) Its obsolescence explains why the word is glossed *eyen*, ' eyes ', in a later hand.

242. The C reading makes sense, and is accepted by C. T. Onions as *þat þu ne sicst boȝ ne rind.* The meaning is, ' By day you are stone-blind, so that you cannot see a branch nor the bark of a tree.'
  Three words call for comment. (1) The spelling **sichst** with *chst*, presumably for *cst* [cf. *hecst* 687, 699; *necst* 688. Cf. Jordan, § 198, Anm. 2 and 3)], is not to be paralleled in C. The nearest parallel is *chan* (1793) for *can* [cf. C. T. Onions, Bib. 59. The spelling *þurch* (1401) for *þurh* is less relevant, since the guttural spirant is written ȝ in this part of the MS (except once, *noht* 549)]. (2) **bov.** The original reading was *bos*, with a round *s* longer than normal and extending well below the line. Perhaps it was written in error for ȝ [cf. *þurs* 823; *mist* 78, and see note; and *nuȝte* 1751, and see note]. A form *bos* would have been incomprehensible to the corrector [see Introduction,

p. 14], who altered it by expuncting *s* and writing a shallow *v* over it, resulting in *bov*, with which we may compare *snov* 430. (3) Originally C read *strind*; but *st* is expuncted, by whom we cannot tell. C. T. Onions accepts *rind*; and there is evidence that *rind* (literally 'bark of a tree ') could by synecdoche take on the wider meaning 'tree' [see E. Björkman in *Minnesskrift af forna lärjungar tillägnad Professor Axel Erdmann*, 1913, pp. 51f, note on *Morte Arthure*, 921 (and cf. 1884, 3363) *þat ryuer . . . Þare þe ryndez ouerrechez with reall bowghez* (' the river . . . over which trees extend with splendid branches ')]; so that *bov ne rind* might mean 'branch nor tree'. The original reading *strind* is perhaps to be explained as dittography, the scribe's eye having caught the *st* of *stare* in the line above. Atkins restores *strind*, taking it to be *NED*'s *strind²*, 'a stream' [cf. A. H. Smith, pt. ii, pp. 163f (Wells's and Gadow's defence of *strind* cannot be accepted)]. The reason why the corrector altered *strind.*to *rind* would then presumably be that he could not understand *strind*; or that he simply expuncted *st* in error, much as he expuncted *dd* in *raddest* 159.

J's *þat þu ne syst bouh of lynd* confirms C's *bov*; but where it differs from C it is weaker. Thus it has smoothed away the *ne . . . ne . . . ne* construction to the detriment of metre and meaning. But worst of all, there seems to be no reason whatever why the Owl should be able to see the branch of a lime-tree. It seems to be a further example of J emending what he cannot understand (see Introduction, pp. 6f).

245–52. The unrighteous man who sees nothing for any good purpose is compared and joined with those that are of the tribe of the Owl. *so doþ* (251) answers to *ri3t so hit farþ* (245) [cf. Stanley]. With 245–6 Atkins [Bib. 32] compares a passage in the *Ancrene Riwle* [p. 94, 12–16] about wretched men of malice (*uniselie ontfule*): ' For if any man says well or does well they may by no means look there with the straight, right eye of a good heart, but blink in another direction, and look asquint to the left. And if there is anything to be blamed or anything hateful, then they squinny with both eyes.'

248. atprenche, the form in C here (J *aprenche*) and in C and J at 814, occurs only in O&N. Stratmann (but not Atkins, q.v.) emends to *atwrenche* here and 814. The error *þ* for *wynn* is not common in either OE or ME MSS (but cf. 1125, note), and it seems most unlikely the blunder should have been made six times, here and at 814 in C and J and in their common antecedent. Moreover, though he is not free from mistakes, the J scribe does not copy blindly what he cannot understand. The word *atwrenche occurs only in one text, in *Seinte Marherete,* as *etwrenchen* and *edwrenchen* [EETS (O.S.) 193, pp. 32, 5 and 36, 4]; it is etymologically transparent as a derivative of OE *wrenc, wrencan*, whereas *atprenche* is obscure. As Grattan (doubting the tenuous etymology suggested by Atkins) says, ' If the *þ* is to be regarded as original, and the word as etymologically connected with MnE *prank*, both the force of the prefix *at* and the development of meaning in the simplex need explanation.' Whether we read *atprenche* with the scribes or emend to *atwrenche* with the etymologists, the meaning remains virtually unaffected.

249. þurste. [J has *þustre*.] There are a number of unusual spellings involving *r* in C: *schirchest* 223, *wercche* 564, 1503, *worþ* 1218, *þorte* 1721; and *unwerste* 178, and *worþ* 1642 are shown to be wrong by the rhymes. It is likely that some of these are scribal errors (cf. the erratic examples of *l*-metathesis, *blod* 317, *hlad* for *halt* 1576); others may represent genuine forms, for apparently erratic examples of *r*-metathesis are not uncommon in OE and ME. Thus the form *þurste* finds some support in the Kentish Hymn's *ðriostre* (28) [Dobbie, *A.S. Poetic Records*, vi, 88]. In the present edition such forms have been retained.

256. Galegale. ' A ludicrous perversion of *nightingale* ' (*NED*). The word is derived, as is the second element of *nightingale*, from OE *galan*, ' to sing '. To recapture the force of *galegale* in translation it may perhaps be permissible to make up a word like *gabble-gale*.

258. spale. *NED* derives this word (which occurs here only) from OE *spala* [found once, in the *Laws of William the Conqueror* (Liebermann, i, 484, 2.1)], with the meaning ' a substitute ', related to MnE *spell* (*NED*'s *spell*, sb.⁵), some of the meanings of which would fit here, especially the Australian [and New Zealand] ' cessation from labour ' [and perhaps the Somerset meaning ' relaxation ' given by Hall (but cf. *EDD* s. *spell*, sb.³)]. As Gadow suggests, the Owl is saying to the Nightingale, ' Give your tongue a rest.' Wells (and Grattan with some hesitation) sees in *spale* the Northern English word *spale* ' a splinter '; Wells suggests, ' a splint, a cleft stick in which the tongue is caught '. But the area of distribution of the word as well as its meaning are not really satisfactory, and *NED*'s derivation is to be preferred.

259. þat þes dai bo þin oȝe. Translate, ' that the day is yours.'

273f. The rhyme **cunde/schende** is best explained [with C. L. Wrenn, Bib. 41] by assuming SE provenance for the poem. But cf. 1725f, note.

274. In ME it was not necessary to express an object that was clearly understood. [Cf. 310, 601, 726, 1309, 1326, 1628, 1741.] Here *me* is understood.

276. Vor riȝte cunde. Translate, ' because of my very nature.'

277f. foȝle/þuuele. This rhyme will be discussed first in conjunction with *vuele/fuȝele* 63f, secondly in the context of the assonances in O&N, (1) dissyllabic, (2) trisyllabic.

E. J. Dobson [*E&GS* 1 (1948), pp. 56f (and also cf. Dobson, *1500–1700*, p. 182)], discussing the rhyme 277f (but not the related 63f) adduces evidence that the sounds ȝ and *v* were growing alike in ME, making the consonants in these rhymes more nearly true. The vowels of 63f, however, cannot give a true rhyme: in the dialects of the extant MSS short *ü* rhymes in 63f with short *u*, the same imperfect rhyme as in 277f, if *þuuele* is taken as directly <OE *þȳfel* [see A. H. Smith, s. *pȳfel* and cf. *pȳfelett; for the short vowel *u* in *þuuele* cf. Luick, § 353]. Dobson seeks to establish that 277f was a true rhyme, the vowel *u* in *þuuele* having the quality of OE *þūf* ' a tuft ' [which may have influenced OE *þȳfel*, or, less probably, there may have been an OE *þūfel (presumably by suffix-ablaut)]. This agrees with C. T. Onions's reconstruction of 277f, *fu(ȝ)le/þuvle* (i.e. *þuvle* with *u* not *ü*). Dr Onions's reconstruction of 63f is *fule* (for *vuele* of both MSS) rhyming with *fu(ȝ)le*. [But cf. Luick, § 402 Anm. 1, for retention in late Middle Kentish of ȝ; and note Dan Michel's *uoȝel(es*, Wallenberg, p. 265. (Dobson offers a preferred alternative explanation of 277, which similarly involves reduction of ȝ.)] The best solution is perhaps to be found in G. V. Smithers's suggestion (quoted by Dobson) that a true rhyme is not intended in 277f; and to treat 277f and 63f [with S. T. R. O. d'Ardenne, Bib. 50] as examples of trisyllabic assonance.

The following real or apparent assonances occur in O&N: (1) dissyllabic, *honde/schomme* 1651, *singinge/auinde* 855, *ibolwe/isuolȝe* 145, *worse/mershe* 303, *flesche/cwesse* 1387, *wise/ire* 1029, *iwone/frome* 475, *kume/iwune* 1319, *itrede/icwepe* 501, *worde/forworpe* 547, *worde/iworpe*

659, *oflonged/ongred* 1587 (cf. note), *wiue/ischire* 1531, *heisugge/stubbe* 505, *wepen/forleten* 987; (2) trisyllabic, *ȝoepe/duȝeþe* 633, *vuele/fuȝele* 63, *foȝle/puuele* 277, *cradele/apele* 631, *togadere/betere* 807, *gidie/ȝonie* 291, *luuieþ/schunieþ* 791. Obviously, some of these were originally true rhymes: for 1651 and 855, cf. J's *honde/schonde*, and *singinde/avynde*; for 633 J has *youhþe/duhþe* [OE *iuguþe, duguþe*]. Others are less obvious. (1) The OE p.ps. *bolgen/swolgen* rhyme in 145 [with ȝ>w (Jordan, § 186 and Anm. 1) in J's *tobolewe/iswolwe* (in J *w<ȝ* is the rule), and in C's *ibolwe* (in C *w<ȝ* is exceptional)]. For 303 the original may have had a near-true rhyme, *werse/mersse* [see C. T. Onions's note to 83f, C. L. Wrenn, Bib. 41, and Jordan § 181; but, for the quality of *s, ss*, cf. Wallenberg, pp. 314ff]; for *flesche* (1387) the original may, similarly, have had *flesse*; but *cwesse* [which does not appear to be recorded in *NED*] remains obscure [Bradley, Gadow, Breier, and Atkins take it as from OFr *quasser*; they do not attempt to explain the stem-vowel, which is perhaps due to the semantically close OE *cweccan* with which the OFr verb may have been crossed (in ME, forms of the past of the verbs would have been similar: **quaste* and *cuahte*—cf. *NED*, s. *quash*, v. and s.v. *quetch, quitch*, v.)] For 1029 Stratmann restored the original *ise* for *ire*; this considered with the place-name evidence may help to establish the provenance of the poem; A. H. Smith (s. *isern*) says, ' The form *isen* survives in regular use through the ME period especially in the SE dialects, and is found in that area in place-names. In other parts *iren* is in more normal use and ultimately ousts *isen.*' [See also Dickins and Wilson, p. 186, and S. T. R. O. d'Ardenne, Bib. 50.] Some of the remaining assonances may have been recognised licences [cf. Gadow, pp. 29f], thus 475 and 1319 on nasals, 501 and perhaps 547 and 659 on dentals. 547 and 659 may, however, have been true with the p.p. *-worde*, though the best evidence that this form [direct <OE p.p. *worden*] survived in ME is, perhaps C's *forwurde/borde* 1491 (J *forwurþe*). [Cf. *NED*, s. *worth*, v.[1], A3.; *MED*, s. *forworthen*, 2.(b).] 1587, 1531, 505, 987 were no better in the original than now, and show that the poet was not careful about rhymes. (2). S. T. R. O. d'Ardenne has called attention to the greater degree of licence in trisyllabic rhymes. 63 and 277 have been discussed above. 631 is an example (like 501) of assonance on dentals; and so is 807, which was originally *togedere/betere* [cf. Luick, § 363 Anm. 3, on *a* and *e* in *togadere* (807 is different from *betere/chatere* 283, which would give a true rhyme only in SE and West Midland dialects—cf. Luick, § 180)]. For 291 C. T. Onions has *gedie/ȝenie* [Kentish *e* (<*y*) in *gedie*, and non-Western *e* (<*eo*) in *ȝenie*]. 791 is simply an assonance on *v* and *n*. One other imperfect trisyllabic rhyme, *ȝomere/sumere* 415, further illustrates the degree of licence.

279f. Cf. 65–8 and note on the mobbing of owls.

283f. For the rhyme see 277f. note. **Yif.** Cf. *underyat* 1091 also with *y* for *ȝ* [S. R. T. O. d'Ardenne, Bib. 48]. J's *Þeyh* also makes sense.

289. Wells translates, ' It is in the judgment of wise men ', i.e. less literally, ' It is the opinion of the wise.'

291f. For the rhyme see 277f, note. See Appendix, pp. 162f on the proverb.

293. **At sume siþe** goes with *Alured sede* rather than with *herde i.*

294–7. Cf. Appendix, pp. 160–3. *The Proverbs of Alfred* have a similar proverb, lines 449–53 (J): ' Thus says Alfred, " Do not chatter, nor consort (?), nor chide with any fool, nor with tales of many kinds, chide with no madmen." '

299. an oþer side. The original may have had *an oþer siðe* [cf. Atkins and C. T. Onions] answering to *At sume siþe* 293 ; the assonance *siðe/wide* would not be impossible, cf. 501f and 631f [and see 277f, note]. *Side* does, however, also make sense, though not as good; Atkins, ' in another place '; Hinckley (Bib. 40), ' on another page ' (but this implies too early a use of the sense ' page '—cf. *NED*, s. *side*, sb.¹, 9.a.); the best meaning is probably *NED*, (17.b.) ' on the other hand '.

301f. For the proverb cf. Appendix, pp. 160–3.

303f. For the rhyme see 277f, note.

304–8. C. T. Onions restores the original singular meaning of **crowe** in this passage. The Wise Man and the Fool of the proverb 294–7 are represented by the Hawk and the Crow. There is, therefore, no question of crows mobbing the hawk [but see Atkins]. It appears that the MSS were not familiar with the SE **hi** (' she '), and interpreted it as pl. (' they ') [cf. 10 note, and the emendation 1439], leading to the correction in C of the acc. fem. *hi* to *hem* (308, see footnote), whereas J took this *hi* (308) to be acc. pl. To remove the erratic form **hore** (305) we should perhaps emend to *hire* or *hure* [cf. Glossary].

309f. þu me seist of. Translate, ' you speak to me about,' (and cf. 363); **telst** with object pronoun *me* not expressed (cf. 274, note). Possibly we should read

> ʒet þu me telst of oþer þinge,
> & seist þat ich ne can noʒt singe.

telst would then mean ' blame '.

317. bold. See 249, note.

322. on Irish prost. Perhaps because Irish priests jabber in Irish [Hinckley, Bib. 39 and 43].

323–8. riʒte time. The Owl lists the canonical hours of the night rather than those of the day. ' The Owl takes credit for singing, not all night like the Nightingale (331), but only to call the religious to their hours: **an eue,** Vespers (*æfen-sang*); **bedtime,** Complin (*niht-sang*); **ad middel-niʒte,** Matins with Lauds (*ūht-sang*),' Hall (giving the OE equivalents). **dairim** (presumably with final *e* elided) means ' the dawn ' and does not refer to a canonical hour (as Hall thought); but (like J's *dayrewe*, 'the first streak of day ') it goes very well with *daisterre*.

333. leist. We should perhaps read *lest*. The scribe first wrote *seist* (' you are saying '), and then corrected initial *s* to *l*. Perhaps he did not think it necessary, or forgot, to cancel the *i*.

335. crei. The word occurs only here. (1) The early editors derived it from OFr *cri*, ' cry '; but the rhyme is against this etymology. (2) There is an OE gloss [Wright-Wülcker 208, 10] *cra*, ' the sound of frogs or crows', and Atkins suggests *crei*<ON *krei, an erroneously hypothesised cognate of *cra*. There are, however, only a very few Scand. loan-words in O&N [viz. *bondeman, griþ, ille, nai, skente (skentinge), skere, sckile, triste, truste*,]; and, other things being equal, an etymology assuming native origin is to be preferred. (3) Atkins's further suggestion seems best: he derives *crei* from a hypothetical OE *cræg, neuter, related to the hypothetical OE weak masc. *craga which underlies ME *craw(e*, ' throat, crop of birds', cognate with Middle Dutch *crāghe*, cf. *NED* s. *crag*, sb.². [The related Scand. words are loans from Middle Low German. (For a pair similar morphologically to *cræg and *craga, cf. Icelandic masc. *múli* and Middle High German neuter *mūl*, both meaning ' mouth '.)]

338. Þas monnes, 'of man'.

340. of þar, 'thereof', i.e. 'of your song'. Translate, 'That one sets no great store by it.'

345ff. The construction is difficult. Perhaps translate (assuming ellipsis), ' However joyous the song may be, it is never so joyous that it will not seem very miserable if it. . . .' *he* in lines 346f refers to *song*, a masc. n.

347. oure unwille, <*ūrum unwillum* (' against our will, in our despite '), at the price of a very slight emendation, gives excellent sense. The exemplar of C's and J's common antecedent probably had (like the emendation) *ou* for more normal *u*. [Another example of *ou* for *u* in the common antecedent probably underlies C's *houdsiþe*, J's *houþsype* (cf. 1586, note).] Cf. Hall, Hinckley, Bib. 40, and C. T. Onions (note).

The MS reading may be defended, though not convincingly, (1) by interpreting *ouer unwille* as ' beyond what displeases, beyond the point of displeasure ' (cf. Atkins); or (2) by interpreting *ouer* as ' anywhere, in any way ' (<OE *ōhwær*—thus Holthausen, Bib. 38) and presumably taking *unwille* to be some form of adverbial dat. construction, i.e. *ower unwille* =' to displeasure in any way ', or more freely, ' to anyone's displeasure '. Both (1) and (2) ignore that *unwillum*, *unwille* (etc.) in OE and ME, except where specifically qualified otherwise (e.g. by a possess. adj.), refers to the subject of the sentence, here *he*; i.e. unless a word like *ure*, ' our ', qualifies it, *unwille* would mean ' in despite of the song '.

349f. seide/rede, and 1781f, *sede/grede* 473f, *sede/bede* 549f, *seide/dede* 707f, *seide/swikelede* 837f, *erede/sede* 1295f, *ised/red* 395f; *misrede/maide* 1063f, *grede/maide* 1337f, *ȝene/isene* 845f. These rhymes depend on the sound-change by which in WS (or perhaps all Saxon) and OK, palatal *g* before *d* and *n* was lost and the preceding vowel lengthened [cf. Luick § 251, Jordan § 191 and Anm.]; this sound-change is reflected in the spellings *sede*, *ised*, and *ȝene*. [J's spellings are diphthongal in every case, except *yene* 845 and 893, a rare word (cf. *NED*, s. *yain*, v.) which the scribe may not have known, and so could not alter to conform with his system of spellings.] Cf. 1381–4, note.

351f. On the proverb see Appendix, pp. 160–3. There are very many proverbs on the theme of excess, but none of them is identical with that in the text. Cf. such sayings as *Ancrene Riwle* (p. 129), *Euerich þing me mei . . . ouerdon: best is euer imete.* [' Everything may be done to excess: moderation is best in all things.']

357–62. Here and 879–86 the Owl speaks in the manner of a homilist; lines 716–20 show that the Nightingale is capable of the same language.

362. Here and in lines 512, 704, 801, 1056f, 1072, 1230, 1344, 1432, 1569f, 1602, 1699f, 1706, 1741, the subject, though clearly understood, is not expressed. [Cf. L. Gebhardt, *Das unausgedrückte Subjekt im Mittelenglischen* (1922); for examples of unexpressed objects see note to line 274.] It is just possible, however, that Þat is a rel. pron., and not a conjunction.

369f. þusternesse/lasse. The rhyme requires *lesse*, with *ĕ* for *ă* probably by analogy with *lēste* ' least ' [Luick §§ 205, 231, 363, Anm. 6.], so that the rhyme cannot be used as evidence to establish the provenance of the poem. So also 1227f and 1406f; but *masse/lasse*, 481f would, if the poet knew only *lesse*, presuppose an original rhyme *messe/lesse*, where *messe* could be either a French loan-word or a SE dialect form of *masse* [cf. Breier, p. 62; Jordan § 32 Anm. 3], or the poet may have known both *lesse* and *lasse*.

373–82. The description of the hare naturally agrees in many ways with the details expressed and implied in the ME poem *On the Names of a Hare* [edited by A. S. C. Ross, *Proceedings of the Leeds Philosophical and Literary Society* 3 (1935), 347–77]. One of the names of the hare is *louting* ' skulker ' (26), cf. *luteþ al dai* (O&N, 373); another is *couearise* ' get-up-quickly ' (42), cf. **stard suþe coue** (O&N, 379).

378. Translate, ' is ready with his tricks '; literally ȝarewe (adj. acc. pl.) qualifies *blenches*.

379. **stard.** J's *start* and *bistarte* (for *bistart*), ' leaps at ', 1438, confirms that *start* (syncopated 3 sg. with assimilation of *t* and *þ* under *t*, written *d* in *stard* in C) must be the verb from which MnE *to start* is derived. The vowel, however, is etymologically unexplained [cf. *NED*]; it cannot be an exceptionally early example of the late ME sound-change *er* > *ar*, of which there is not a trace in the MSS. It cannot be the same ablaut grade as in the inf. forms C *misstorte*, J *myssturte* (677; rhyming with *horte*). The grade of the related late OE *steartlian* [cf. *NED*, s. *startle*, v.] may be the same as in *start*, but it is difficult to see how, except as the result of some analogy, this could be found in *start*.

388. **doþ gode node.** The idiom, established by G. V. Smithers [Bib. 45], is found also in *Kyng Alisaunder* (EETS (O.S.) 227, line 2340; cf. EETS (O.S.) 237, p. 99).

389f. The Owl may be going to battle in the company of, or in the place of, the hawk, for lines 271–6 (and cf. 1674–7) show her to be proud to be of the *haukes cunne*; and in the OE poem *The Battle of Brunanburh* (64) the *gūþhafoc* (' battle-hawk ') accompanies the conventional satellites of battle, the raven, the eagle, and the wolf [cf. F. P. Magoun, *Neuphilologische Mitteilungen* 56 (1955), 81–90; E. G. Stanley, *Anglia* 73 (1956), 442f]. Otherwise there seems to be little evidence that the owl was thought of as flying by night with the troops, though a Danish *folkevise* [quoted by Margaret Ashdown, *MLR* 18 (1923), 337f] has the owl in the company of the eagle and the raven hovering over the field of battle.

394–6. Cf. 667f and 1792, note (and Introduction, p. 22) on the poet's sympathy with the Owl's side. **ised/red**, see 349, note for the rhyme.

396 and 401. For **he** meaning ' she ' see Glossary.

405f. **fliȝst** (without unetymological final *e*) is required by the rhyme and is supported by J's *flyhst*. *fliȝst/isvicst* is a true rhyme, for in southern dialects of ME χ > *k* before -*þ*, -*st*, -*t* of verbal endings [cf. Jordan § 198 Anm. 2, and C. T. Onions, note on line 89]. Both MSS (and, therefore, their common antecedent) agree in the rhyme-word **i-svicst** (J *swykst*; *sv* is a normal spelling in C for *sw*—cf. Glossary under *sw*-). Neither gives sense. A corrector in C hoped to restore sense by reading ȝ*if þu vicst*, ' if you fight '. This makes sense, but has no more authority than a modern emendation; and if the text must be emended it is better to retain *isvicst* (a reading not likely to be invented by a scribe who has *vicst* before him), and assume that a negative has been omitted. Grattan thinks the reading ȝ*if þu nisvicst* ' rather weak '. It is hard to see why. There are people who grow bold if you take flight, the very ones who, if you don't leave off, will run away themselves. Grattan's own suggestion to read ȝ*if þu ne wīcst* [< OE *wīcan*

' to give way '] involves tampering with *isvicst* (*swykst*) plus the intro-
duction of a negative, and convinces as little as Hall's suggestion *ʒif
þu biswicst*, ' if you deceive ', contextually, ' if you delude by a show of
fight ', which Grattan rightly condemns.

411. **Hule.** C's directing letter *H* must be the original reading. Cf.
955. The rubricator misread C's directing letter, and so wrote a
capital rubric *Þ*.

413. **H.** Savage [*JEGP* **40** (1941), 283f] believes that the poet's know-
ledge of the hen's frenzied behaviour in the snow was the result of
observation, not reading. Cf. Introduction, p. 32.

415f. **ʒomere/sumere.** See 277, note [and cf. the same rhyme in *On
God Ureisun of Ure Lefdi* (39f) adduced by C. T. Onions].

417–19. **niþe** and **onde.** For the legal implications see Introduction,
p. 29.

421–6. Cf. 244f and 1402, note.

427f. ' " Nor would he mind though flocks (coarse felted stuff made
of refuse of wool . . .) were muddled up with fine carded wool and hair ",
that is, he would take a perverse delight in a confusion which would
be troublesome to sort out ' (Hall). This homely comparison seems to
fit the context at least as well as ' He cared not though companies
[<OE *flocc*] were mingled (huddled together) by heads and by hair ',
i.e. were fighting and pulling one another by the hair [R. Morris and
W. W. Skeat, *Specimens of Early English* (1886), i, 347]. Both explana-
tions involve *imeind bi* which cannot be paralleled (*wiþ* or *mid* are the
normal prepositions, as in 131 and 870).

437–49. Here the words of the Nightingale are reminiscent in subject
matter and style of medieval lyric poetry. **wlite** (439) and **rude** (443)
are ambiguous, for they mean face as well as radiant beauty, face as
well as red hue; and this ambiguity is made use of in a context where
the Lily and Rose speak.

440. **þat þu hit wite.** For the spelling *C wte* cf. *w[i]se* 54 note. [The
meaning of the phrase is discussed by C. T. Onions, *RES* **4** (1928), pp.
334–7.]

446. **Vor hire luue,** ' for love of her '.

453. Translate, ' When what I came for is done.'

458. **winteres.** Cf. 489–94, note. **reue.** The common antecedent of
C and J presumably had, like C, *rene*. The J scribe writes *teone*
(' trouble '), and produces sense, but mars the rhyme.

459f. **harde/erde.** <OE *hearde/earde*. The normal development is:
short OE *ea* before *rd* is lengthened [Luick § 268]; this long *ea* is
monophthongised to *ǣ*, written *e* [as in erde] or *ea* [as in *earding*-
(28)]. But lengthening did not take place in every case. There is
evidence that *heard* was not always lengthened [Orm has *harrde*].
Where lengthening did not take place the development was *ea>ǣ>a*,
as in the spelling *harde*. The rhyme originally was presumably *herde/
erde* with long vowels, but an original rhyme *harde/arde* with short
vowels is not impossible.

469. For **he** =' she ' see Glossary.

473f. For the rhyme see 349, note.

475f. For the rhyme see 277, note.

481f. For the rhyme see 369, note.

483. **cundut.** The glossarial equivalent ' carol(s) ' is no more than a convenient approximation. The modern carol is not descended direct from the medieval *conductus*. A *cundut* (Latin *conductus*) was a two, three, or four-part song of which not all the parts were furnished with words. Its distinctive feature was that the melody of the tenor, if not an original theme, was taken from popular song and not from ecclesiastical music as in most other part-songs, such as rotas or motets. Originally a *conductus* was sung while the priest proceeded to the altar. See R. L. Greene, *The Early English Carols* (1935), ch. i; *The New Oxford History of Music*, ii (1954), edited by Dom Anselm Hughes, 171-4. The singing of *coundutes* is mentioned also in *Sir Gawain and the Green Knight*, 1655: *coundutes of Krystmasse & carole3 newe*.

489–94. Summer is here personified; **he** (491) and **his** (492) refer to Summer. For if these words are taken as referring to ' the man ' (of *monnes ponk*) the behaviour of the animals (493f) is not suitably introduced, and **Vor** (493) becomes meaningless. It is likely that some degree of personification is intended also with *winteres* (458). See Introduction, pp. 25f, and Appendix, pp. 167f; [and cf. Stanley; Hässler, pp. 21f]. On the meaning of **wlonc** (489) see 1400, note.

499–501. **teme** is properly of the female, **itrede** of the male bird. Cf. 515–23, where there is a similar conflation of the sexes.

501f. For the rhyme see 277, note.

505f. For the rhyme see 277, note.

507f. and 519f. The (factually mistaken) belief that the nightingale loses its voice after copulation is ascribed (wrongly) to Pliny by the German philosopher Albertus Magnus (1193?–1280). There is evidence that the belief was held more widely. It is alluded to in a poem of the minnesinger Heinrich von Morungen (died 1222), and in the French proverb, *Quand le rossignol a vu ses petits, il ne chante plus* [W. Gottschalk, *Die bildhaften Sprichwörter der Romanen*, i (1935), 223]. [Cf. Hinckley, Bib. 42; and Stanley.]

510f. For the rhyme cf. 1383f and note.

512. The subject ' it ' is not expressed. Cf. 362, note.

515. The inversion, **habbe he**, expresses the conditional. So also in 567, 975, 1683.

523. **longe** probably qualifies **ni3tes**. It might, however, be adverbial, ' when nights come on long '.

528. i.e. who goes forward in action, who stays behind in idleness.

529f. For this widely distributed proverb, cf. Appendix, pp. 160–3. Kenyon [Bib. 29] translates line 530, ' whom one may lay hard tasks upon '.

541f. **inume** means ' refuted in argument, answered ' as well as ' captured ' [cf. *nimen* 607]. In the context of legal procedure the vocabulary of trial by battle is used metaphorically, even where, as here, there is no thought of battle. See D. Everett and N. D. Hurnard, *MÆ* **16** (1947), 12–14. Cf. 656, 1197f and notes, and Introduction, p. 29.

547f. For the rhyme see 277, note.

549f. For the rhyme see 349, note.

567. For the inversion see 515, note.

571–4. It is impossible to say what constitutes the proverb, 571f or 573f; in neither case has a satisfactory parallel been found. [Cf. Appendix, pp. 160–3.]

590. **An** means ' and '; **stede** is acc. pl. rather than sg. [Kenyon, Bib. 29].

591f. **muse/huse.** The rhyme is true [OE *mūsum* (dat. pl.) and *hūse* (dat. sg.)]. So also 609f.

596. **bihinde.** The Glossary follows H. S. V. Jones, *JEGP* 24 (1925), 452f.

601. The object is not expressed. See 274, note.

609f. For the rhyme see 591, note. The lines mean, ' I love the church, and love to cleanse it of loathsome mice.'

614. **wnienge** with *eng* for *ing* (cf. J *wunying*). The ending is Kentish. [See J. R. R. Tolkien, *E&S* 14 (1929), 119.] Cf. *heriinge* 981.

620. **sniuþ.** A clear *wynn* (not *thorn* as printed) in C. J has the subj. *snywe*, which might be taken as confirming a subj. in C; *sniuw*, however, is not a possible spelling in C. [See Stanley.]

630. A translation might be, ' Just do their business wherever it drops.'

631–4. For the rhymes see 277, note.

635. **Wat** may either mean ' how '; or it may be the exclamation ' what ', and should be followed by *!*.

637f. **ivvrne/urne.** A true rhyme: <OE *gefyrn* (with adv. *-e*) and *yrnan* [cf. Gadow].

638. The proverb, ' Need makes the old wife trot ', is well known also in languages other than English. See Appendix, pp. 160–3. The pun on **node** is only here, but since it accurately describes a condition in old women, thus giving a point to the proverb, it may serve to explain its origin.

641f. **idiȝt/miȝst.** *miȝt*, the normal form in C, is required by the rhyme. [Cf. W. Horn, *Anglia Bbl* 36 (1925), 166.]

645f. Probably, ' It is built by plaiting in all directions, from inside to a long way outside.'

651. **iwende.** The etymology is obscure. and *NED*'s sense ' contrivances ', though it fits the context well, is difficult to justify. Grattan says, ' As the prefix *i* had no definite meaning at this date, there would seem to be no objection to equating this word with the OE noun *wend*; so " course, alternative ".' Atkins emends to *ihende* (<OE adj. *gehende* ' close at hand ') to which he gives the meaning ' conveniences ' (pl. adj. used as n.); he adduces no parallel.

656. **ibunde.** Here again the vocabulary of trial by battle is used metaphorically. Cf. 541, note. A possible MnE rendering might be ' tied up in knots '.

658. **Hong up þin ax.** Cf. Appendix, pp. 160–3. A proverbial expression, of which the fullest version is perhaps that in Richard Hill's *Commonplace-Book* of 1536 [EETS (E.S.), 101, p. 132]: *When thow hast well doo, hange vp thy hachet*. The general meaning in the O&N context is ' give up ! '

659f. For the rhyme see 277, note.

660. Translate, 'hardly knew what to do', or 'was driven almost to her wit's end'. [Cf. Kock, Bib. 27.]

667f. Cf. 394–6, note, and 1792, note. **strong**, 'hard, difficult, tough' [the meaning is discussed by O. S. Arngart, *ESts* 30 (1949), 165; cf. Hall, p. 299.]

669. **gon to.** Cf. 838, note.

670. **winne.** C has a clear *thorn*, not *wynn*, and J similarly reads *þinne*. Probably the common antecedent of C and J had also *þinne* (for *winne*, i.e. *thorn* for *wynn*), which was retained in the two MSS [J does not use the *wynn* rune]. The meaning of *winne* is 'strife', and this fits tolerably well here; but a case might be made out perhaps for the retention of the MS reading *on þinne*, with some such meaning as 'in straits, having a thin time', *toȝte* is used similarly in line 703. [Cf. *NED* s. *thin*, adj. 4, for figurative uses of the word.]

679f. **Without emendation.** **upe þon** is derived <OE *uppan pām (? 'as against that'—cf. Wells and Atkins), and may perhaps be translated 'even so' (in contextual extension of 'as against that'). Gadow's interjectional *upe þon!*, 'up and at them!', 'into the fray!' ['drauf los'] also seems a possible interpretation; but he too fails to provide a parallel use. The lines are probably best translated, 'But nevertheless, yet even so, here is a possible way out for him who understands it', or, less convincingly, 'But nevertheless, still up and at them! Here is, etc.' **is to red** means 'is an advisable or possible course of action' (see *NED* s. *rede*, sb.¹, 3.b.). **hine** refers to *red*<OE *ræd*, masc.

With emendation. Grattan makes much of the evidence of scribal difficulty. Of C he says, '*nopeles, þ* altered from *ȝ*, same hand. *ȝut*, the *ȝ* is strangely shaped: the scribe was evidently copying a doubtful letter in his MS.' Describing J (which reads *Ac nopeles þ- hyet upe þon*) he says, 'Both scribes [C and J] have edited this line, J after starting to copy his original. He writes *þ* for the unfamiliar *wynn*, puts a dash after it, and then makes a new attempt. The correct reading I assume to have been *Ac nopeles wit upe þon her is to red*, etc., "But nevertheless thereupon is Wit at hand as a help, if one but know him."' It seems unlikely that both MSS would have misread Grattan's hypothetical original, which in any case gains nothing in smoothness, and only little in sense.

681f. Translate, 'For Wit is never so keen as when knowing what to do is a matter of doubt to it [i.e. to Wit].' The sense of these lines is that wit is sharpened by emergency, as in 689f.

687f. and 699f. See Appendix, pp. 160–3; the same proverb also occurs in Icelandic and Dutch.

694. **redpurs.** Though this particular compound occurs only here, the idea ('a bag of tricks') is found in a number of versions of the fable of The Fox and the Cat [Cf. Appendix, pp. 164–6; and K. Warnke, *Die Quellen*, pp. 250–3].

696. **uolde**, i.e. of his *redpurs*. The figure, that the bag of tricks must be explored, is found also in the *Peterborough Chronicle*, A.D. 1131 [J. Earle and C. Plummer, *Two of the Saxon Chronicles Parallel*, 1892, i, 262; ii, 306]: *Nu him behofed þæt he crape in his mycele codde in ælc hyrne gif þær wære hure· an unwreste wrenc* ['Now he had good reason to creep into his big bag (of tricks), into every corner, (to see) if there might be just one vile trick'].

699f. hecst/nest. The rhyme requires the forms of 687f (where J has *hekst/nest*). The forms without *c* or *k* are of the dialect of the MSS, not of the original if that was SE. [Cf. Jordan § 198 Anm. 3.]

701-4. Translate, ' The Nightingale had with sound sense made good use of all her anxious care; in her time of hardship and strain she had collected her thoughts very well with good sense.' [Cf. 362, note for the syntax of 704.]

707-836. In this speech of the Nightingale the purpose is to prove that her one talent is worth more than all the many gifts of the Owl. It seems possible that the Nightingale is echoing, and applying to herself, an important aspect of a problem that was in the foreground of scholastic discussion in the twelfth and thirteenth centuries, the connexion of the virtues. It was held that one virtue sincerely exercised could, since all the virtues were interconnected, embrace all other virtues. The devoted exercise of one virtue could, therefore, surpass the weak or indifferent exercise of all the virtues. [Cf. O. Lottin, *Psychologie et morale aux XIIe et XIIIe siècles*, iii (1949), pp. 195–252.]

707f. For the rhyme see 349, note.

709. sumere. The *er* mark has been omitted in both MSS.

716-20. See 357-62, note.

720. ' Who knows any good '; **of** is used partitively.

722. ginneþ is (as is common in ME) used periphrastically with the inf. **wirche.** It may be omitted in translation. [See Hall.]

724. After **shal** the verb of motion is not expressed (cf. 824 and note). Before **bon** *he shal* is understood: 'to what place he must go, and where he must be for long.'

726. The object of **biȝete** is not expressed. Cf. 274, note.

729. kanunes. *NED* defines a *canon* in the pre-Reformation sense as, ' A clergyman (including clerks in minor orders) living with others in a clergy-house (*claustrum*), or (in later times) in one of the houses within the precinct or close of a cathedral or collegiate church, and ordering his life according to the canons or rules of the church. This practice of the *canonica vita* or canonical life began to prevail in the 8th c.; in the 11th c. it was, in some churches, reformed by the adoption of a rule (based upon a practice mentioned by St. Augustine) that clergymen so living together should renounce private property: those who embraced this rule were known as *Augustinian* (*Austin*) or *regular*, the others were *secular canons*.'

730. wicketunes. A. H. Smith (s. *wīc-tūn*) adduces evidence from place-names that the meaning is ' dwelling-places ', a compound of OE *wīc*. Outside place-names *wic-tun* twice translates *atrium* in the *Paris Psalter*, 95, 8 and 99, 3 (Dobbie, *A.S. Poetic Records*, v). The final *e* of *wicke* is to be explained, perhaps, as the result of late OE weak forms of the word, a development perhaps due to the frequency with which *wic* was used in the dat. pl. *wicum* (cf. A. H. Smith, Pt. ii, p. 261, and esp. pp. 225f); an example is *ii hina wican* from *Hemming's Cartulary* of the late eleventh century (B. Thorpe, *Diplomatarium Anglicum Ævi Saxonici*, 1865, p. 446; for the form *hina* cf. A. H. Smith s.v. *hīwan*). The *ck* in *wicke* is an example of sporadic *ck* for *k* in the Cotton text (J has *wike*); cf. *eck* 174, *bileck* 1081. An alternative etymology (the only advantage of which is that it avoids difficulty with the -e of *wicke*) is to derive *wicke*<OE weak fem. *wīce* ' service ' (*wicketunes*, therefore, places where monks said their offices). No other compound of *wīce* is recorded.

732. to midelniȝte. See 323–8 and note. In the hymns sung during the midnight service (Matins and Lauds) reference to the coming of light is often made [e.g. in Ambrosius's ' Æterne rerum Conditor ' (see *Breviarium ad usum insignis ecclesiae Sarum*, edited by F. Procter and C. Wordsworth, fasc. ii, 1879, col. 34); in ' Ecce iam noctis tenuatur umbra ' (*ibid.*, col. 35); in Prudentius's ' Ales diei nuntius ' (*ibid.*, col. 111; and in Prudentius's ' Lux ecce surgit aurea ' (*ibid.*, col. 148)].

733. prostes upe londe. The priests referred to here may simply be those living in the wilds of the country; but it is more likely that secular parish priests were meant, in contradistinction to the regular *clerkes, munekes, & kanunes.* The services of secular priests were confined to the daytime (cf. 734), those of the regular priests are held during the night also.

735f. Cf. 483f.

741. bidde. Either 1 sg., or (less probably, but in agreement with J's *bidden*) 3 pl.

745. we. The common antecedent of C and J presumably had *þe* with thorn for *wynn*. C reads clearly *þe* (retaining the reading of his exemplar); and J reads *þu* (emending the *þe* of his exemplar); *we* fits the context better than *þu*, since both birds will be involved in the *dome.*

746. þe sulfe þe Pope. J omits the second *þe*. It is perhaps possible to retain it (with the early editors and Gadow), assuming a substantival use of *sulfe*, ' before that very one, the Pope of Rome '. An OE parallel is provided by *sylfes þæs folces* of *Riddle* 64, 6 [Dobbie, *A.S. Poetic Records*, iii, 230; and cf. F. Tupper's note (in his edition of *The Riddles of the Exeter Book*, 1910, p. 206); ' Either simply *þæs* or *þæs sylfan* is in better accord with idiom.'] On the legal implications of this line see Introduction, p. 29 [and Stanley].

747f. noþeles/an oþer þes. C has *wes* rather than *þes*, presumably from confusion of *wynn* and *thorn*. In J there was a blank after *oþer* until a fifteenth-century hand inserted *bles* ' blast ' (for which there is no more authority than for a modern guess). Gadow's suggestion to read *þes*, gen. sg. of the dem. pron., (a virtual retention of the C reading), and to translate ' you shall hear something else about this ', seems best. For the rhyme cf. 881f. For the meaning of *þes* cf. *þes* 882 and *þas* 1442; for *an oþer* cf. the use of *an oder* 903. The only other possible suggestions involve emendation: to *hes* ' behest, judicial pronouncement, sentence ' (Atkins); or to *res* ' onrush ' (Grattan). [C. L. Wrenn (Bib. 41) seeks to derive *þes* from OE **þys*, OK **þes*, ' storm '; but that is a ghost-word. See B. T. *Suppl.* s. *þys*.] See Stanley.

759f. mani eine/oþer maine. In this part of the poem *kan* is construed with *iwit* and nouns of similar meaning in the sense of ' to know a trick '; cf. 774, 794, 797, 799, etc. Line 757 has *For ich kan craft & ich kan liste* and this is echoed here, in *Ich kan wit & song mani eine.* The rhyme is best explained [with E. Björkman, *Archiv* **126** (1911), 237] thus: *enne* < OE *ēnne* (WS *ǣnne*) rhyming with *mēne* <OE *megne, mægne*; the vowels provide a true rhyme (if *e* of *enne* remains long by analogy with *ān*, but the *nn* of *enne* only assonates with *n* of *mene* (cf. *anne/uenne* 831f and note). The MS spelling *maine* (J *mayne*) is from uninflected *main* (<OE *mægen*); and this form may in turn have influenced the spelling of the rhyme word *enne*.

To the alternative suggestion that *mani eine* [J has *mony eine*] be emended to *manteine* (translating, ' I know what is wise, and I keep up my song ') Professor d'Ardenne (*Iuliene*, p. 151) rightly objects that, whether the provenance of the poem be SW or SE, verbs in *-teine* should have final *i* not *e*: *manteini* [cf. Breier, p. 140]. [See Stanley.]

762. That strength is of no avail against cunning is the subject of much proverbial wisdom. See Appendix, pp. 160-3.

763f. **liste/sholde miste.** The rhyme confirms the difficult form *miste; mist* (825 and 1640) is, of course, normal 3 sg. pres. of *misse* [with *eþ* > *þ* by syncope (Sievers-Brunner § 358, 2), > *t* after *s* (Sievers-Brunner § 359, 8)]; and *imist* 581 is the normal p.p. of *misse*. The least unconvincing explanation of inf. *miste* is probably that of Mätzner and *NED* (s. *mist*, v.²); the inf. *miste* is (for the rhyme) formed on the p.p. *mist*, a development with which that of the similar Swedish and Danish v. *mista* should be compared.

Less convincing is the assumption made by Kenyon [Bib. 29] that *sholde* conceals in its *-e* ' one of the not infrequent instances [Kenyon quotes no other example] in which unstressed *haue* is phonetically reduced and absorbed in the *e* of *sholde* '. Atkins (without discussing the difficulties, syntactic and semantic, involved) regards *sholde* +active p.p. as a development of OE *sceal* + passive p.p. [e.g. *Beowulf* 2255f, *sceal se hearda helm . . . fætum befeallen* (' the hard helmet must <be> deprived of ornaments '); with which Klaeber in his edition (1936), p. 210, compares 3021f, *Forðon sceall gar wesan . . . mundum bewunden* (' therefore the spear must be grasped by hands ')]; Atkins translates the words, ' would (should) have missed, or gone astray '. Stratmann takes J's *solde* as <OFr *solde* ' wages, reward ' with *miste* a 3 sg. p.; but *s* is a normal spelling for *sch, sh* in J (and not uncommon in C): e.g. *solde* 975 C and J, 977 C ; Breier (pp. 22f) records 4 other examples from C, and 27 from J. In any case the sense of the suggestion is weak: ' missed (its) reward ' for ' failed '.

769-72. On the text see footnotes. The sense of these lines is a development of the proverbial wisdom discussed in 762 note. Cf. *Proverbs of Alfred*, 192f (J), *wit and wisdom, þat alle þing ouergoþ* [' Wit and wisdom which surpass all things ']. Cf. 787f.

776. **biuore grete temes.** Translate, ' in front of great teams '. Teams of horses were hitched one in front of the other, and the first referred to in this line is the leading horse. [Thus Kenyon, Bib. 29; he refers to Chaucer's *Troilus and Criseyde*, i, 218-24, and the team of horses depicted in the *Luttrell Psalter* (see E. G. Millar's partial facsimile (1932), *f.* 181*b*–182*a*, and cf. *f.* 162*a* and *f.* 173*b*).] The J variant *bi sweore*, ' by the neck ' (for *biuore*), may describe the horse pulling against its collar.

781f. **ne . . . þat . . . n(e.** The second negative is required by ME syntax, but should be omitted in translation.

783-8. The point of the argument is that wisdom (**wit**) or skill (**craft**) overcomes brute force. But the poet's logic is faulty : he endows man not merely with wisdom and skill, but also with strength, which is more than is necessary to set him above all other creatures, and weakens the force of the poet's statement (773-82) that the strong horse must obey the weak child.

790. **al þe ȝer.** Because the Owl sings all the year round, and has accused the Nightingale of singing only in summer (481-508).

791f. For the rhyme see 277, note.

793f. Translate, ' Do you think the worse of me because I have only one talent? '

795–804. The manner of wrestling was that a prize-fighter issued a general challenge, and took on, one by one, all comers, till at last, if at all, he was thrown; the new champion challenged the rest, till he was thrown, and so forth; in the end the victor, whom none, who had tried, could throw, and none, who had not, dared to challenge, won the prize. The passage in O&N should be compared with accounts of great wrestling matches, like that in *Gamelyn* [W. H. French and C. B. Hale, *Middle English Metrical Romances*, 1930, pp. 216f, 235–66, W. W. Skeat, *The Complete Works of Chaucer*, iv (1894), p. 651].

801. The subject is not expressed. See 362, note.

804. **genge.** The meaning here appears to be that of OE *gegenge* (*Genesis*, 743; Bib. 68, vol. i) ' convenient ' [a meaning that does not seem to be part of the Old Saxon element in *Genesis B*].

807f. For the rhyme see 277, note.

808. **min on on horte.** Grattan's translation of *on horte* as ' radically, essentially ' fits the context well; yet of the many similar uses of OE *heorte* listed in B.T. *Suppl.* none quite corresponds, and the phrase as such is not in *NED*. G. V. Smithers [*E&GS* 3 (1950), 78–80] compares lines 712, 789, and 836, in each of which the Nightingale's one talent is contrasted with the Owl's many. This also is the drift of Atkins's free translation, ' Put thy crafts all together, yet is my wit alone the better.' The emendation here suggested assumes haplographic omission of *on* in the common antecedent of C and J (and, therefore, in C and J), and adopts Grattan's *on horte*. The reading thus obtained points the antithesis of ' one ' and ' many '; it may, however, be thought an unnecessary emendation, since the line as it stands gives sense, though weak: ' yet is mine radically better '. [Smithers proposes a different solution; he takes *horte* (J *heorte*) to be a unique example in English of Middle Dutch *hort*, ' thrust, onslaught ', synonymous with *sweng*.]

809–34. For the fable of The Fox and the Cat see Appendix, p. 164.

809f. **driueþ/him sulue liueþ.** None of the suggested meanings and etymologies of *liueþ* seems entirely convincing. (1) <OE *liefeþ* ' believes, trusts ' (Mätzner), which in SE areas would provide the form *leueþ* (with long tense *e*), in SW areas *luueþ* (with long *ü*) ; (2) < OE *liofaþ* ' lives ' (Wells), which in SE would give *leueþ* (short), in SW *leoueþ* (short *ŏ*); (3) <OE *be)lifeþ* ' remains ' (Atkins), which (unlike the other two suggestions) provides a true rhyme, but there is no evidence that the verb existed in OE or in ME without the prefix *be-*. The present edition, like Grattan's, follows Mätzner. It is probably an imperfect rhyme of *ī* with tense *ē*. There seems to be no example of a rhyme in O&N of SE long tense *e* derived from PrGmc *aⁱ* rhyming with SE long tense *e* derived from PrOE *ȳ* or *īe*, or it would be tempting to suggest that the original had *dreueþ* [<OE *drǣfeþ*, OK *drēfeþ*, ' drive '], leading to a true rhyme in Kentish.

812. **fox.** Both MSS have *for*; presumably their common antecedent had left off the hairline and stroke that turn one type of *r* into an *x*. Palaeographically this seems more likely than that a SE original had been confused, even if it were assumed that a SE original had *fos*. [But see S. R. T. O. d'Ardenne, Bib. 48.]

813. **wrenche** is best regarded as gen. pl. governed by **uele.** See 20, note.

814. atprenche. See 248, note.

816. There is evidence that foxes are still treed [C. Brett, Bib. 36, on English foxes; K. Huganir, pp. 17f, on American foxes]; that foxes were treed in the Middle Ages is shown by a fourteenth-century miseri-cord in Gloucester depicting a fox on the branch of a tree [reproduced in F. Bond, *Wood Carvings in English Churches*, i (1910), 99; (see Bruce Dickins, Bib. 37)]. Alexander Neckam (p. 204) writes about it [see B. J. Whiting, *Anglia* **58** (1934), 368–73], as does the author of the OFr *Roman de Renart* [see Whiting, *Anglia* **61** (1937), 126–8]. The Fox (for in line 816 it can only be the Fox, not the Cat), hanging from the bough has come to occupy a central place in the discussion about the use made by the poet of ' sources ', so much so that the chief point, made by F. P. Magoun Jr., *California Folklore Quarterly*, **4** (1945), 390–2, escaped comment, namely that it is robbing the fable of its point to include the Cat's one, but supremely effective, shift, the life-saving ability to climb trees, among the many tricks in the Fox's bag; it is a blunder in the art of narrative. Cf. 783, note.

824. Weþer . . . þe. In O&N it is only in this construction that *þe* meaning ' or ' occurs (1064, 1360, 1362, 1408). [See *NED* s. *the*, particle, l.c. (to the examples cited there must be added the fourteenth-century *Sir Beues of Hamtoun*, Auchinleck MS lines 2852, emended away by Kölbing, EETS (E.S.) 46, p. 130).] After **shal** the verb of motion is not expressed (see 724, note).

831f. anne/uenne. The original presumably had **enne/uenne**, (an in-dication that the *n* in *enne* was long and the stem-vowel short; cf. 759f). **bi dune ne bi uenne** is obviously used vaguely to mean ' everywhere, anywhere ', like the more usual tags, such as the alliterative *bi dale and bi doune*, or *bi feld and fen, bi friþ and fen*, etc.

835. mi solue. See 869, note.

837f. For the rhyme see 349, note.

838. Þu gest al to. The explanation provided by *NED* (s. *go* 91.a.), leading to, ' You get to work wholly with treachery ', seems far better than Atkins's view that *al to* here means ' altogether to ', or Grattan's view that *gest al to* means ' approachest everything '. (Cf. line 669.)

845f. For the rhyme, ȝene [< OE (-)*gegnian*]/sene, see 349f, note.

849f. For the rhyme see 1725f, note.

852. alre wnder mest, ' the most amazing thing of all '.

854–92. G. G. Coulton (Bib. 33) suggests that the Owl echoes in this passage ' that sentence so dear to St Bernard ', that a monk has his duty not in teaching but in weeping. 854f seem reminiscent of *Ancrene Riwle* [p. 164, 12f]: ' Either we are fools that hope to buy eternal bliss with trifles [?], or the holy saints are fools that bought it so dear.' Atkins (Bib. 32) shows that the Owl's teaching about man's duty to weep is the stock teaching of the time: man must weep for his own sins (865), and for the sins of others (885); he must weep on account of his longing for Heaven (881), and because of the sorrow everywhere around him (884). With these lines Atkins compares the ME sermon on Psalm 126, 6 (Vulgate 125, 6) [Bib. 71, p. 159]: 'The tear(s) that man weeps for his own sins . . ., the tear(s) that man sheds for his fellow-Christian's sins . . ., the tear(s) that man weeps for hatred of this world . . ., the tear(s) that man weeps for longing of Heaven. . . . And what reward shall they have for this sending forth (of hot tears to Heaven)? Eternal salvation, everlasting light, and life without end.'

855f. For the rhyme see 277, note.

858. Eggers well translates **bidde bote** by ' seek grace '.

861. **more wepe þane.** Translate, 'weep rather than '.

863f. For the rhyme see 1725, note.

868. **foliot.** In English, the word occurs only here; in OFr and early MnFr the word occurs as a fowling term, some sort of foolish trick to catch foolish larks, consisting perhaps of a device, roughly in the shape of a bird, with glistening mirrors, which, to the enticing sounds of skilful whistling, drew the larks into the fowler's net. [See Stanley.] Atkins has suggested that a pun is intended on the name of Gilbert Foliot, Bishop of Hereford to 1163, of London 1163-87, the adversary of Thomas Becket [cf. David Knowles, *The Episcopal Colleagues of Archbishop Thomas Becket* (1951), passim]. The word is sufficiently rare for such a pun to be not unlikely; even so, its significance remains obscure.

869. **mi.** C's *me* may reflect the pronunciation in positions of reduced stress; cf. the inverse *mi solue* 835, described by Wells as an ' early occurrence of *myself* '.

882. ' Those who are here, they have sorrow for it.' This line is similar to *The XI Pains of Hell*, 207f (Bibl. 70, p. 153):

> Ac trichurs and lyeres and les
> Þat weren her, wo is ham þes.

[' But cheats and liars and false men who were here, they shall have sorrow for it.'] Cf. Introduction, pp. 32f [and Stanley, Bib. 51, and *Archiv* **192** (1955), 23]. [In view of the parallel use in *The XI Pains of Hell* (as well as *þat boþ* 251) Grattan's belief that *þat* is a conj. and that the subject ' they ' is not expressed (' That they are here, woe is them thereof ') seems unlikely.]

883f. **iborȝe/sorwe.** A true rhyme <OE *geborgen/sorge*. Cf. 431f.

901. The two spelling systems in C are discussed in the Introduction, pp. 6-11. The second system of spellings makes its first appearance here.

905-10. It was common knowledge that nightingales do not sing in some countries. Alexander Neckam [pp. 102 and 458] in his *De Naturis Rerum* as well as in his poem *De Laudibus Divinæ Sapientiæ* tells how the nightingale is heard on one bank of a river in Wales but not on the other, and K. Huganir, p. 99, quotes Giraldus Cambrensis, who says, in his *Topographia Hibernica*, I, xxiii [*RS* (1867), v, 56], that there are no nightingales in Ireland.

909. **Noreweie.** See 999, note.

910. **Galeweie,** almost certainly Galloway (not Galway), for the fierce independence of the Gallovidians was notorious [cf. A. L. Poole, *From Domesday Book to Magna Carta* 1087-1216, 1951, pp. 272 and 278; J. MacKinnon, *The Constitutional History of Scotland*, 1924, p. 84].

913. **preoste,** to the priests. The Owl is answering the Nightingale's claim (733-5) to give what help she can to secular priests, or to priests in the country [thus Mätzner].

917-20. The meaning of the simile is this: The Nightingale, in lines 716-42 (summarised by the Owl at 849-51), had claimed that she was helping priests to instruct man how to reach the everlasting song of heaven. But she sings only in the civilised south where priests are intent on the same end with more formal, and therefore more forceful, teaching than the Nightingale's. Her weak teaching is like the bubbling of a little spring, useless when it is next to the vigorous stream of the priest's teaching, though it might be of some use if it were on the hill-side, which is now parched (i.e. without any form of instruction). **floþ** (920). In *floh*, the MS reading of C, *h* probably stands for *þ*. In Cii *þ* is written sufficiently often for *h* (cf. 1256 note) for an inverted spelling, *h* for *þ*, to be possible. The spelling *floh* seems to be related to *þunch* (1649 and 1651), with *h* probably for *þ*, i.e. *puncþ*.

921. soþ. C occasionally has *o* for *ū*: *fole* 104, *bote* 884, *flores* 1046.

923f. meoster has the accent on the second syllable. The rhyme requires the usual C form *ner*, not **neor**.

932. deoulene, gen. pl. weak ending *-ene* <OE *-ena*. In early ME weak forms of this word are not uncommon; OE *dēofol* was strong. Cf. 1412 and 1616.

933f. igremet/ofchamed. OE has two related verbs, *gremian, gegremod*, and *gramian, gegramod*; the second, > ME *igramed* is required here. In C, *t* for final *d* is not uncommon [cf. Breier, p. 32; Luick, § 713]. In C, *ch* for *sch* occurs here and in *ich chadde* 1616, *cliures charpe* 1676, *his chelde* 1713; in each case the preceding letter or letters may have led to this error, which should perhaps be emended: *ch* after *ch*, *s* omitted after *s*, or here *s* omitted after *f* which is like long *s*.

936–8. It is strange that the Nightingale should only now be thinking of the Owl's words at 592–6. She has had her chance to answer this charge in her last speech, 707–836.

936. For **he**='she' see Glossary.

941. For the proverb see Appendix, pp. 160–3. Þe is regarded by *NED* (s. *the*, particle, 1) as a conj. and compared with OE *þe* in constructions like *Heo þa fæhðe wræc þe þu . . . Grendel cwealdest (Beowulf*, 1333f) ['She avenged that enmity in that thou didst slay Grendel.'] [Cf. B.T., *þe* III.] This view leads to a preferable sentence structure here than Hinckley's view, quoted by Grattan, that *þe* is an example of the use of the def. art. before abstracts [Hinckley thinks it a Gallic use, but cf. B.T. *se*, I (6), *NED* s. *the* B.3.d.] It is preferable also to Grattan's view that both MSS follow their common antecedent which had wrongly expanded contracted *þat*, to which Grattan wishes to emend, unnecessarily if *NED* is accepted.

943f. Bruce Dickins, *TLS*, 1927, pp. 250f (and see J. P. Gilson's complementary letter, *ibid.*, p. 408), quotes from MS British Museum Additional 35116 *f.* 24c (a Yorkshire book, containing French and Latin pleas at law mainly between 1300–12) the marginal entry:

Selde erendeȝ wel þe loþe
And selde pledeȝ wel þe wroþe.

['The hated man rarely intercedes successfully, the angry man rarely pleads successfully.'] The meaning in the context is perhaps: When you plead that your client should be shown mercy you will not succeed if you are hated by the judge; but if you plead that your client shall have justice you will succeed only if you have a cool head to put his case clearly. The scribal error, *endeð* for **erendeð** [J *endeþ* for *erendeþ*], is best explained by the omission of the *re* mark in the common antecedent of C and J. [See S. T. R. O. d'Ardenne, Bib. 50; her interpretation of the proverb is somewhat different: 'It is no good sending as a messenger (ambassador) a man who is disliked', or, less probably, 'Seldom is he a good messenger (advocate) he to whom it is hateful', or, 'Seldom does he obtain by intercession he to whom it is hateful.']

951. hi understod is, according to the editors, refl. ' bethought herself, took thought '. (So also, with the pronoun in the dat., not acc., at 1297). But the dictionaries do not record a refl. use of *understand* with the meaning suggested, and perhaps (though the meaning is weaker, and fits lines 951 and 1297 less well) all that is meant is that the Nightingale understood the full import of the Owl's words.

952. lette. A weak past derived from the strong OE verb *lǣtan*, past *lēt* [not, as Gadow thinks, <OE *lettan* ' hinder from ', which in ME requires *to* or *for to* when it governs an inf.].

953f. ' A contrast is here intended between speaking in anger [**mid wraþþe**] and speaking with an unclouded mind ' [**a sele** (q.v. in the Glossary)] (Atkins).

953. For he =' she ' see Glossary.

955. Hule. (1) The easiest solution, and, in view of the similar confusion at line 411, the most probable, is to emend MS *þule* to *Hule*. (2) A mistaken attempt was made in the first impression of this edition to defend MS *þule* as an elided use of the def. art. preceding a noun in the voc. But in OE, ME, and early MnE the def. art. is so used only (*a*) when its noun follows a noun in apposition to it [*A God þe heyȝe Trinite* (C. Brown, *Religious Lyrics of the 14th Century*, 13²⁵); *Socoure vs, Darrie þe Kyng* (*Kyng Alisaunder*, 2380)]; or (*b*) when its noun is followed by a dependent gen. or qualifying phrase introduced by *of* [*se mæra maga Healfdenes* (*Beowulf*, 1474); *þe prince of hell* (*Cursor Mundi*, 18077 MS. Vesp.)]. (3) Grattan also takes *þ* to be an elided *þe*, but dat., not voc.: ' To the Owl she said.' In view of the vocatives at 217, 411, 707, 1298, 1638, and at 33, it would be surprising to have a dat. here. (4) It is not impossible that *þule* might be an elision of *þu ule*. There are many examples of *þu* preceding a noun in the voc. in ME [e.g. *Thow deiþe, thou come to me* (*Ipomedon*, 4688, and cf. 4697); see *NED* s. *thou* I. b); but it is far from certain that the *u* of *þu* could be elided in such uses before *u* of the following word.

961-4. The general meaning is: Just as those who are wise go on along the right road even though it has muddy patches, so the sun follows its course punctually even though its course is such that it must shine on the Owl's foul nest. The Nightingale seems to have adapted the proverb which in ME is found in *Handlyng Synne*, 2299f:

> Þe sunne hys feyrnes neuer he tynes
> Þoghe hyt on þe muk hepe shynes

[' The sun never loses his radiance though he shines on the muckheap.'] See Appendix, pp. 160-3.

Atkins takes **for** (962 and 965) with **forlete**, ' leave (something) for (something else)', a usage not recorded in ME; Brett [Bib. 30 and 36] rightly takes *for* to mean ' because of '. **venne** may here mean either ' fen, marshland ', or, more probably, ' mud, mire ' [cf. A. H. Smith, s. *fenn*]. Two improvements have been suggested (but are not accepted here, because they are not strictly essential): in conformity with J and as an improvement in metre and morphology **ine nest** has been emended to *in neste*; P. G. Thomas [in *YWES* 3 (for 1922), 35f] suggests that *neuer* should be inserted after *sunne*, a metrical improvement which would have the additional virtue of conforming to the wording of the proverb.

965f. Like the sun, that follows its course regardless of what it shines on, the Nightingale will not leave her rightful place by the bed-chamber of the lord and lady on account of the privy next to the house. **hole brede** does not mean (as Atkins thinks) ' hollow log ' (the dwelling-place of the Owl), but [as Brett, Bib. 36, says] ' a plank with a hole in it '.

970. hexst. C has *r* for *x*; cf. J's *hexte* and 812, note. The lord and lady are ' the highest ', and *hexst* is dat. pl. with final *e* elided before *ich* [cf. Gadow's glossary]. [Attempts (like those of Wells and Grattan) to defend the MS reading *herst* (<OK *herst* ' hillock, copse, wooded eminence '—cf. A. H. Smith, s.v. *hyrst*—in contrast with *fule venne*, 962) are based on a misinterpretation of the whole passage.]

975. For the inversion cf. 515, note.

978. prost. Atkins renders C's *brost* acc. pl. neuter by ' souls '. The word is, especially in OE, often used of the seat of the affections. Yet there is no convincing parallel to *brost* meaning in effect ' themselves ', and the emendation to *prost*, though weak, is safer.

981f. heriinge. Cf. *wnienge* 614 and note.

987f. For the rhyme see 277, note. [Hinckley (Bib. 40) emends **wepen** to *greten*, without discussing the other assonances.]

991f. of twere twom. *twere* (J *tweyre*) is perhaps gen. of *two*, equal in meaning to *of two*, comparable with the OE pleonastic *bām twām* (dat. pl. ' both ') ; or perhaps the phrase means, literally, ' of two of two ', i.e. ' of two of a set of two ', i.e. ' of two alternatives '.

Atkins emends *twere* to *twene* (<OE *twēona*, gen. pl. of *twēo*, ' doubt '), translating the line, ' which is the better of two doubtful things? ' But there is nothing of doubt in *blipe oper grom*, and it seems best to let the MS reading stand, acknowledging that it has not been explained convincingly. [Other emendations are palaeographically less satisfactory than Atkins's, and do not make better sense than his emended reading or than that of the MS: to *pan twam* or *pinge twam* (Mätzner, comparing the not truly analogous *of twam pinge* 1477), or to *pese twam* (Holthausen, Bib. 38).] The rhyme is inexact, since the *o* of **twom** is long, that of **grom** short.

999–1014. The commentators see a striking resemblance here to Ohthere's description of Norway in King Alfred's *Orosius* [EETS (O.S.) 79; ' pp. 17–21 passim ', says Atkins, including Wulfstan's description of Esthonia, though that is one of many wild countries not mentioned in O&N.] But the links between England and Scandinavia long survive the Anglo-Saxon period, and Dickins and Wilson compare the *Hakonar Saga's* account [*Icelandic Sagas, RS* (1887), ii, pp. 241, 248 (=*RS* (1894), iv, pp. 252, 258f)] of Cardinal William's mission to Hakon the Old in 1247. ' It was told him by the Englishmen for envy's sake against the men of Norway that he would get no honour there and hardly any meat, and no drink but sour whey; and the English dissuaded him . . . against going to Norway and frightened him both with the sea and the grimness of the folk.' At Hakon's coronation feast ' it was told me that I should see few men . . . (and) they would be more like to beasts in their behaviour than men '. But other countries are described in similar terms; Ireland, for example, as described by Giraldus Cambrensis in his *Topographia Hibernica*, III, x [*RS* (1867), v, 151]. The description of the wild land in O&N is an example of the medieval, non-realistic, wild landscape and its inhabitants (cf. E. R. Curtius, *European Literature and the Latin Middle Ages* (1953) pp. 200–2).

1001f. **houentinge/genge.** The second element of *houentinge* is from OE *getenge* (+dat.), ' close to ', and the rhyme requires the *e* derived direct from *-tenge*. The first element must be from a dat. sg. or pl. (*heofene*, *-um*), and we should expect *houene itenge*, perhaps elided to *houenetenge* (cf. J's *houenetinge*, to which Atkins emends the C reading).

1007f. For the rhyme see 1381–4, note.

1007. Dickins and Wilson compare William of Malmesbury, *Gesta Regum Anglorum*, IV, § 348 [*RS* (1889), ii, 399], who refers to the Norwegian habit of eating raw fish.

1010. I.e. ' they know no better '.

1011. **noþer.** The common antecedent of C and J must have omitted the *er* mark, and so was misunderstood by the J scribe, but copied faithfully in C.

1013f. The inhabitants of the barbarous north looked like devils, who were frequently depicted as of human form, either covered with fur like beasts, or clad in furs like savages. For illustrations see the Victoria and Albert Museum's *Small Picture Books*, No. 15 (1950), Romanesque Art, Pl. 21 (showing an English Last Judgement plaque of about 1150–60); and *Archæologia* **60**, Pt. 2 (1907), Pl. 34 (the Judgement Porch, about 1270–80, of Lincoln Cathedral). [Cf. further Stanley.]

1016. Presumably a topical reference, but who the good man from Rome is remains obscure. The names of three men who undertook papal missions have been invoked : (1) Atkins favours Cardinal Vivian, who in 1176 undertook a mission to Scotland, Ireland, Norway, and the adjacent islands; (2) K. Huganir (pp. 108f) believes the wild country must be Norway, and the man from Rome Nicholas Breakspear (who visited Norway in 1152–4, a time that might well be referred to as *wile* in the poem); if right we should here have an allusion to the only Englishman ever to become Pope (Adrian IV); (3) Börsch, p. 7, thought Cardinal Guala's mission to the Scots was meant, but its date, 1218, makes it too late (cf. 1092, note).

1021f. ' This rather fantastic illustration may have been suggested by the poet's reading of Neckam's *De Naturis Rerum*, ii. ch. 129. where an account is given of a jongleur who trained two apes to fight in a mimic tournament, armed with shield, sword and spear. In the chapter immediately following the bear is described as a type of cruelty, and this idea may have suggested itself as adding point to the illustration ' (Atkins). **bore/spere.** The original must have had *bere*; *bore* (with *ŏ*) is <OE *beora* with non-WS back-mutation.

1024. Between **hi me** and **wolde** C (but not J) has *segge*, which gives no sense. The editors omit it (often silently). Mätzner emends to *hi masse wolde*, i.e., ' They would do better to teach a bear to wield both shield and lance, than that one should induce that wild people that they would wish to hear mass being sung.' This emendation would be palaeographically more convincing if the original is assumed to have had SE *messe*, misread as *me segge*. Even so, the sense gained by Mätzner's emendation is less good than that gained by omitting (without satisfactory explanation) *segge* in agreement with J.

1025. MnE syntax requires that in translation ' do ' is supplied after *sol[d]ich*.

1027f. The poet forces **bridel** into a rhyme with *del*, although in normal pronunciation the second syllable is unstressed, with short *e*.

1028–30. Halter and bridle and the man with weapons of steel typify means of restraint, all of no avail here.

1029. **wode wise.** Dickins and Wilson defend C's *wude wise* as a unique adjectival use of the noun derived from OE *wudewāsa*, ' wild man of the woods ' (of which ME forms in -*wise* are recorded). In their Glossary *wude-wise* is translated ' barbarous ways ', which is very near in meaning to the more obvious (and more likely) *wode wise* in J. **wise/ire,** for the rhyme see 277, note.

1036. **of.** Probably the meaning of *singe of* is ' speak in song about ', i.e. ' I sing of hymns ' ; but possibly *of* is used as a partitive [cf. *NED* s. *of*, 45], ' I sing something of hymns.' There is a further possibility: to take *singe songe* together, ' sing songs ', with *of chirche*, ' about the church ', giving the subject-matter of the songs; but, in view of *chirche song*, ' hymn-singing ' (984), this is less likely.

1037. **olde laȝe.** The usual meaning of this phrase (cf. Atkins, Bib. 32) is ' the old dispensation ' (as opposed to Christ's new dispensation); but (as K. Huganir, pp. 51f, says) this cannot be meant here, for the proverb of 1039f is based on New Testament as well as Old Testament texts (cf. Galatians 6 : 7–8; Job 4 : 8; Proverbs 22 : 8, etc.). Perhaps the phrase is used more loosely here, with some such meaning as ' an old dictum '. Mätzner suggests emending to *in olde daȝe*, ' in days of old ', which is common enough in ME [cf. *NED* s. *day*, sb. 13.a], and provides a convenient way out, if that is felt to be necessary.

1039f. This proverb is found also in *The Proverbs of Alfred*, 78f:

> Hwych so þe mon soweþ,
> Al swuch he schal mowe.

Cf. Galatians, 6 : 7–8, and Appendix, pp. 160–3. **man,** even where used like an impersonal pron., is the regular antecedent of *he*.

1043f. **rad/abrad.** Atkins derives *abrad* from OE *abrǣd, abrǣgd,* p. of *abregdan*, ' move suddenly ', here ' raise the eyes '; this explains J's reading *abraid*, but leaves the rhyme imperfect, the *a* in *rad* being short, that in *abrad* long. Bradley, followed by *MED*, takes C's *abrad* to be the past of the OE weak verb *abrǣdan*, ' dilate '; but that should have a past *abradde* in ME. Grattan suggests *abrad* may be the p.p. from OE *abrǣdan*, here used in an absolute construction, ' with dilated eyes '; this is morphologically more satisfactory than Bradley's suggestion, and provides a true rhyme.

1046. **flores.** For the spelling see 921, note.

1048. **biclopt.** The scribe seems to have made two errors in this word. He has left off final *t*; and he has written *o*, an impossible spelling for *ü* (cf. J's *iclupt*). Atkins suggests *biclopt* may be a genuine form (not otherwise recorded) < hypothetical OE **cloppian*, instead of < the normal OE *beclyppan*. **bihedde.** Grattan thinks that the verb here and at 102 may not be the same as at 635, but derived from the past of the Kentish form (with *ē* for *ȳ*) of OE *behȳdan* ' conceal '. This meaning would fit well here; but the meaning ' watched over ' fits better at 102 and is not impossible here. The most likely view is perhaps to assume that the original here had SE *behedde* ' concealed ', and that the scribe who transposed O&N into the Western dialect of the common antecedent of C and J took this form, and pressed it into service in his dialect (where it belongs to a different verb), with the meaning 'watched over ', i.e. the Nightingale, who guards houses (1045), also watches over the couple. [Cf. 273, note and 1725, note.] Since this edition is of the extant text C, and not of its putative original, the Glossary does not give a meaning other than ' watched over '.

1049–1110. See Appendix, pp. 165f for Marie de France's *Lay of the Austic* and allied stories, which underlie this passage.

1049f. ware/lere. The rhyme requires the form *were*<OE *hwǣr*; *ware*, the normal form in C, is from OE *hwār*, *hwāra*.

1056f. grine & wel. C reads clearly *grineþ wel*, with thorn for ampersand; cf. J's *grune & wel*. [Grattan suggests that the original had *grine þe*, ' snares or '; in O&N, however, *þe* meaning ' or ' occurs only in conjunction with *h)waþer* (see 824, note); and in any case the J reading gives better sense.] The subject of **sette & lede** is not expressed (see 362 note). C's *ledde* is an impossible form; J's *leyde* is better; probably the form miscopied by the C scribe is *lede*, with loss of palatal *g* before *d* (cf. 349, note). The lines mean, ' Bird-lime and snares, and all kinds of things he set and laid to catch you.'

1063f. For the rhyme see 349, note.

1071f. tunge/songe. These rhymes, *ung/ong*, have been discussed by M. S. Serjeantson, *RES* 7 (1931), 450–2. [Cf. L. Morsbach, *Mittelenglische Grammatik*, 1896, §§ 88, 93 Anm. 1, and 125 Anm. 1; Dobson, *1500–1700*, § 92, Note 1; Luick, §§ 367, and 429, 1 and Anm. 3; Jordan, § 31 Anm. and Nachtrag.] It appears that these rhymes are not confined to any one area, though their exact distribution is not fully established.

1072. This proverb seems to occur only here, though it has been suggested that a somewhat similar idea is found in *The Proverbs of Alfred*, 458–60: ' A wise man can enclose much in few words: and a fool's bolt is soon shot.' (Cf. Appendix, pp. 160–3; and cf. O. Arngart's Explanatory Note to the passage in his edition of *The Proverbs*, where further parallels are adduced.) **songe.** There is no evidence to determine whether a specific song is referred to, or whether, as seems more probable, the exigencies of the rhyme determined the choice of word, with *seiþ in þe songe* meaning vaguely, ' as is said and sung '. The subject of *seiþ* (' it ' in MnE) is not expressed; cf. 362, note.

1075. shome/grame. A true rhyme: <OE *sc(e)ame* or *sc(e)ome* and *graman* or *groman*. In ME the forms with *o* are confined to the West Midlands, i.e. the dialect of the MSS; all other areas have *a*. (Cf. Jordan § 30.) See 1089f.

1081–6. Atkins sees a reminiscence here of Marie de France's *Lay of Yonec*. A young lady is locked up by her old husband in a tower to which, called by her prayer full of ardent love, a knight, Muldumarec, flies in the shape of a falcon. But there the resemblance ends. He consoles her, though not with a song, and of their union Yonec is born; the falcon is mortally wounded by spikes fixed to the lady's window by the lord.

1088. riȝte niþe. For the legal implications see Introduction, p. 29.

1091f. The prayer, **Iesus his soule do merci !**, can only refer to a dead man. [Thus the early commentators (summarised by K. Huganir, pp. 70f, note); D. Everett, *YWES* 12 (for 1931), pp. 117–19; F. Tupper, Bib. 44; L. de la Torre Bueno, *Anglia* 58 (1934), 122–30; Atkins, *MLR* 35 (1940), 55f; and conclusively, C. T. Onions, *MÆ* 17 (1948), 32.] Hinckley's view [Bib. 39—and *ELH* 4 (1937), 299f; followed by

K. Huganir, pp. 70–80] that the prayer can refer to a living person is untenable. Four kings bearing the name of **Henri** might be meant: Henry I (1100–35); Henry II (1154–89); Henry III (1216–72); and the Young King Henry (1170–83), crowned to secure the succession in 1170; during Henry II's absence in Normandy and Ireland in 1170–2 the *rex filius suus* (as the Young King Henry was officially described) was virtually king of England. Yet it is unlikely that he should be referred to here [as is thought by Hinckley (Bib. 43) and, more fully, by S. T. R. O. d'Ardenne, *ESts* 30 (1949), 157–64]; for at all times, whenever there could be any doubt who was meant, Henry II or the Young King, the Young King's title was qualified, in Latin, French or English, as the case might be, by 'young' or 'son'. Henry III's death comes too late, Henry I's too early (and he could not be referred to simply as 'King Henry' after Henry II's accession); and so the opinion of the poem's first editor, Stevenson, still seems the best, that the reference is to Henry II. He was respected as a monarch on account of his firm rule after the anarchy under King Stephen; and he was a generous patron of literature. (Cf. C. H. Haskins in *Essays in Medieval History presented to T. F. Tout*, edited by A. G. Little and F. M. Powicke, 1925, pp. 71–7.) See Introduction, p. 19.

1093. let forbonne, ' "caused (the knight) to be outlawed'. This sentence [of outlawry], at the date of the poem, does not necessarily mean " banishment or exile ", i.e. a substantive punishment, but merely a criminal process, a means of compelling accused persons to stand their trial (see Pollock and Maitland, vol. ii, p. 459) ' (Atkins). [See also C. T. Flower, p. 324.]

1096. niþe & . . . onde. For the legal implications see Introduction, p. 29.

1100. wunne. Perhaps the meaning wanted here is ' possessions ', something rather more concrete than ' happiness '; cf. the phrase *worldes wunne*, ' worldly joys '. Otherwise, however, this extension of meaning cannot be paralleled, and may be felt to be inadmissible.

1101. an hundred punde. Gadow and Atkins point out that the amount is excessive [by the standards of wergeld; see Liebermann, vol. ii, Pt. ii, pp. 731–4]. But this is too literal a view; the poem is not bound by facts, and a hundred pounds is, simply, as large a sum as you could wish.

1111. ereming. The omission of *n* here and in *murninge*, 1598, is probably simply a scribal error. But cf. A. McIntosh, *RES* (N.S.) 2 (1951), 70

1115. children. Here possibly ' girls ' in antithesis to **gromes**, ' boys '. [Thus Atkins, who compares the use of the word at 1453 and 1463.] Another explanation seems, however, more probable; A. H. Smith, s. *cild*, says, ' Compounds like *leorning-cild* " pupil " and *munuc-cild* " boy training to be a monk " point to more precise applications [than "young person "], and the use of the latter meaning, " young monk ", in place-names is confirmed by the somewhat later [thirteenth century] statement in *Gesta Abbatum Monasterii S. Albani* [*RS* (1867), i, 54], that Child-wick, Hertfordshire, was so named because the place provided suste-nance for the young monks of St Albans.' The antithesis of *children* to *gromes* remains; for *gromes* may here have the more specific meaning of ' lads in service '. Together *children* and *gromes* may, therefore, mean ' boys of the cloister and serving lads '. **heme & hine** is translated ' villagers and farmhands ' by S. T. R. O. d'Ardenne [*Iuliene*, pp. 157f (and cf. J. R. R. Tolkien, *RES* 1 (1925), 215, and A. F. Colborn, *Hali Meiðhad* (1940), pp. 112f)], who suggests that this might be a weakened meaning of a phrase that had its origin in the distinction between religious and lay inhabitants of a village or town; for *heme*, 'inhabitants of a place, householders, dwellers', is a derivative of OE *hām*, 'a dwelling-place, a household' [see A. H. Smith, s. *hāme*]; and *hine* (which in OE could mean simply 'household, a family and its dependents') came to mean 'a religious community' (see A. H. Smith, s. *hīwan*) and that is the sense required here [rather than 'farmhands' (cf. *NED* s. *hind*, sb.²)]. In *Hali Meiðhad* (edited by A. F. Colborn), 146f, the antithesis of *heame* and *hine* is used in conjunction with that of foe and friend: . . . *þe maked of eordlich mon & wummon heouene engel, of heame hine, of fa freont.* [. . . 'which makes of earthly man and woman an angel of heaven, turns *heame* into *hine* and foe into friend'.] In O&N, the line means that, when they pursue the Owl, people forget all their traditional enmities; the monastery boys run with the lads of the castle and the village, the village-folk are at one with the monastics.

1125f. swore/dore. The rhyme requires J's word, *sweore*, spelt *o* for *eo* (as often in C), [<OE *swēoran*, *dēorum*]; so that C's *spore* [<OE *sporum*] is impossible, even though the meaning 'claws' [a meaning first recorded in early MnE (see *NED* s. *spur*, sb.¹, 5)] fits better than 'neck'.

1127. blod is here 'the vital principle, that upon which life depends' [*NED* s. *blood*, sb. 4]; so that the line is circumlocutory, 'As a living thing of flesh and blood you are worthless.'

1128. shueles. *NED* (s. *shewel*), followed by Atkins, tentatively derives the word from a hypothetical OE **scīewels*. A form **shuueles*, or J's *sheules*, or Atkins's emendation **sheueles*, might be better. But the word is difficult [*schawles* (1648) is not to be explained (as Atkins attempts) by 'analogy' with ME *scheawen*, *schawen* (<OE *scēawian* 'to look'—translated 'show' by Atkins)]; and the form in C is best left unemended.

1132. at þan ende. Grattan asks: 'Does this mean "at last" (Hinckley), or "near by" (Atkins), or "at the boundary" or "at the end (of the pole)"?' Though *MED*, s. *ende*, n. (1), 23 (1), provides many examples of the meaning 'at last', it does not fit the context as well as 'at the boundary', or 'at the far side', which is perhaps the best.

1133. *NED* (s. *year*, 7) translates a ʒere here by 'every year', but the meaning 'in spring, in the warm season' [suggested by Bruce Dickins (quoted by Atkins), with reference to B.T. *Suppl.* s. *gēar*, IIIb] is more appropriate.

1145–1330. A. C. Cawley, has given careful consideration to the astrology in O&N, and uses it as supporting evidence for the dating of the poem by reference to the planetary conjunction of 16 September 1186, a conjunction predicted for that date as early as 1184, and regarded as an evil omen. The prediction of that pestilential season and the fears it inspired in all, clergy and laity, rich and poor, are vividly described in the 1184 annal of Roger of Hoveden's *Chronicle* [*RS* (1869), vol. ii, pp. 290–8 (translated in Bohn's *Antiquarian Library* (1853), by H. T. Riley, ii, 36–45)].

The birds' debate on astrology would, Cawley believes, have had special point at any time after 1184; even after 1189 [the date suggested by lines 1091f (cf. note, and Introduction, p. 19)] the conjunction of

1186 was well remembered. The debate must be seen against the background of that age; and Cawley says, ' By the end of the twelfth century there cannot have been much danger in making an outspoken defence of the new astrological theories, judging by the fact that we find Alexander Neckam openly supporting a Christianized astrology with arguments which are basically similar to those used by the Owl.' Of the Nightingale, on the other hand, Cawley says, ' It is her want of learning that makes her out-of-date on the subject of astrology and unaware that it can be defended on orthodox and thoroughly respectable grounds.'

1149-60. Cawley suggests that the Nightingale's charges are to be directly associated with the evil planetary influences of Mars and Saturn, such as were predicted for 1186 (see 1145, note).

1156. þoues rune. See 1215, note.

1166f. *NED* (as was pointed out by the anonymous reviewer of Atkins, Bib. 34) records *tobuneþ* only here and in William of Shoreham (EETS (E.S.) 86 p. 82, *The Hours of the Cross*, line 85]; and *clut* only here and again as *clout*, in the nineteenth century, a Kentish dialect word meaning ' a clod, or lump of earth, in a ploughed field '; [according to *EDD* s. *clout*, sb.³ the word is also found in Yorkshire]. See Introduction, pp. 17f.

1174. All socially respectable people, lay or clerical, but not the poor, nor the peasantry (nor, for that matter, monks), wore linen (i.e. underclothing). [See G. G. Coulton, Bib. 33.]

1177-9. The right to pronounce a curse in the divine name is a part of the priestly office; and outside the priesthood no man has authority to do so. The Owl's remarks are occasioned by the Nightingale's invocation of God's wrath, 1169-74.

1183. On the legal implications of **alde niþe** see Introduction, p. 29.

1186. Drah to þe! The phrase has not been explained convincingly. Perhaps *þe* is an ethic dative, *to* then being adverbial, as in MnE *go to!* (thus Atkins). Grattan tentatively suggests as another possibility that ' *þe* is a corruption of some ancient form of " gee! " ' Gadow takes *to þe* to mean ' to your side (of the road)' shouted to a road-user coming the other way; but this hardly fits the context unless it is taken to mean something like, ' Mind your own business! ' In the context the phrase seems to be a cry to slow down somebody who is going too quickly. ' But,' as Grattan says, ' this still leaves the carter unaccounted for.'

1191. The collocation of **hunger** and **hergonge** is discussed by Bruce Dickins [*LSE* 4 (1935), pp. 75f] in connexion with the alliterative phrase *here & hunger.*

1193. luste is to be derived (with Gadow) from WS *līest, lȳst*, pres. ind. 3 sg. of *lēosan* ' to lose '; the final *e*, which would in any case be elided before *h*, is inorganic. The line repeats the argument of line 1159 (thus Kenyon, Bib. 29). [Wells's interpretation of *luste* as a personal use (3 sg. pres. subj.) of the impersonal verb *luste* (<OE *lystan*), with some such meaning as ' have joy in, desire ', is inferior in sense and very difficult in syntax (see *NED* s. *list*, v.¹).]

1197f. Bruce Dickins, *LSE* 5 (1936), 68-70, translates these lines, ' if men have undertaken to fight a judicial combat, I know which of the two is doomed to defeat.' See 541f and note; and Introduction, p. 29.

1204. **eorne oþer erne.** As Hinckley (Bib. 40) says, the meaning is probably ' run or ride '. This is the meaning of the similar collocation in Layamon's *Brut*, 6138f:

> Eorneð and eærne[ð]
> and al þis lond bearneð!

[' Run and ride and burn all the land! '] Those who run are the poor, as in *Havelok the Dane* [EETS (E.S.) 4], 101, *Poure þat on fote yede* [' The poor that went on foot ']; and those who ride are the rich, i.e. the Owl can foretell people's poverty or prosperity. Gadow (writing before Hinckley) connects the phrase less plausibly with the OE *Laws of Alfred* [Liebermann, i, 51]: *Gif hie* [i.e. *frið*] *fáhmon geierne oððe gearne. . . .* [' If a *fahmon* (i.e. a man exposed to the vengeance of a slain man's kin because of the murder) reaches it (i.e. asylum) by running or riding. . . .'] Gadow suggests, therefore, that in O&N the Owl knows if people shall run or ride, i.e. seek asylum; in other words, the Owl knows when a crime is going to be committed. [Grattan suggests that the meaning is ' compete or win ', but (though he also refers to the passage in the *Laws of Alfred*) he does not justify his interpretation, which, in any event, is less satisfactory in meaning than Hinckley's suggestion.]

1206. **smiþes schal.** (1) The C reading is [as Gadow, Grattan and Hinckley (Bib. 40) say] clearly *smiþes*; J has *smithes*; the reading *snuwes* of the earlier editors could only be the product of emendation (as it is in Gadow). But *snuwes* would not be an improvement: it is unlikely in form and syntax; and the Owl's list of forebodings is of events that affect creatures more directly with catastrophe than do ' snows '. (2) Hinckley takes line 1206 together with the preceding line, interpreting *smiþes* as ' carpenters ', and by extension as ' shipwrights '. It seems, however, that in English the word *smith* never meant ' worker in wood ' [except in so far as it may render Latin *faber* (see *NED*)]. The meaning ' workers in metal ' fits the context, and (as Cawley has shown) the astrology. *Smiþes* here means ' armourers ', who are subjects of Mars, and who, if they bungle their riveting, will bring about calamity, which the Owl forebodes.

The pl. *smiþes* with the sg. *schal* is difficult. J has *smithes sale*, so that the common antecedent of C and J must have had the solecism. (1) G. V. Smithers (Bib. 45) suggests that the original had sg. *smiþ*, and that this was altered under the influence of the pl. *schipes*. (2) Grattan tentatively suggests that the *es* of *smiþes* is not the pl. termination, but ' an isolated instance of the unstressed pronoun, =" them " '; but that would be a dialect peculiarity unknown in the areas with which the poem (or the MSS in which it is extant) has been connected. In any case, it is difficult to see what ' them ' would refer to, unless it is to *schipes*, with *smiþ* as ' shipwright '. (3) A possible explanation is perhaps to be found in early pl. uses of *schal(e* for the normal *schule*. *NED* (s. *shall*, A. 3ε) has *we scale* as early as the *Lambeth Homilies* of the late twelfth century. J's *sale* is dissyllabic, but the final *e* would be elided before the vowel of *uuele*, which explains C's monosyllabic *schal*. The metre of the C reading is not, however, as smooth as that obtained by emending to *smiþ*, so that Smithers's explanation may be felt to be more attractive. [See Stanley.]

1210. **nule.** (J has *wile*.) In comparative constructions a negative was at times introduced pleonastically. [Cf. Einenkel, pp. 76f]. In translation it must, of course, be omitted: ' more than I wish to tell you '.

1213. tacninge. Atkins takes this to mean ' symbolism ', the allegorical interpretation of Scripture, ' presumably ', as Cawley says, ' with reference to the knowledge of the Gospel which the Owl has laid claim to in lines 1209–12 '. Cawley advances an alternative interpretation: that *tacninge* means ' betokening, presaging ' (cf. *NED*, s. *tokening*). In this he follows Gadow's translation ' Zeichendeutung ' (i.e. the interpretation of signs). Since *tokening* does not anywhere else mean ' the symbolical principle ', but something more immediate, Cawley's seems the better explanation. He translates the line, ' I know all about presaging or prognostication.'

1215. rem. To raise a ' hue and cry ' is the legal duty of everyone who sees a felon; and whoever hears it must arm himself and join in the pursuit. [Cf. Pollock and Maitland, ii, 578f; Secular Laws of King Cnut, in Liebermann, i, 330.] Cf. 1683, note.

1218. worþ. On the spelling see 249, note.

1225f. her [for *er*, with inorganic initial *h*, as often in the MSS, especially in J (see Breier, p. 22)] is supplied from J, where it has a point before and after it. This may indicate that the common antecedent was difficult here; perhaps, like C, it had a space, perhaps it had *her* (like J), which a scribe might not have understood. In these lines *he*, *his* and *him* refers to some word like ' calamity ' [or ' trouble ' (Atkins), or ' harm ' (Eggers)] which must be understood: ' If you see it coming, calamity is almost deprived of its strength.' There are many proverbs with the general sense of 'Forewarned is forearmed', or ' A danger foreseen is half avoided '; but none has been adduced that is really close to that here ascribed to Alfred.

1227f. For the rhyme see 369, note.

1229f. flo. Both MSS read *fleo*, so that the common antecedent may have been that. The context requires *flo* ' arrow ', suggested by Gadow (who retained the impossible MS form). As Kenyon (Bib. 29) says, ' Since each scribe was copying from a MS that in different parts had both *o* and *eo* (from OE *eo*), it is not surprising that *flo* (<OE *flā*) should be changed to *fleo* in the neighbourhood of two occurrences of *fleo* [1230 and 1231].'

schal toward misȝenge. *misȝenge* (J *misyenge*) occurs only here; by some it has been taken to be a noun, by others a verb. If a noun, it seems to be a doublet of *misgang* ' going astray '; if a verb, it is presumably a derivative of OE *gengan*, and (like *misgo*) means ' go astray '. [Cf. the similar pair, OE *misfēran* and *misfaran*,] The etymology is difficult in either case. Some support for a form of the ME verb *genge* <OE *gengan* with initial *ȝ* or *y* is perhaps given by the inf. *ȝinge*, quoted by Bradley from John Mirk [EETS (O.S.) 31 (1902), line 1851; Mirk wrote about 1400 in Shropshire]. Similarly, there may be support for the noun *gang* with initial *ȝ* or *y* in the form *ȝong* quoted by Bradley from Layamon, *St Katherine*, and other early ME texts of the West Midlands; a noun *ȝenge, however, is not recorded, so that it seems more likely that *misȝenge* is a verb.

The syntax of the phrase is easy if *misȝenge* is a noun, and more difficult if a verb. (1) Those editors who take it as a noun simply assume that, as elsewhere (cf. 724, note), a verb of motion is not expressed after *schal*; and they translate ' shall fly towards misfaring ' (Wells). Some may wish to assume haplographic omission before *toward* of the verb *to* ' proceed ' [cf. *teo* in Glossary]. (2) Those who follow *NED*, s. *misyenge*, in assuming it to be a verb must take *toward* as an adv. meaning ' onward ', a considerably earlier example than any given in *NED* (s. *toward*, adj. and adv., B.2.), where the earliest is dated 1426, from Lydgate. [The emendation *schal* [*þe*] *toward misȝenge* ' shall miscarry toward you ' (suggested by the anonymous reviewer of Atkins, Bib. 34) avoids the syntactical difficulty, but has not been accepted here because the emendation can be avoided by the first alternative explanation.] **hu fleo** (J *hw fleo*). The subject pronoun (MnE ' it ') is not expressed here. See 362, note.

The lines may be translated, ' An arrow flying on its way shall miss its mark if you see how it flew from the string ', the assumption being that ' you ' is the mark, who will have time to move out of the way.

1232. **heo** refers to *flo*, which is fem.

1233. As Wells says, this line is in apposition to *sor* in the next line. The construction in J, with *þauh* ' though ' (where C has *þat*) may be the original; cf. 1235 footnote. **odwite.** Atkins and Grattan think that the *o* is miswritten for *e*; J has *edwite*. But Gadow is right to defend the C reading, connecting it with OE *opwītan* which exists side by side with *ætwītan* and (with a prefix not related to *op-*, *æt-*) *edwītan*; all having the same meaning, ' blame, reproach '. The noun *odwite* is not recorded elsewhere; it has the same meaning as *edwite*, ' blame, reproach ', here perhaps ' shame '.

1241f. Cawley suggests that the Owl's refutation, that she is to blame for the calamities she foresees, is reminiscent of a passage in Boethius's *Consolation of Philosophy*, v, 6 [Loeb Classical Library, p. 405]: ' " For doth thy sight impose any necessity upon those things which thou seest present? " " No." " But the present instant of men may well be compared to that of God in this: that as you see some things in your temporal instant, so He beholdeth all things in His eternal present. . . . As you, when at one time you see a man walking upon earth and the sun rising in heaven, although they be both seen at once, yet you discern and judge that the one is voluntary, and the other necessary, so likewise the divine sight beholding all things disturbeth not the quality of things which to Him are present, but in respect of time are yet to come." '

1246. **summe men** is dat. sg., ' to some man ', i.e. the man of 1247–50. [See Kenyon, Bib. 29.]

1256. **þurþ** for *þurh* and similar uses of *þ* for *h* have been retained in the present edition since such spellings are not uncommon in late OE and ME. [See C. T. Onions, Bib. 59 ; A. Napier, *Compassio Mariæ*, EETS (O.S.) 103, pp. 80f, and *OE Glosses*, p. 94 (3532), p. 3 (66), and p. 16 (552); W. Skeat, *William of Palerne*, EETS (E.S.) i, p. 310; Hall, p. 238 (*þupte*), p. 302 (*woþ*); Wells, Bib. 62; E. Dobson, *1500–1700*, p. 182².] Cf. *þurþ* 1405, 1428, *neþ* 1267, *heþ* 1405, *hopful* 1295, *noþt* 1391, 1395, 1552 [to which must be added from the poem immediately following O&N in C, *Long Life* line 50, *noþt* (EETS (O.S.) 49, p. 158)], *napt* 1470, 1620, 1740, (and cf. *innoþ* misread *inoh* in J; 1317–20 note). [S. R. T. O. d'Ardenne (Bib. 48) wishes to read *wynn* for *thorn* in *noþt* (and presumably also *napt*); confusion of *wynn* and *thorn* is, of course, very common in C (see Introduction, pp. 9f), yet each time the word *noþt* or *napt* occurs in C the shape of the letter *thorn* is unmistakable. These spellings are related to the spelling *noyt* in MS Digby 2 (*A Song of Sorrow for the Passion*, 57, in Carleton Brown, *English Lyrics of the XIIIth Century*, p. 124) rhyming with *hiboyt* (i.e. *iboht* ' bought '), *soit* (i.e. *soht* ' sought '), and *þoit* (i.e. *þoht* ' thought ') ; in the last two rhyme-words *i* is written for *y*, which may have been indistinguishable from *þ* in the exemplar (as it is in C, where *y* and *wynn* are distinguishable); the letter *wynn* does not occur in Digby 2. In the *Ayenbite of Inwyt* (see Wallenberg, p. 166) *napt* for *naȝt* is also found.]

1267. neþ. On the spelling see 1256, note.

1270. his worde was goddspel. According to *NED* this is the earliest example of *gospel* meaning ' something as " true as the gospel "'. The next is from Chaucer (*Troilus and Criseyde*, v, 1264f).

1271–80. A number of proverbs are here joined together into one gnomic utterance. See Appendix, pp. 160-3. The proverb at 1271 is to be found also in the *Proverbs of Hendyng*, I, 17:

> So þe bet þe be,
> So þe bet þe bise!

' The better things go with you, the better you must look to yourself.' The meaning is presumably: ' The richer you are, the more you must look to your spiritual welfare.' This is joined to the idea that the things of this world do not last, which is expressed in the proverbs that follow it in O&N. The proverb at 1273f is at least reminiscent of that in *The Proverbs of Alfred*, 138–41:

> Yf þu seoluer and gold
> Y[h]efst and weldest in þis world,
> Neuer vpen eorþe
> To wlonk þu niwrþe.

[' If you possess and control silver and gold in this world, never become too proud on earth.'] The proverbs at 1275-8 are also found in OE proverbs. See Appendix, pp. 160-3.

There is perhaps a parallel to the whole passage in *The Proverbs of Alfred*, 173–86: ' Thus spoke Alfred: " Put not thy trust too much on the sea that flows. If thou hast many treasures and gold and silver enough, it shall crumble to nothing, it must pass into dust. The Lord shall live forever. Many a man has God's anger for his gold, and for his silver he neglects and forgets and ruins himself. It would have befitted him better if he had never been born.' The punctuation adopted by the C scribe for lines 1275-8 is different from that of the rest of O&N: he has a point in the middle of each line, before *þat*. A point in the middle of the line is used several times in the punctuation of lists, or to indicate a pause or change of voice, but nowhere else is pointing in the middle of the line used so regularly as here.

1285f. A wrestling metaphor. Cf. 795–804 and note.

1295f. hoþful. On the spelling see 1256, note. For the rhyme see 349, note.

1297. hire understod. See 951, note.

1301–30. wicche crefte. Cawley points out that the Nightingale in her original charge (1145–74) had made no reference to sorcery (although she claims at 1309 to have done so). He suggests that she was ' dismayed by the thoroughness and competence of the Owl's defence '. Cawley's analysis of the Nightingale's motives and course of action seems convincing: ' When the Owl puts up her successful defence of astrology . . ., the Nightingale is able to fall back on an overt accusation of sorcery.' He goes on to say, ' Rather than try to refute the learned arguments that the Owl has advanced in support of astrology, it is easier for her to admit the validity of the astrological art as such, but at the same time deny that the Owl knows anything about it. The substance of her thoughts may be summarised as follows: " A man who is learned in astrology can foretell the future from the stars; but you know nothing about the stars, so it follows that you must get your ' strange wisdom ' by practising necromancy." '

1305–16. The Nightingale's argument may be summarised thus: She had authority for cursing the Owl (1169–74), for the priestly authority, which the Owl (1178–82) had taken to be necessary, had been exercised long ago in condemnation of witchcraft; yet even if that had not been so, cursing has become so universal that the Nightingale is not alone in doing so.

1309. The object of *seide* is not expressed. MnE requires ' so '. See 274, note.

1310f. a bisemere is construed with askedest.

1312. þe mansing. Börsch (p. 7), followed by Dr Huganir (p. 123), suggests that this is an allusion to the great number of excommunications in the poet's lifetime. It may well be that it is a topical allusion; but excommunications and interdicts are too common in the late twelfth and early thirteenth centuries to allow us to infer more definitely some specific historical event.

1315f. Perhaps, to recapture the lively style of the poem, **fule** and **a wrecche hule** should be regarded as direct speech.

1317–20. As these lines stand in C they do not make sense. Two emendations have been thought necessary. *An* (1319) has been emended to *þat* (following Stratmann); *þ*' (i.e. the contraction for *þat* or *þer*), 1320, has been emended to *þe*. [Palaeographically neither is difficult. At 1319, where C has *An*, J has *&*, and *&* may well have been, in the common antecedent of C and J, a misreading of *þ*', the contraction for *þat*. At 1320 both MSS have the contraction *þ*', which, presumably, was in the common antecedent, a misreading of *þe*.] **þinge** (1319) is probably prepos. sg. or pl., *of wucche þinge* having the meaning ' of whatever thing(s ' or, less literally, ' of whatever '; or possibly *þinge* is gen. pl. dependent on *wucche*, ' of whichever of things ', or, less literally, ' of whatever '. **kume** is pres. subj. sg. or pl. ' may come ', the relative not being expressed [cf. *NED* s. *that*, rel. pron. 10]. The meaning is: ' I have heard, and it is true, the man must be very learned in astrology, if he is to know [*literally*, that he may know] the inner source of whatever may come, as you say is usual with you.' **innoþ**, literally, ' inside, inside of the body, womb ', is taken to mean ' inner source ' (following Wells); J has *inoh* ' enough ', which may be an attempt on the part of the J scribe to make sense of the passage: *innoþ* was obsolescent, and the change to the familiar *inoh* would be made easier by the scribe's awareness that in his exemplar *þ* was a possible spelling for guttural *h* (see 1256 note); and C's *innoh* at 1220 shows that double *n* need not have stopped J from thinking *innoþ* a spelling of *inoh*. Some editors accept J's *inoh* as the correct reading, although it conflicts with the editorial principle that the more difficult of two variant readings is more likely to have been the original. The following are some of the more important alternative views. [Some of the translations in which they are summarised are inferred from the editorial discussions, and are not supplied by the editors.]

(*a*) Wells (i) accepting J's *inoh*, ' and [must] know very well from what things may come: thus thou sayest, that [pron.] is customary [*either supply* with thee, *or* customary = in the course of nature] ';

(ii) accepting *innop*, ' and know the hidden source from which things come '; (iii) taking *wucche pinge* as adj. and pron. dat. sg. or pl. ' from which thing(s) ', with *pat* (' that which ' or ' what ') as subject, ' and know . . . from what thing(s) comes what is customary. . . .'

(*b*) Gadow (accepting J's *inoh*), ' The man may well be skilled in astrology and know sufficiently from what things (i.e. causes) that, which you maintain is common (i.e. quite natural), may come.'

(*c*) Atkins, emending *An* (1319) to *Þat*, accepting J's *inoh*, and emending *pat* (1320) to *pe*, ' I have heard, and true it is, (that) the man who really knows what things are coming, must be wise in star-lore, as thou sayest is true (i.e. usual) of thee.'

(*d*) Grattan takes *pinge* as gen. pl., *cume* as a noun [with stem-vowel short, due to analogy with the verb, for the sake of assonance], and *wucche* as an indefinite adj., resulting in the translation ' of whichsoever things' arrival '. More freely, he renders the whole line, ' If he know the inner sources of the coming of any and every event.' In his footnotes he makes the further suggestions that *An* (1319) is the first occurrence of *an(d)* = ' if ' (*An wite* being ' if he know ' with omission of subject pronoun), and that either *pat* (1320) was miswritten for *pe*, or *iwune* for *pi wune* ' your habit ' [following Stratmann's *pat is pin iwune*]. He accepts *innop*. From this the following translation may perhaps be reconstructed, ' The man must be very learned in the stars, if he know the inner sources of the coming of what thing soever, as you say that it is your custom.'

1319f. For the rhyme see 277, note.

1322. bihaltst. Thus Grattan. Mätzner [in his footnote to line 852] first suggested that *bihaldest* may underlie the *bihaitest* of the two MSS. Kenyon (Bib. 29) suggested that in Southern English *bihaldest* would be syncopated to *bihaltst*, which might easily be written **bihaltest*, and then misunderstood, because it is an anomalous form, resulting in the form *bihaitest* of the MSS. This explanation seems more likely, and the meaning ' behold ' fits better than any other suggested. Other suggestions include Stratmann's emendation to the otherwise unrecorded *biwaitest* ' beholdest ' (<OFr *waiter* ' watch '), Wells's derivation from OE *behatan* (with the vowel influenced by the p. *beheht*—cf. such ME spellings as *biheyhte*), to which he gives the contextual meaning ' makest vows to ' or ' threatenest with thy cries '. Gadow has the same etymology, but translates tentatively in this context ' adorest '. Atkins emends to *bihauest* (<OE *behāwian* ' to gaze at '); he assumes that the error occurred because in the MSS *it* is not dissimilar to *u*, and *u* might be a spelling for *w* (at 1202 the C scribe alters *groue* to *growe*).

1325–8. Atkins points to Neckam's *De Naturis Rerum*, II, chaps. 128–9 which treat of the ape's natural talent for mimicry. K. Huganir (p. 46) refers to the *Dialogus Creaturarum* of Nicholaus Pergamenus [edited by J. G. Th. Graesse, *Die beiden ältesten lateinischen Fabelbücher des Mittelalters*, Bibliothek des litterarischen Vereins in Stuttgart, vol. 148 (1880), p. 246], where a fable is told of an ape who wrote books.

1326. The object of **folde** (MnE ' them ') is not expressed. See 274, note.

1328. top ne more. Cf. 1422. The literal meaning is ' neither top nor root ', i.e. the ape is ignorant of learning, from beginning to end. [Related phrases, found outside O&N, are *crop and more* and *top and rote* (see *NED* s. *more*, sb.[1], 2; s.v. *top*, sb.[1], 5; and Bradley s. *crop*).]

1334. Normally OE *tǣcan* is construed with the person taught in the dat ; exceptionally acc. appears to be possible: *and tæhte hi þa geryna* (sic), ' and instructed them in the mysteries ' Ælfric's *Lives of the Saints*, xxx, 93f. [EETS (O.S.) 94, p. 196; (cf. B. T. *Suppl.* s. *tǣcan*)]. *wif* may, therefore, be acc., and, since *wif* is historically a neuter with sg. and pl. forms uninflected in the nom. and acc., it is possible that the word is acc. pl. here [*NED* s. *wife* records uninflected pl. forms as late as the thirteenth century, though there happens to be no certain example in O&N (the existence of the pl. *wiues* (1562) does not preclude the possibility of an uninflected pl. in the text)]. Wells takes *wif* to be dat. pl., but (without final *e*) that is impossible; Gadow takes it to be acc. sg.; Atkins acc. pl.; Grattan notes that after the *f* of *wif* a *t* is cancelled, and wonders if the exemplar has *wife* (J has *wiue*), which may be a dat. sg. or pl., and would probably give the happiest reading.

1337f. For the rhyme see 349, note.

1340–2. The Nightingale's view that there may be true love between husband and wife commends itself so readily to the modern reader that it is important to remember that it runs counter to the tenets of the stricter doctrine of courtly love, which one might have expected the Nightingale to sympathise with. Andreas Capellanus in his *De amore* [translated by J. J. Parry, *The Art of Courtly Love*, Records of Civilization, vol. 33 (1941), pp. 105–7, 175] reports the ruling of Marie, Countess of Champagne, quoted as authoritative in a judgment given by the Queen of France herself: ' We declare and we hold as firmly established that love cannot exert its powers between two people who are married to each other; for lovers give each other everything freely, under no compulsion of necessity, but married people are in duty bound to give in to each other's desires and deny themselves to each other in nothing.' There is, however, no evidence to suggest that this most rigorous doctrine of courtly love was ever followed in real life in England; and, more important here, it seems to have had no place in English vernacular literature. An account of happy marriage is given by the author of the *Ancrene Riwle*, p. 97 (in a parable), who describes how the husband, when he is sure of the love she bears him, may correct his wife's ways, and so not diminish, but increase and strengthen the love that is between them. And even the author of *Hali Meiðhad*, p. 24, cannot deny that a wife may have much comfort of her husband, each always finding delight in the other; but he goes on to say that this ideal picture is only rarely seen on earth.

1342. **awer.** In C *t* is confused with *r* a number of times (see footnotes 1106, 1221, 1222, 1341, 1353, 1360, 1449, 1471), so that it is reasonable to emend the meaningless *awet* of the MS to *awer* < OE *āhwǣr*, ' anywhere ' (thus Wells); OE *ōhwǣr* (> *ower*), a parallel form of *āhwǣr* with the same meaning, presumably underlies J's *oþer*, improved to *on oþer* ' another (one) '. This seems more likely than that the J reading was the original, since its construction is awkward, ' than another one, her husband '. Grattan's suggestion that the original may have been *a were* ' a man ', in apposition to *hire copenere* involves the same awkward construction, as well as the clumsy repetition of *were*, the two meanings of which, ' husband ' and ' man ', would be confusing in the context.

1344. The subject of **forleose** (MnE ' she ') is not expressed. Cf. 362, note.

1350. C's **wummon** is properly a sg. form, and Atkins emends to *wummen*, a more probable pl. form. J's *wymmen* is pl., and *beoþ* is not recorded as a sg. in O&N. But a pl. with *-mon* for *-men* occurs in *wimmon* 1357, and C's *wummon* should be left unemended [as the editors (except Atkins) do]. [At 1387, however, the sg. is used in a very similar context, and it might perhaps be possible to take *wummon beoþ* to be sg. here.]

1352. **bit.** See 1388–90, note.

1356. **Hwi witistu** in the original would explain C's *Hwitistu* more readily than the assumption that capital *wynn* of *Witistu* has been misread as *H*. Since J reads *Witestu* the error must go back to the common antecedent.

1357. **wimmon.** See 1350, note.

1358. **Ne ne mai ich.** Though dittography is common enough, Grattan defends the *ne ne* of both MSS as an example of doubling for emphasis, and points to *Poema Morale*, 102 [Hall, p. 37] where the Trinity MS has *Þeih we hes ne niseien* [' Though we did not know of it ']. Perhaps *ne* in these instances is a form developed from OE *nā* ' by no means ', with other negatives ' at all '.

1360, 1362. On *weþer . . . þe*, and *hwaþer . . . þe* see 824 and note.

1366. **gold & seoluer** together form one concept, and can take a singular verb as late as early MnE: *When gold and siluer becks me to come on*, Shakespeare, *King John*, III, ii, 24 (=III, iii, 13) [cf. W. Franz, *Die Sprache Shakespeares* (1939), § 673]. In ME such lack of grammatical concord is common, even in cases where the compound subject forms a less definite single concept than here; cf. *Lef & gras & blosme springes*, ' Leaf and grass and blossom(s) springs ' (Carleton Brown, *English Lyrics of the XIIIth Century*, No. 86, line 2). The function of **hit** is that of a resumptive pronoun, like *hi* in *Vor children, gromes, heme & hine, hi þencheþ alle of þire pine* (1115f), but, since the force of what it resumes is felt to be sg. in the sg. here.

1373–5. **songe** is prepos. sg. here. The word is historically masc., and **hine** 1374 and 1375 refers to it. It seems that *heo* (in both MSS) for **he** (1374) is due to the anticipation of the *eo* in *beo*; the error must go back to the common antecedent of C and J. *he*, of course, also refers to *songe*.

1377–81. Some degree of personification, i.e. reference to the god of love, inheres in **luue**. The word is historically fem., and **ho** (1378) and **heo** (1380) refer to it. So does **he** (1381) which in this text is a possible fem. form (cf. Glossary, s. *he*; and see 1389 and note).

1378. **vich.** As Atkins says, this form is derived from OE *gehwylc* ' each, every '. In the Glossary it is recorded with *hwuch* (<OE *hwylc*, without prefix) ' what sort (of) '.

1380. **atbroide** is obviously derived from OE *ætbre(g)dan*, pp. *ætbro(g)den*; but the meaning is not quite clear. Of the meanings given for the OE etymon in B.T. *Suppl.* two might fit: ' taken away from ' with the idea of spoliation, and ' taken away from ' with the idea of seduction. Grattan (following Bradley) gives the meaning as ' snatched away '; the other editors have ' stolen ', wishing to imply perhaps ' stealthy ', a sense which *atbroide* cannot bear. *MED* has ' diverted ' (only here); presumably they mean ' diverted from its lawful course ', which fits the context, and may, like the more suitable rendering ' extorted ', be interpreted as comprising the aspects of seduction and rape.

1381-4. Forms in C from the OE verb *bregdan* are: pres. stem *upbreide* (1414) rhyming with *bigrede*, *uorbredeþ* (510) rhyming with *awedeþ*, **forbreideþ** (1383) rhyming with **nawedeþ** [see also *bretst* 1633 note]; the p.p. *broiden* (645), *atbroide* (1380), *tobrode* (1008) rhyming with *unsode*, **forbrode** (1381; corrected from *forbroide*) rhyming with **rode**.

The rhymes at 1414, 510, and 1383 depend on the OE sound-change discussed in connexion with *seide/rede* 349f (see note), by which, in WS (or perhaps all Saxon) and Kentish dialects, palatal *g* was lost before *d*, and the preceding vowel lengthened. The OE p.p. in these areas is *brōden<brogden* with exceptional loss of guttural *g*, probably by analogy with the regular loss of palatal *g* in the pres. stem [see Sievers-Brunner, § 214 Anm. 9]; this explains the rhymes at 1008 and 1381. The rhymes reveal the phonology in the original dialect; the occasional C spellings with *-eid-* and *-oid-* (and the correction of *forbrode* here) show that C was written in an area where the sound-change resulting in the loss of OE *g* in these positions did not take place. J's spellings are *-eyd-* or *-oyd-* in every case (cf. 349 note); except *uorbredeþ* (510) and *tobroude* (1008). At 510 the J scribe has ' edited ' the text unintelligently; he has *awey deþ* for C's *awedeþ* (509), either by mechanical substitution of *-eyd-* for *-ed-* of his exemplar, or because he cannot make sense of the exemplar, and somehow interprets it as meaning ' does away '; his *tobroude* is regular, *<tobrogden*, without levelling of the palatal *g* of the pres. into the p.p.

The rhyme *unsode/tobrode* (1007f) is not true. The *o* of *-brode* is long (by compensatory lengthening after loss of *g*) as in 1381. The *o* of *-sode* is short.

1387f. For the rhyme see 277, note. On **Wummon** cf. 1350, note.

1388-90. Stratmann emends **lustes**, 1388 and 1390, to **lust**; but Wells rightly defends the reading **lustes** of both MSS; taking *is strong* as impersonal, and translating, ' It is difficult to destroy the lusts of the flesh.' At 1390 no difficulty arises with *lustes*. Atkins follows Stratmann at 1388 because of Wells's further difficulty: that *he* (1389 both MSS) refers to *lustes*, i.e. is a unique pl. form. But it is simpler to assume that *he* here means ' she ' (cf. 1377-81, note) and refers to *wummon* 1387. *MED* (s. *abiden*, 9a) suggests that *abide* (subj. sg.) here has the meaning ' persist '; ' It is no marvel that she persists [in lusts], for carnal desires make her slip.' Grattan believes that *he* 1389 refers to the man of 1351f; and he would presumably translate, ' It is no wonder that he persists [in begging and sighing] '; it seems very unlikely, however, that a mere ' he ' would recall *sume sottes lore* many lines ago. [Is it possible perhaps that Grattan at one time wished to interpret *bit* as ' waits ' (*<OE bīdan*), so that *he abide* might recall *sume sottes lore þe ȝeorne bit?* Grattan's Glossary (like that of the other editions) lists *bit* s. *bidde(n.*] Grattan's view might have seemed more acceptable if he had taken *he* to refer to *wepmon* (1379); the lines would then have some such meaning as, ' It is no marvel that he is patient, for carnal desires will make her slip (i.e. yield to him in time).'

1391, 1395. **noþt.** See 1256, note.

1395-1416. In lines 1387-94 the Nightingale has treated of woman's frailty, and this leads naturally to an analysis of sin here. The passage has been discussed a number of times, most helpfully perhaps by Kenyon (Bib. 29; summarised by Atkins in his footnote to these lines). A more recent treatment is to be found in M. W. Bloomfield (Bib. 49;

the work has been used extensively in the notes to these lines). In the order of Gregory the Great's list, usually followed at the time, the sins are *Superbia* (Pride), *Ira* (Wrath), *Invidia* (Envy), *Avaritia* (Covetousness), *Acedia* (Sloth), *Gula* (Gluttony), and *Luxuria* (Lust). Each of these sins manifests itself in many ways, and the Nightingale, whose treatment is not formal, at times refers to branches of sins rather than to the sins themselves. Sins and branches of sins referred to by her are *drunnesse* 1399, ? *wrouehede* 1400, and *golnesse* 1400, described by her as sins of the flesh; and *niþe an onde* 1401, *murhþe of monne shonde* 1402, *ʒeoneþ after more* 1403, and *modinesse* 1405, described by her as sins of the spirit. (For difficulties concerned with the sins individually, see the notes below.) The ascription of sins to the flesh or spirit was not always the same in medieval theology: Gluttony and Lust were always taken to be sins of the flesh; Pride, Wrath, Envy, and Covetousness were usually taken to be sins of the spirit, and so was Sloth in the early Middle Ages, but there is evidence [e.g. in the *Ancrene Riwle*, p. 86, 15] that in England, about the time when O&N was written, Sloth could be regarded as a carnal sin. The identification of the Nightingale's list with the traditional list of the sins is not always easy. Obvious equivalents are : *golnesse*, Luxuria; *ʒeoneþ after more*, Avaritia; and *modinesse*, Superbia. Probable equivalents (see notes below) are : *drunnesse* ' drunkenness ', a branch of Gula; *niþe an onde*, Invidia or Ira, or both; and *murhþe of monne shonde*, ' Schadenfreude ', a branch of Invidia. The reading *wrouehede* (and its meaning) is in doubt. If the Nightingale's list were complete the word would have to stand for Sloth, the sin otherwise missing from the list. But medieval lists were not always complete, and J's *wlonkhede*, ' Luxuria ' probably, parallel with *golnesse*, would fit well. The following ME lists are incomplete: *Vices and Virtues* [EETS (O.S.) 89, p. 7] omits Envy, and a MS note in Latin says, ' Here ought to be put *Inuidia*, which this soul seems to forget in its confession. *Nith* should not be forgotten. . . .'' In the same text there is a further list [p. 89]: *ʒiuernesse* [Gluttony], *galnesse* [Lust], *ʒitsinge* [Covetousness], *wraðð* [Wrath], *nið* & . . . *ande* [Envy], *idel ʒelp* [' vain boasting ', i.e. Vainglory, a branch of Pride], *modinesse* & *priede* [Pride]; Sloth is omitted. An incomplete list comes in the lyric *An Old Man's Prayer*, 52–63 [G. L. Brook, *The Harley Lyrics*, p. 47; Carleton Brown (revised by G. V. Smithers), *Religious Lyrics of the XIVth Century*, p. 5]: ' My life used to be evil and false. Gluttony was my minstrel; he was staying for a time with me; Pride was my playmate, Lechery my private washerwoman; with them is Mocking Deceit, and Guile; Covetousness carried my keys ; *Niþe ant Onde* were my comrades, who are vile folk; Liar was my interpreter, Sloth and Sleep my bed-fellows, who entertained me at times.' Here Wrath appears to be missing (unless it is part of *Niþe ant Onde*). The Nightingale's informal treatment of the sins is as unsystematic as that in the Harley lyric.

1399. drunnesse. The spelling with omission of the middle consonant (*c* or *k*) in a group of three is paralleled in: *strenþe* (for *strengþe*) 781, 1674; *sprinþ* (for *springþ*) 1042; *golfinc* (for *goldfinc*) 1130; *ʒunling* (for *ʒungling*) 1433; and *þunþ* (for *þuncþ*) 1592. [Cf. Breier, pp. 43f.; Irene Williams, pp. 129f.; A. Napier, *OE Glosses*, p. 33.] *NED*, s. *drunkness*, records the ME form *druncnesse* in *Lambeth Homilies* [Bib. 71, p. 33]. Drunkenness is a branch of Gula (cf. Chaucer's Parson's Tale, 821f.).

1400. wrouehede. The fourth letter in C may be read *u* or *n*. Stevenson and Wright read *wronehede* which has no satisfactory etymology: the *o* makes it impossible for it to be <OE *wrǣne* ' libidinous, wanton ' (for which reason Hinckley, Bib. 40, emends *o* to *e*; his **wrenehede* would be exactly parallel in meaning to *golnesse*). Wells, Gadow, and Atkins read the MS as *wronchede* [but see footnote], i.e. a form of an otherwise unrecorded **wronghede* ' error, wickedness ' [which may perhaps be taken (cf. Bloomfield) to mean ' malitia ', a branch of Sloth (as in the *Ayenbite of Inwyt*, p. 31)). Atkins's interpretation is the best in every way. He ' emends ' to *wrouehede* (in fact the reading of the MS), which he connects with ME *wrowe*, *wrawe* (?<an unrecorded OE **wrāh*, **wrāg* (thus *NED* s.v. *wraw*)] with *u* for *w* (as in *siueþ* 1526); in C *ow*<OE *āg-*, *āh-*, is normal (cf. *owe* 100, *þrowe* 478, *wowes* 1528). The adj. *wraw* means ' angry, peevish, contrarious '; the noun is the abstract of the adj., ' irritability, peevishness '. The word, and its derivatives, come under the head of Acedia in Chaucer's Parson's Tale, 677ff: *Accidie maketh hym* [i.e. man] *hevy, thoghtful, and wraw* [variant *wrawful*]. . . . *He dooth alle thyng with anoy, and with wrawnesse, slaknesse, and excusacioun, and with ydelnesse, and unlust.* J reads *wlonkhede* glossed by the editors as ' pride '. But B. **v.** Lindheim [*Anglia* **70** (1951), 33–9 (a reference for which I am indebted to Mr G. V. Smithers)] adduces firm evidence from OE and ME that the adj. *wlonc* can have such connotations as ' wanton ', and its derivative nouns ' wantonness ' [thus, *Lambeth Homilies* (Bib. 71, p. 9, line 26), *festen, þe swiðe ouerkimet þes flesces wlongnesse* (' fasts, which easily overcome the lust of the flesh ')]. The objection to J's *wlonkhede* that it cannot come in a list of the sins of the flesh, therefore, falls to the ground: the word is parallel to *golnesse*, and equal to it in meaning. It may be another example of J substituting a familiar for an unfamiliar word (cf. Introduction, p. 6).

1401f. niþe an onde. Either word can mean either ' ill-will, enmity ' (when either word may be coupled with *wrappe*), or ' envy '. The two words in collocation can mean either Wrath or Envy, or both at the same time. [Cf. Bloomfield, p. 429.]

An example of the difficulty in ME is *Cursor Mundi* 1069 describing the ill-will which Cain bore his brother Abel. The Cotton MS has *Vntil his broþer nith he bare*; the Fairfax MS has *enuy* for the Cotton MS's *nith*; but MSS Göttingen and Trinity have *ire*; in the context of Genesis, 4: 5–8 (on which the passage is based) envy fits well, though, in fact, Cain is described as wroth (*iratus* in the Vulgate). On the other hand the description of Hate in the Chaucerian *Romaunt of the Rose* (148) has *onde* with *wrathe* and *yre* in a context that has no trace of envy; while the West Saxon translation of the Gospels [edited by W. W. Skeat, *The Four Gospels in Anglo-Saxon, Northumbrian, and Old Mercian Versions*, 1871–87] *anda* (variant *ande*) renders 'invidia ', Mark, 15: 10, and Matthew, 27: 18. It is possible that *niþe an onde* at 1401 refer only to Invidia (so that 1402 is merely an amplification of 1401, as Superbia at 1405 is amplified by 1406); if so, the list of sins lacks Ira. But it seems equally possible that, as perhaps in the *Harley Lyric* referred to in the note to 1395–1416, both Invidia and Ira are meant by the phrase.

1402. murhþe of monne shonde. Both MSS read *monnes honde*. What is wanted is a sin of the spirit, so that it seems very doubtful if Hinckley's view (Bib. 40) can be maintained, that *honde* means ' side, party ' [*monnes honde* being contrasted with *Godes honde*; Grattan, however, thinks that the interpretation ' mirth arising from worldly pleasure ' would well suit the context]. But Schadenfreude was very commonly regarded as an aspect of Invidia, as Kenyon (Bib. 29) has shown.

Kenyon's emendation to *monne shonde* is very slight, for the division of words in the MSS is at times erratic. To Kenyon's parallels, of joy at another man's shame as a form of Envy, may be added *Cato's Distichs* [Bib. 96, p. 580] lines 335f:

> Of oþer mennes euel fare
> Envye makeþ him gleo.

['Of another's wretched fortune Envy has his joy.'] That is all he says of Envy, except to tell the reader to shun it. In view of the connexion between *The XI Pains of Hell* and O&N [cf. Introduction, pp. 39f] it may be worth noting that in *The XI Pains* (107), among the sinners punished, is *He þat is glad of oþres harme*. The idea remains a commonplace for a long time; cf. Spenser's *Faerie Queene*, I, iv, 30; and Thomas Lodge's *Rosalynde*, edited by W. W. Greg (for *The Shakespeare Classics*, 1907), p. 38. [See Stanley; Atkins, Bib. 32.]

1404. The covetous man in his desire for more shows no mercy. Though the phrase **milce & ore** is often applied to divine Grace, it is not used exclusively so; cf. 1083.

1405. On the spellings **heþ** and **þurþ** see 1256, note.

1405f. For the rhyme see 369, note.

1406. This line amplifies the description of the proud man in 1405.

1410. It is unusual in the Middle Ages to regard the sins of the flesh as less than those of the spirit. But, as Atkins (Bib. 32) says, a similar idea comes in the *Ancrene Riwle*, p. 86: 'Temptation of the flesh may be likened to a foot-wound; and spiritual temptation, which is more to be feared, may, on account of that peril, be called a breast-wound. But to us carnal temptations seem the greater, because they are easily felt; the others, though we have them often, we do not know them, yet they are great and terrible in God's bright eyes, and are, therefore, much more to be feared.'

1412. Historically **imene** takes the dat., and Grattan sees a dat. in **deouel** (miswritten for *deoule*). [Atkins takes *deouel-imene* as a compound; which, though not impossible, is not etymologically as satisfying. Pronunciation, meaning, and metre are not affected, whichever view is adopted.] Atkins compares this line with a passage in the *Lambeth Homilies* [Bib. 32, p. 103]: 'Pride: it is the beginning and end of all evil. It turns angels into foul devils; and it makes man also, if he grows too proud, the *deofles ifere*, companion of that Devil, who had fallen out of heaven through his pride.' Some of the meaning 'pride' seems to survive in **mode** in this line.

1413f. On the rhyme see 1381-4, note.

1415f. **Swuch** here means 'the one who has just been described', i.e. 'woman'. The lines mean, '[If he does so] a man may reproach a woman with Lust, who himself sins worse through Pride.'

1422. Cf. 1328 and note. The poet has inverted the normal order of **more** and **toppe**, presumably for the sake of the rhyme.

1428. On the spelling of **þurþ** see 1256, note.

1432. E. J. Dobson says: '**þat** is the subject of *stal*, and *to* is adverb not preposition (cf. *OED* s.v. *To*, D.1): the meaning is " who stole to [her] by dark night ".' The solution is happy, though morally unsound. The Nightingale's analysis of the sins was orthodox, but now she has fallen into error. That is what the Owl thinks, 1512-14.

NOTES 147

1434f. **his** and **hit** (1435) refer to ȝunling, which is here neuter (though historically masc.), even when (as here) it refers to a girl.

1437–9. **ouersid** is a spelling for *ouersit* (cf. 1587); in order to rhyme with it the original must have had *bit* (cf. 445, 1352), not **bid**. [See Sievers-Brunner, § 359. 3.] J's line 1438 as a whole is obviously unsatisfactory; but if Grattan's interpretation of J's *bistarte*, viz. ' springs at ' is right, and if it here has a sexual connotation, the C reading (with the very weak **heo bistant**, ' harasses her ') could be much improved by the slight emendation to **heo bistart**. C's *bi-sehþ* [=*bi-sekþ* in J], ' beseeches ', has been emended to **hi sehþ**, ' she sighs '. [The original *sikþ* may have become *sihþ* either by analogy with the p. *sihte*; or the sound-change in *sicte*>*sihte* also affected the syncopated forms: *sicþ* >*sihþ* (cf. Luick, § 717.5). The development is part of the general development of OE *sīcan* into MnE *sigh*. Cf. *biluþ*, 1557 (<*bilukþ*, ? by way of *biluhþ*). For *sehþ* with *e* for *i* cf. *rehte*, 1602. The fem. pron. *hi* (here miswritten *bi*) occurs as nom. elsewhere, cf. 10, note.] After the man neglects the maiden what is expected is that she sighs, and not that he beseeches, especially if we read *bistart*. The meaning of the lines would then be, ' He comes and goes, commands and begs, takes possession·of her, and neglects her, and she sighs often and long.' This would serve as a logical introduction to what follows (especially 1446f). It is the commonplace of the deceived maiden. [See Stanley.]

1442. **þas** is gen. sg. dem. pron. after **fondi**; literally, ' to make trial of that thing ', i.e. ' to try it '.

1447. **bringþ**. Stratmann's emendation is essential, and Holthausen (Bib. 38) is right in rejecting Atkins's view that *bring* (of both MSS) is subjunctive. [Cf. W. Ebisch, *Zur Syntax des Verbs im ae. Gedicht Eule und Nachtigall*, 1905, pp. 45f.]

1448. For **him** referring to ȝunglinge see 1434f note. **ne**. In OE and ME after a negative main clause *ne* was at times used pleonastically in consecutive clauses (cf. Einenkel, p. 76, § 22ε). 1445–8 may be translated, ' When I see the strained face which love bestows on the young thing, I cannot, for pity, leave off, so that I sing to her of joy.'

1451f. The rhyme is satisfactory: **ilest** is the normal syncopated form of *ilesteþ*, **rest** the syncopated form of *resteþ*, 3 sg. pres. ind. (thus Kenyon, Bib. 29). **bute** is conjunctive here, and the meaning is, ' and love only rests for a moment on such maidens ' or, more literally, ' and love does nothing except that it rests for a moment ', etc.

1454. **breþ** is the subject of **falþ**.

1461. **breþ** means both ' breath ' and ' passion ', and the poet skilfully exploits the two meanings.

1463f. **bi me**, by my example. **understond/vvend**. As Atkins says, the syncopated 3 sg. pres. ind. is *understent* which rhymes with *went*; the final *d* of the MSS being probably only scribal [though possibly the original had *understend/(i)wend*, cf. the rhyme at 1519f (thus Grattan); it should be noted, however, that the scribe of J first wrote *rede iwent* and then altered it to *rede iwend*]. The original was probably *understent/rede iwent* (with final *e* of *rede* elided).

1467f. **wite/utschute**. If the original was SE, the rhyme must have been *wite/utschete* (SE *e* for WS *y*). C. T. Onions (in his note on the rhyme at 9f) says, that in O&N it is normal to rhyme short *e* with short *i*; he compares his reconstructed rhyme *keste/wiste* (9f) with his reconstructed rhyme *stede/mide* (1767f), and cf. *ofligge/bugge* (1505f). [Cf. S. T. R. O. d'Ardenne, Bib. 50.]

1470. On the spelling **naþt** cf. 1256, note.

1473. Translate, ' it seems a very great and shocking surprise to me '.

1478. A weak line, presumably merely to supply a rhyme-word; it adds nothing except to say that two is not three.

1483. **Hure** has some such meaning as ' at all ', or ' least of all ' [cf. Gadow, p. 188]. The punctuation in J is instructive: a stop after *Hure*, which is a most unusual position, and presumably an indication that the word was felt to be intrusive, perhaps even exclamatory. The sense is, ' If he is an honourable and valiant man, nobody that is wise will want to bring shame on him, least of all through his wife.'

1485f. There is evidence in the thirteenth century that the outraged husband who found his wife in the act of adultery was no longer allowed to slay the guilty pair or either of them, as he might in Anglo-Saxon times, but was allowed to emasculate the adulterer. Cf. Pollock and Maitland, ii, 484.

1491f. For the rhyme see 277, note. **at bedde & at borde** (cf. 1579), a legal formula corresponding to Latin *a mensa et thoro*; the meaning is ' full marital relations '. The phrase was enshrined in the bride's response in the marriage service, of which no early ME forms are extant. The following is from the northern Brough MS of 1403: ' Here I take þe to my wedded housband, to hald and to haue at bed and at borde, for fayrer for layther, for better for wers, in sekenes and in hele, till dede ws depart, and þare-to I plyght þe my trowth ' [*Publications of the Surtees Society*, **63** (1875), p. xvi.] The version of the *Sarum Manual*, printed by Pynson in 1506, is: ' I, *N.*, take the, *N.*, to my wedded housbonde, to haue and to holde fro this day forwarde, for better for wors, for richer for pouerer, in sykenesse and in hele, to be bonere [' meek and mild, affable ' (<*debonnaire*)] and buxum [' obedient '] in bedde and atte borde, tyll dethe vs departhe, if holy churche it woll ordeyne, and therto I plight the my trouthe.' [*Ibid.*, p. 19*]

1493–6. **ley.** In C the forms of the letters *y* and *þ* are often identical, and it is difficult to decide if the reading here is *ley* or *leþ*. The meaning of the lines is that there can be no true love between the adulterers when the man remembers the low fellow whose bed the woman has been sharing. The general sense requires the past *ley*, and this is confirmed by J's *lay* and by 1509. **swuch man** must refer to **swuch cheorles**, i.e. to the husband, and so we might expect the past instead of the pres. **gropeþ**; but, as Atkins points out, the past *ley* follows the past **miȝte** (1493), whereas the pres. *gropeþ* follows the pres. **mai** (1495), i.e. lines 1495f repeat the sense of 1493f with only a change of tense.

1498. **aren.** Holthausen's suggestion (Bib. 38) that the C reading is a spelling of *harm* seems the best. Three of the most common orthographic peculiarities of C [see Introduction, pp. 9–13] have come together in one word: omission of *h*, paragogic *e*, and final *n* for *m*. Harm is found in collocation with shame at line 1733. The difficulty probably goes back to the common antecedent of C and J, for J's version is worse than C's (except that it has *is* for C's **his** with unetymological *h*); the meaning of the J line is ' the one is at the other's shame ', which omits the alternatives required by the context. These alternatives, stated in lines 1477–80, are: **þat on**, that the husband is a man of valour, and harm will ensue from adultery with his wife (1481–6); **þat oþer**, that the husband is weak and impotent, and a feeling of disgusted shame (cf. 1506) will rob adulterous love-relations with his wife of their full satisfaction.

The C reading may be *areu*, the last letter may be either *n* or *u*. (1) Stratmann reads *a reu* ' in sorrow ', and Atkins translates this in the context, ' that in one case there is sorrow, in the other disgrace '. (2) Wells reads *areu* (<OE *earg* ' cowardly, base '), ' the one thing is base, the other a disgrace '; but, as Atkins says, an abstract meaning ' cowardice, baseness ', is required as a suitable alternative to ' shame ', not an adjective. (3) Grattan thinks that possibly such an abstract may have been some form of the noun *areȝþe*, the *þe* being apocopated before *þat*, and *areȝ* written *areu*.

1500. It seems likely that the common antecedent of C and J had (like J) *hire ibedde* where C has **hire bedde**. The final *e* of *hire* would be elided before the *i* of *ibedde*.

1503. **wercche.** On the metathesis see 249, note.

1505f. **ofligge/bugge.** For the rhymes 1467f note; a SE original may have had *ofligge/begge*. The meaning of line 1506 is, ' You may well buy pleasure for yourself with disgust ', i.e. ' You may well pay with disgust for your pleasure.'

1507. **freoman.** Cf. *bondeman* 1577, note.

1509. **he** =' she '; for other instances see Glossary.

1509f. **lai/awai** (<OE *læg, on weg*) and *mai/wai* 1601f (<*mæg, weg*) might be regarded as Kentish rhymes on OK *e*: i.e. *lei/awei* and *mei/wei*. But there are no other examples of rhymes of original PrGmc *a* with original PrGmc *e* in the poem; it seems, therefore, more probable that the explanation is to be sought in the development of *wei* > *wai*. See Introduction, p. 9.

1512–14. See 1432, note.

1516. That the Nightingale's sympathies are not confined to maidens is shown in 1083–6.

1519f. **iwend/send.** Of the two possible forms of the p.p. of OE *wendan, gewend* and *gewended*, the former is more common in OE southern dialects [cf. Sievers-Brunner, § 406, Anm. 3.; Irene Williams § 241], and *iwend* is more likely to have been the reading of the original than *iwended*. The rhyme-word would then be *send* (which is the reading of both C and J). But the context requires a pl., which ought to be *sendeþ*. Two explanations are possible: either the rhyme forced the poet to use *send* for *sendeþ* [cf. Atkins], or, as Grattan believes, there is a change from pl. (*lauedies beoþ*) to sg. (*heo . . . send*, ' she sends '). The latter view seems unlikely (but cf. 1569, note). The alternative is to depart from the MS evidence, and to assume that the original rhyme was *iwended/sendeþ*, a rhyme of the type discussed in the note to line 277. **mode.** J's *mone* [' moan(s) ', i.e. ' to me they send their plaint(s) '] gives perhaps somewhat better sense than the C reading, as it agrees better with 1563 [see Holthausen, Bib. 31]; but *mode* is not impossible, either with the usual meaning ' to me they send their thought(s) ', or ' to me they convey their grief(s) ' [see *NED* s. *mood*, sb.¹, 2. c. for the meaning ' grief '; and cf. Grattan]. The metre seems to require a dissyllabic form of *mode*, which may be a plural form.

1521–1602. The Owl's tale of the man who spends all that he has on a paramour, while his rightful wife is ill provided for and sits at home longing for him loyally, is in some ways reminiscent of *The Penyworth of Wytt* (see Appendix, pp. 165f). The principal difference is that in the Owl's account the ill-used wife cuckolds her husband. The most important similarities are: the reference to merchants at line 1575, the account of the treasures given to the paramour, and the anxious care with which the wife awaits her husband. [E. Schröder, *EStn* 55 (1921), 474–8, suggests that *The Penyworth of Wytt* is Anglo-Norman in origin. (See Stanley.)]

1523f. gulte/pulte. The normal form of the 3 sg. pres. ind. is *gult*, and it is unusual for the poet to alter the form of the first rhyme-word to give him an easier rhyme, but that is the best explanation here (thus Atkins).

1524. over can probably be construed with **pulte** (cf. 63f and note); but J's *oper* is an easier construction.

1527. attom is presumably a sandhi development of *at hom* (J has *atom*).

1529f. A better reading would be obtained by inverting the order of the lines in this couplet; since J's order is the same as C's the common antecedent of the MSS must have had the same order.

1531f. On the rhyme see 277, note.

1543f. heo nah iweld þah. The meaning is, ' she cannot help that ', or, ' it is not her doing that '. See *NED* s. *wield*, sb. 4.b.

1548. Wi ! J has *Þi* (? for *forþi* ' therefore '), and this is what the editors read here (Atkins even amends to *forþi*). It seems more likely that *Wi* is *NED*'s interjection *wi*, ' An exclamation used to introduce an anxious question or a statement of something regrettable.' [See Stanley.]

1552. On the spelling of **noþt** see 1256, note.

1553–62. With this passage should be compared *Proverbs of Prophets, Poets, and Saints*, 227–32 [Bib. 83, p. 537]: ' If you have a beautiful wife and wish that she should be faithful all her life, do not jealously find fault with her for keeping company with any man; in that way you may encourage her to love him, though she would not have looked at him before.' [See Stanley.]

1555f. lokeþ/spekeþ. It is probable that in the original dialect, whether SE or SW, this was not an exact rhyme [but cf. S. T. R. O. d'Ardenne, Bib. 50]. The syncopated form of *spekeþ*, i.e. *spekþ*, would be more regular in this text, but *preteþ/tobeteþ* (not *pretþ/tobet*) 1609f shows that unsyncopated forms are possible. [Gadow attempts tentatively to derive an exact rhyme from a ME *leken (<OE *lōcian* +the stem-vowel of the noun *lēc* ' look '), i.e. **lekeþ/spekeþ*; but there is no evidence that such a verb existed.] **manne** is probably prepos. sg.; but pl. is not impossible.

1557. biluþ. It is possible that C has missed out a *c* or *k*; J has *bilukþ*. But there may be a phonological explanation; see 1437–9, note.

1560. he here means ' she '. See Glossary for other examples.

1568–70. Since the Owl is not encouraging actual adultery (though she has shown that she does not take a very serious view of that sin, 1543f) she is not strictly immoral here; even so, she does seem to be invoking divine mercy for very questionable ends.

1569. The subject (MnE ' he ') is not expressed; cf. 362, note. There is a change of number from pl. to sg. here, from *lauedies* 1563 and *heom* 1567f to *lauedi* 1569 and *hire* 1570.

1575. For a connexion between **chapmon** and a possible analogue see 1521ff note. On cniht see 1577, note.

1576. On **hald** cf. 249, note.

1577. **bondeman.** The meaning of the word changes in ME as social conditions change the bondman's status. In early use the word [a Norse loan-word, cf. OIcel *bondi*] probably had the same meaning as OE *ceorl*. But the ceorls' status was depressed from that of free men, acknowledging no lord below the king, to one of servitude in a strict routine of labour on the estates of private lords. The change had begun before the Conquest. As a result the words *ceorl* and *bonda* came to mean 'unfree peasant, villein', and, by a further change of meaning, *bonde* came to mean 'a tiller of the soil, a husbandman'. In ME, therefore, a *freeman* (cf. 1507) is of a higher rank than a *bondman*; yet, though a freeman is born free, he is still not of the gentry. In early use the *knight* typifies not so much a social class as the military profession, and is often contrasted on the one hand with the merchant (as at 1575), and on the other with the clerk. [Cf. F. M. Stenton, pp. 274–9, 463–5; A. H. Smith, s. *bondi*; and *NED* s. vv.]

1579. Cf. 1491f note. The line, rendered freely, means, 'and serves him in every way, as she had vowed in marriage'.

1586. **houdsiþe.** Probably the best explanation is Stratmann's, that *houd-* combines three of C's occasional spellings: unetymological *h-*, *ou* for *ū*, and *-d* for *-t* [cf. Introduction, pp. 9–13; and 347, note], so that *houd-* = *ūt-*. The wife's anxious care for her husband out on a distant journey is a stock topic of medieval literature, both didactic and romance. *Hali Meiðhad*, lines 450f, tells of a wife who in addition to having a bad time when her husband is at home, *hwen he bið ute, hauest aʒein his cume sar care & eie* ['when he is away, you have anxious care and fear for his return']. The *Ancrene Riwle*, pp. 166f, has: 'Listen to this parable: A husband was away on a distant journey; and people came and told him that his dear wife grieved so much for him that, without him, she took no pleasure in any thing, but was, through thinking of his love, looking haggard and pale and wretched. Would that not please him better than that people should say to him that she made merry and was full of sport and raged lustily with other men, and lived in worldly pleasures?' An example of this topic coming in romance is Dorigen's great sorrow for her husband [Chaucer, Franklin's Tale, V (F) 815–36]: *For his absence wepeth she and siketh* (817). The J reading, however, is *houpsype*, a form which defies explanation as a misreading of *utsiþe*, except by an unlikely chain of further scribal errors: *houdsiþe* miscopied as *houðsiþe*, copied into J as *houpsype*.

Atkins takes J's *houpsype* as his starting-point. He assumes that the common antecedent of C and J had *houþsiþe*; in C the *d* represents *ð*, not uncommon for *þ* in this part of the MS. He takes *þ* in *houp-* to be written in place of *h* [a spelling common in C (cf. 1256, note); but not found in J (cf. *innoþ* 1319, note); this fact makes the explanation seem improbable]. Atkins derives *houh-* < OE *hoh-*, *hog-*, a first element in compounds, with the meaning 'sorrow, care' [but Grattan rightly objects that this would be the only case in C where OE short *o* + *ʒ* is not kept] ; *houhsiþe* he takes to mean 'sorrowful, anxious journeyings'.

Grattan also begins with *houp-* (with *d* for *ð* in C), which he derives from the rare OE prefix *ūð-*, 'away, beyond' [with which he compares Northern *outh* 'above, over' of unknown eytmology (cf. *NED* s. v.)], translating the compound ' super-journey, long journey '. Since the use of this prefix was already exceedingly restricted in OE, and survives in ME only in Orm's *upwite* (' prophet ') it is not likely that it should have given a new ME compound.

1587f. oflonged/ongred. On this rhyme see 277, note. As they stand in C the lines may be translated, ' and sits, and sighs, seized with very sorrowful longing, grieved at heart in her sorrow '. But J has *ongreþ*, which may be the original reading [C's *ongred* having *d* for *ð* (cf. Introduction, p. 10); for the rhyme cf. 501f, 547f, and 659f]. J's line 1588 may be translated, ' and she is sorely troubled at heart ', *hire . . . ongreþ* being refl., ' troubles herself, vexes herself '. Either C or J makes good sense.

1598. murninge. Cf. 1111, note.

1601f. For the rhyme see 1509f, note.

1602. The subject of **hoзeþ** (MnE ' she ') is not expressed; cf. 362, note. This accounts for the C reading and J's *howeþ* (cf. 455). Gadows' emendation to *ho goþ* ('she goes ') is unnecessary, and results in inferior sense. [Wells reads *зeþ* for *goþ* without emendation; but the form is not possible.]

1610. tobusteþ & tobeteþ. This alliterative phrase is discussed by F. P. Magoun, Jr., *MLN* **40** (1925), 408–10. [Cf. S. T. R. O. d'Ardenne, *Iuliene*, p. 82.]

1616. ich chadde. On *ch-* for *sch-* see 933f, note.

1618. unneaþe. The C reading is clearly *inmeaþe*, which may well be a scribal attempt to copy exactly a badly written *unneaþe* [<OE adj. *unēaþe* (or *unīeþe*), ' difficult, hard, troublesome '; cf. 1605]. The scribe of J, similarly confronted with *inmeaþe* in his exemplar, tried to make sense of it by reading *unmeþe*, adj. ' unequal, unfair, ungentle ' (cf. *NED* s. *unmethe*). The passage as it stands in C means, ' I do them good by my death. That is why you are having a very difficult time, for though . . .' [*þe is* is impersonal, ' it goes hard with you ']. The meaning of the J reading is the same in effect (since *unmeþe* here means ' ungentle '), i.e. ' you are having a very harsh time '. The Owl's words imply that the Nightingale is in difficulties because of the Owl's cogent argument that her body is useful to mankind, while the Nightingale, alive or dead, is useless.

Of the more recent editors, Gadow and Atkins read *unneaþe* (adj.). Wells follows J, deriving *unmeþe* from the OE noun *unmǣþ* ' transgression, wrong '; so that the line must mean something like, ' wrong is indeed with you', i.e. ' you are quite wrong '. Grattan unconvincingly suggests that *wel* (for *wele*) is a noun, and translates (with *unneaþe*, adv. ' scarcely ') ' to thee is weal scarcely ', i.e. ' It is your condition that is scarcely a happy one.'

1620. naþt. On the spelling see 1256, note.

1624. þe зet is, as Atkins says, <OE *þā gīet* ' even then ' [see B.T. *Suppl.* s.v. *git*, ' yet ', I. (2)].

1625–30. ' The meaning of the passage is that the Owl, as scarecrow in the cornfields (cf. lines 1611–14), preserves the wheat from crows and other birds, while in the wood its corpse attracts inquisitive small birds and brings about their capture ' (Atkins).

1628. The object of **iuo** (MnE ' them ', i.e. little birds) is not expressed. Cf. 274, note.

1631f. mon. A form of the oblique case would have been more regular here, like the pl. *monne* (proposed by Atkins), or the sg. *men* (proposed by Holthausen, Bib. 38; cf. 1246); the word is governed by *to gode* (+dat.), and by *stal . . . stode* (+dat.). But inflexions are not sufficiently regular in O&N to be sure that *mon* must be emended. **stal ne stode** means ' afforded no help, were of no use ' (see *NED* s. *stall*, sb.¹, 2.b.). It seems not unlikely that, in addition to this basic meaning, the poet intends a punning reference to *stal*, ' decoy-bird '. [See *NED* s. *stale*, sb.³, and *stall*, sb.². The word is not recorded in English before the fifteenth century. It is from French, and appears to occur only (as *estal, estale*) in Anglo-Norman, in *Les contes moralisés* by Nicholas Bozon (Bib. 90, p. 169), of a pigeon used as decoy to entice a hawk into the net. [The Central OFr form is *estalon*. It occurs, for example, in Jean Lefèvre's translation of *La vielle ou les dernières amours d'Ovide* from the Latin of Richard de Fournival, in the same piece (edited by H. Cocheris, 1861, p. 41) as contains the word *foliot* (cf. 868, note).] The meaning of the lines is, ' But, alive or dead, you were never any use for the good of mankind ', perhaps with the punning implication, ' But you never helped mankind as a decoy-bird, alive or dead.'

1633. bretst. Holthausen's suggestion [Bib. 38 (improving Breier's, p. 43)], that an original *bretst* was copied into the common antecedent of C and J as *breist*, is the best solution; *bretst* is the syncopated 2 sg. pres. ind. of OE *brēdan* (' breed ') with *d > t* (see Sievers-Brunner, § 359.2). But it could also be *<bregdan* (' wrench, pull, move quickly '), with *d > t* (as for *brēdan*), and southern loss of *g* before *d* (see 1381-4, note). The final consonant group of *breist* (for *breitst* or *breidst*) is like *chist* (1331, both C and J, for *chitst* or *chidst*), or *atwist* (1332, both C and J, for *atwitst*). The C scribe copied his exemplar: *breist þi brod*; this did not make sense to the J scribe who, therefore, tried to improve it: *breist þi word* (meaning perhaps ' draw forth your speech ', or ' cunningly entangle your speech '; or, if *breist* is from OFr *braire*, ' cry your words out harshly '—cf. Wells). In doing so he has marred the rhyme.

1639, 1649. On the Nightingale's claim that she need not continue the debate, since the Owl has lost the case at this point, see Introduction, pp. 26f.

1640. Translate, ' For your true learning fails you here.'

1641f. On the rhyme and the spelling *worþ* see 249, note.

1649, 1651. þuncþ. On the spelling see 920 note and 1256 note. **game** here has the same force as it has in the MnE idiom *the game is up*.

1651f. honde/schonde. The correct rhyme is provided by J's *schonde*; cf. the repetition in rhymes of *schame* and *schonde* at 1731-4. As Grattan suggests, the scribe had written *scho'* (for *schon*) when his eye caught *schame* at 1650; he, therefore, added *me*, producing the impossible reading *scho'me* for *schonme*, or *schonme*.

1653f. icwede/stude. The rhyme requires the form *stede*, cf. 590 and especially 966 and footnote. [The forms are etymologically distinct, and, since *stede* occurs in all areas, this rhyme cannot be used for establishing the provenance of the original.]

1658-60. Atkins gives some account of the gathering of the birds at the end of the debate; it is a literary convention, found both in the literary genre of the dialogues between creatures, animate or inanimate (e.g. Golias's *Dialogue between Water and Wine*). and in the debates who is more worthy of love, a cleric or a knight (e.g. in the French *Florence et Blanchefleur*, in which a nightingale speaks in favour of loving a clerk, and a parrot in favour of loving a knight).

1659. **wudewale**. It is not known what bird this is. In early use it seems to be a song-bird, perhaps the golden oriole [Hinckley (Bib. 42) suggests the greenfinch]; later it is the woodpecker. See *NED* s. *woodwall*.

1660. **boþe grete & smale**. See 1668–78, note.

1665. Translate, ' Just as people shout with derision at the man. . . .'

1666. **taueleþ**. The Germanic tribes, at a very early date (before the Anglo-Saxon settlement), acquired from the Romans a number of games using dice and a board variously marked off or chequered. The most popular appears to have been a form of backgammon. Etymologically the verb *taueleþ* [<OE *tæflian*] is derived, by way of the OE noun *tæfl*, from Latin *tabula*, ' the board '. It seems, however, [the evidence of the dictionaries is largely drawn from the OE Glosses *De alea* in MS Cotton, Cleopatra A. III, of the middle of the tenth century (Wright-Wülcker, col. 267, 5–8)] that in English the noun *tæfl* meant ' die ' or ' a game of dice ', and the verb *ic tæfle* ' I play at dice '. Atkins mentions the chapter ' Of Gamblers' in Alexander Neckam's *De Naturis Rerum*, pp. 323f, in which the effects of gambling are described, how standards of decent behaviour are forgotten, and the passions rise with each turn of fortune. [(On the origins) cf. J. Hoops, *Reallexikon der germanischen Altertumskunde*, vol. i (1913), s. *Brettspiel*; and (on the popularity of gambling with dice) cf. Joseph Strutt, *Glig-gamena Angel-ðeod, or The Sports and Pastimes of the People of England*, 1801, pp. xliii f, 229–40, and frontispiece.]

1668–78. The Nightingale's party have come to celebrate the victory which she has proclaimed (1655–64). But they are only little song-birds, and the tag *boþe grete & smale* (1660) has some weakened sense, like ' of every kind ' [cf. 482, and 225, note]; the Owl, therefore, after asking the Nightingale, not without irony, if she has called out the army, reminds her of the fighting-strength of the Owl's party.

1673f. On the rhyme see 1725, note.

1676. **cliures charpe**. On the spelling of *charpe* see 933f, note.

1679. This is among the earliest known references to the fighting qualities of the cock, and, by extension, to cock-fighting. Atkins refers to the account by William Fitzstephen (died ? 1190) in his ' Life of St Thomas ' [*Materials for the History of Thomas Becket, RS*, vol. 3 (1877), p. 9] of London schoolboys indulging in cock-fighting in class on Shrove Tuesday, and to Alexander Neckam's description of the fighting qualities of the cock and a cock-fight in his poem *In Praise of Divine Wisdom*, ii, 801–54 [pp. 391f]. [Cf. Joseph Strutt (see 1666, note), pp. 210f]

1683. **Schille ich**. For the inversion cf. 515, note. **uthest**=*uthes* (with excrescent *t*) <OE *ūt* ' out '+*hǣs* ' command ' [see *NED* s. *outas*]. ME *uthes* was Latinised, and *hutesium et clamor* was the official phrase for ' hue and cry '. See 1215, note.

1685. **ower prude**. Mabel Day, quoted by Grattan, plausibly explains how the C scribe came to write what is distinctly *oþer proude*: he took *ower prude* (presumably with an ambiguous *wynn* in *ower*) in his exemplar to mean ' other proud people '. J's *prude* is correct. The noun *prude* is from OE *prȳda*, the adj. *pr(o)ude* from OE *prūd*.

1687. **eue.** The disputants are night-birds, their debate takes place at night; and Kenyon (Bib. 29) is probably right in taking 1635f and 1655–64 as indicating the Nightingale's song at dawn, with the birds of day gathering around her in the morning (1718), like those that take the nightingale's side in the *Florence et Blanchefleur* debates. But *eue* still means ' evening ' not, of course, ' evening of the approaching day, i.e. morning ' as Kenyon thinks. Evening is the time when, in medieval military practice and in the literary tradition of medieval romances and chronicles, battles end, because the combatants cannot see each other in the dark. The Owl sees hostile forces gathering around her, and she is threatening them; she and her tribe are ready, and before evening comes, and the dark night which must put an end to the battle, she will be victorious. [See Stanley.]

1691f. The agreement, *uoreward* 1689, is literally, ' that we must abide by that through which just judgement would be given us '.

1699. The subject (MnE ' you ') is not expressed. Cf. 362, note.

1701–3. Cf. 51–5, and 54, note on the meaning of **wise.**

1702. **here.** Dickins and Wilson (in their note on line 1790) write: '*uerde.* The supporters of the nightingale, who had joined her when she claimed to have triumphed over the owl. *here* refers to the birds of prey whom the owl had threatened to summon to her aid. It may be that the OE distinction between the two words is here still retained, but if so it need imply nothing as to the sympathies of the poet, since *here* would in any case be more appropriate for the owl's army.' In any case the Owl's army is called *ferde* at 1684. In Anglo-Saxon times the *fyrd* was a form of militia composed, not of professional soldiers, but of men doing military service [see Stenton, pp. 287f]. The *here* in Anglo-Saxon times was a raiding and marauding army of not less than thirty-five men [see *Laws of Ine*, ed. Liebermann, i, 94].

1706. The subject (MnE ' he or she ') is not expressed. Cf. 362, note.

1707–16. The description of the Owl here is reminiscent of that of the Nightingale at 1067–74. The poet is underlining that with both these altercating birds verbal skill, and not deeds of martial prowess, will win the day.

1711. ' Wrongly placed initial in both MSS, the new paragraph should, of course, begin at line 1717 ' (Grattan). [Cf. Introduction, p. 5.]

1713. **& mid his chelde** goes, as Hall says, with *orde.* On the spelling of *chelde* see 933f, note.

1717. **for heo cuþe singe.** As a song-bird the Wren is of the Nightingale's party. Cf. Appendix, p. 167.

1718. **moreȝeninge.** On the time see 1687, note.

1721. On the spelling þorte see 249, note.

1724–6. **wolde.** The meaning here appears to be ' woodland, forest ' as in OE (cf. A. H. Smith, s. *wald* ; *NED* s. *woid*). These lines mean that the Wren is considered wise, because, though it did not teach her about things that matter in the woods, her upbringing among mankind taught her wisdom. As Dickins and Wilson suggest, there is some reference here to a story, now lost, about the Wren.

1725f. **mankenne/þenne.** Atkins (p. 187) attributes to Sir William Craigie the view that, though both MSS of O&N are Western, traces of Kentish forms are found, notably in rhymes which imply the original existence of Kentish *e* for Western and SW *u* (<OE y) [see Introduction, pp. 17f]. In spelling the original Kentish *e* is probably preserved in C's garbled *mannene*, and nowhere else in C or J. [If that is not accepted, Stratmann's emendation *manne/panne* provides an alternative solution. Cf. 131f.] There are other cases where Kentish *e* for MS *u* would provide a better rhyme: *kunne/honne* 65f; probably *wrste* (i.e. *wurste*)/*toberste* 121f [though ME *werste* (<Scand.) exists in areas other than Kent. (Cf. Luick §§ 155.2, 286 Anm. 3; *NED* s. *worst*, a. and sb.)]; *mankunne/honne* 849f; *sunne/honne* 863f; *heonne/kunne* 1673f. The rhymes at 65, 849, 863, 1673, might be inexact rhymes: *ü/ö* [<OE *y* and *eo*]. Atkins refers in this connexion also to *cunde/schende* 273f [cf. *schende/ende* 1287f.]; but *schende* could perhaps rhyme on *ü* [<OE *scyndan* (though there is no evidence that after *sc* OE *y* <*ie* survived into ME; cf. Breier, p. 70; Luick §§ 254a.1, 263; Jordan § 79 and Anm. 2)].

1728f. Translate, ' She could speak wherever she chose, even though it were to be before the king himself '. [cf. E. A. Kock, Bib. 27]. The respect shown here to the Wren is traditional: see Appendix, p. 167. The rhyme **walde/scholde** presupposes an original *wolde*; *walde* is a Western and North West dialect feature (i.e. a characteristic of C); SE and SW dialects have *wolde*.

1730f. þis pes refers to the king's peace. After the Conquest a change took place in the nature of the king's peace. It used to be (the late OE term was *cyninges grip*) a highly exceptional privilege, the grant of royal protection to a favoured few; but, starting with Henry II, the king's peace began to become a form of protection for all, a right to trial which could easily be obtained by simply alleging a breach of the king's peace, for this forced the case to come into a royal court. [See G. O. Sayles, *The Medieval Foundations of England* (1948), pp. 170–2, 336f]. Here this later form of the king's peace must be meant. It may be a general reference to keeping the peace, or it be a reference to a particular, and therefore datable, peace. Even if it is the latter, which is far from certain, there is still the difficulty that the word *kinge* (1731) is supplied by emendation, so that it is not certain that *he* (1732) refers to the king. If the emendation is right (as seems probable), the king who is neither dead nor crippled (1732) must be Richard I [perhaps abroad at the time (for the fact that Henry II was dead see 1091f note)], who (with his officers) maintained either a peace established during the reign of Henry II, or, more probably, a peace established during his own reign. Many dates are possible; but the reading is not certain, and in any case its interpretation need not lead to a definite date. It seems wiser, therefore, not to follow K. Huganir (pp. 80–96) into a discussion about which date, if any, is to be inferred from these doubtful lines, except to say that the date proposed by Hall (p. 566) fits well, that is, 1194–8, when the Justiciar Hubert Walter kept the peace well during Richard's absence from England.

þan kinge. Stratmann, Breier (p. 126), and most of the later editors read *þan* for the anomalous *þanne*, thus improving the metre. The addition of *kinge* is accepted universally.

1732. ʒe. Grattan rightly defends C's *ʒe* as a form of *yea*; the earlier editors emended to *ʒet*; cf. J's *Yet*.

1733f. Hunke (both MSS), may be either 1st dual or 2nd dual; for in C it is followed in the next line by **ʒe**, in J by **we**. In form it seems to be derived from OE *unc* ' us two ', which is what Grattan and C. T. Onions take it to be in meaning also. But the change from *ʒe* (1730) is too sudden; and the meaning ' you two ' seems preferable. *NED* s. *inc* records such ME forms as *ȝunc*, perhaps intermediate between the etymon *inc* and the form here; also, as Dickins and Wilson adduce, *unker* (the possessive adj. 1st dual) is used with the meaning of that of the 2nd dual in *Havelok the Dane*, line 1882 (EETS (E.S.) 4). *Hunke* is, therefore, perhaps to be regarded as a genuine 2nd dual; if it is not, we must either emend *ȝe* to *we* (which agrees with the J reading), or we must emend *Hunke* to some form like *ȝunk*, which would retain C's better sense.

1734. **gripbruche** presumably changed in meaning with the change in the conception of the king's peace (see 1730f, note), so that it simply means ' breach of the peace ' here.

1740. For the spelling **napþ** see 1256, note.

1741. The subject (MnE ' I ') and the object (translate MnE ' so ') of **do** are not expressed. See notes to 274 and 362.

1747f. **schulde/wule**. J's *schulle* provides an adequate rhyme. The original may have had the subjunctive forms *schille/wille*; cf. 1683.

1751. **nuste**. The common antecedent of C and J seems to have had a badly written *nu-* (reproduced in C) which might be read either *nu-* or *mi-*. C's *-ȝt-* presumably goes back to the common antecedent of C and J, where it probably represents a mistaken substitution of *-ȝt-* for *-st-* (an inversion of the spelling *st* for *ȝt* found in *mist* 78—cf. 78 note, and 1300 footnote), thus going back to *nuste*, *niste*, the p. pl. of *wite* (' to know ') preceded by the neg. particle. [Thus in the main Hall and Atkins.] But the present would fit the context better here, and C. T. Onions proposes a present form as an improvement.

ȝe. Since J has *yet*, Dr Onions has made the suggestion that the original had the 2nd dual *ȝit*, which would give better sense than C's *ȝe* (though that is adequate), and than J's *yet* (which does not make sense). [Grattan reads *miȝte ȝe*, which he thinks echoes *mihte we* at 1749, i.e. as the result of some sort of colloquial ellipsis ' where ' and ' find ' are omitted. As G. V. Smithers says (Bib. 45), this seems unconvincing.]

1752-4. Dickins and Wilson are probably right when they say that the poet is accurate enough in his description of the topography of Portesham, which, being less than three miles from the sea may be said to be **bi þare see**. The phrase **in ore utlete** is more difficult; perhaps *in* means ' on ' here [cf. *in one rodde* 1123]; *utlete* presumably refers to the Fleet [see Gadow], which should more accurately be described as an ' inlet ', separated from the sea by Chesil Beach. Possibly (though it is no more than a speculation) Nicholas of Guildford was living in the Abbey of Abbotsbury (less than two miles from Portesham, and about a mile from the sea, less than that from the West Fleet), for Portesham belonged to the Abbey [see Wm. Dugdale, *Monasticon Anglicanum* (ed. of 1849), iii, 54f, for the close connexion between Abbotsbury and Portesham when the Abbey was founded]. A village priest with the title *Maister*, indicative of learning and rank, is not likely to have been dissociated from the Abbey. See Atkins for a different view.

1757f. Translate, ' And through what he says and through what he writes things are the better as far as Scotland.' It seems likely that in this context (cf. 1756) **þurh his honde** means ' through his writing ' (thus Hall and Atkins). **into Scotlonde**. Atkins, and Hinckley [Bib. 42 and *MLN* **48** (1933), 58f], see here some literal connexion between Nicholas of Guildford and Scotland. But to be literal in such references is not characteristic of ME writing; cf. such exuberant words as those in which the poet of the Harley Lyric *In May hit murgeþ when hit dawes* (edited by G. L. Brook, No. 12; Carleton Brown, *English Lyrics of the XIIIth Century*, No. 82), lines 11f, speaks of fair women in the West:

> One of hem ich herie best
> from Irlond into Ynde.

[' One of them I praise as the best from Ireland as far as India.']

1761. The *-en* of **bischopen** preserves more of OE -um (dat. pl.) than the normal *-e*.

1764. **nimen heom to rede,** ' adopt as their decision ' [see *NED* s. *rede*, sb.¹, 2.b.], or, more idiomatically, ' make up their minds ' [E. A. Kock, Bib. 27].

1767f. **stude/mide.** The rhyme requires *stede*. See 1467, note, and 1653, note.

1773–6. As Atkins says [and see F. Tupper, Bib. 44], ' There is abundant evidence as to the contemporary practice of inducting into livings persons of influence whom either ignorance or youth disqualified for such charges. Bishop Grosseteste in the first half of the 13th century tried to put an end to these abuses (see Grosseteste's *Letters*, passim).' On the relevance of these lines to the problem of the poem's authorship see Introduction, p. 21.

1777f. **Swo** (as Hall says) is explained by the subsidiary clause introduced by **þat**: ' Thus . . . in that.' **hi demþ a dwole** means ' condemns them as in error ', or, more freely, ' tells them they are wrong '. **abid,** ' waits ' i.e. for preferment.

1781f. For the rhyme see 349, note.

1785. **ende of orde.** This phrase, which in ME is confined to verse, is discussed by C. T. Onions [*MLR* **24** (1929), 389–93]: it should perhaps be translated ' from end to end ', rather than ' from beginning to end '.

1790. For **here** and **uerde** see 1702, note. The line seems to mean no more than the Chaucerian *withouten any compaignye*, i.e. ' all alone '.

1791. **þat.** C has the abbreviation which may be read either *þat*, or *þer* (J's reading). Either makes sense, ' which they arrived at ', or ' where they arrived '. [But cf. Koch, Bib. 28.]

1792f. The poet here implies his impartiality. But cf. 394–6, note.

1793. MS *chan* has been emended to **can**, though *ch* for *c* is occasionally found in ME [cf. C. T. Onions, Bib. 59].

APPENDIX

EACH section in this Appendix is to be looked upon as in extension of the notes explaining the text. Like the Notes, the Appendix provides comparative material. It is not suggested that the poet need have known any of the material named in either the Notes or the Appendix, though he may have known some of the items named. By giving such material for comparison it is hoped to show that the poet was working in an age the spirit of which is akin to his own spirit. He is not working in isolation, he is not born out of his age.

THE PROVERBS

The poet's use of proverbs has been discussed [see Introduction, p. 34]. A saying is a proverb when it enshrines in pithy form a truth known to all. It is obvious, therefore, that the proverbs quoted in O&N should be found in many collections of proverbs in many languages. The Tables of proverbs provided are designed to facilitate reference to the proverb literature. It is not suggested that the poet used any of the works, even those in ME or Anglo-Norman, as direct sources; though it seems likely that he knew collections of proverbs, there is no means of telling which he knew. Question-marks have been used in the Table to give some indication of the degree of doubt in the connexion between the proverb in O&N and the proverb with which it is compared.

A SUMMARY OF MARIE DE FRANCE'S FABLE OF THE HAWK
AND THE OWL

A hawk and an owl lived amicably upon a tree and laid their eggs in a single nest. One year the hawk had hatched out the owl's as well as her own little birds. She went in search of food, and when she came back her nest was dirty and defiled. The owls had fouled it. The hawk sat down and rebuked her young, saying that she had kept house for twenty years and never had her birds behaved to her so unbecomingly. Her young answered that she should not blame them for it; she should hold herself responsible. [*The next two lines are corrupt, and have not been solved satisfactorily.*] She answered them, ' You are right. I can hatch them, but I cannot change their nature. A curse on such a brood.'
For this, by way of reproach it is said of the apple from the sweet apple-tree: though it falls next to a bitter tree-trunk, it will never roll so far that it will not be known by its taste from what tree it is. One can flee from one's nature, but no one can leave it entirely. [Warnke, Bib. 88, pp. 264–6.]
The version of the Anglo-Latin Romulus Treverensis [edited by Hervieux, *Les fabulistes latins*, ii, 122] helps to fill the gap. The reply of the hawk's chicks was, ' We are wrongly blamed. It is our brother with the big head, who alone did it.'
Odo of Cheriton's fable (in Latin) of a buzzard that laid an egg in the hawk's nest tells how, when the hawk's own chicks reported to the

159

PROVERB LITERATURE

The Owl and the Nightingale	Proverbs of Alfred	Proverbs of Hendyng	Distichs of Cato ME [Latin]	OE Texts, Other ME Texts, and ME Proverbs in Non-English Texts [Anglo-Norman Proverbs]	Bible
99f				Nicholas Bozon, p. 205	
135, 138				MS Faustina, A.x. Nicholas Bozon, pp. 23, 205 (and note) [Marie de France, *Fabeln*, p. 266]	? Matthew vii, 17f ?? Matthew, xii, 33
176		I, 10			
236*					
295–7*	450–3		I, 149–52 [I, 10]		? Ecclesiasticus, viii, 4 ??? Proverbs, xxvi, 4
301*					?? Ecclesiasticus, xiii, 1
351f*				? Ancrene Riwle, p. 129	
529f	? 1640			? Durham Proverbs, 3 ? Handlyng Synne, 2251 [cf. Wm. of Waddington]	
571f*	??? 327f				
638				MS Trinity College, Cambridge, O. II	

687f* 699f*		I, 16		Robert of Gloucester's *Chronicle*, 11771 *Sir Gawain and the Green Knight*, 476 MS Harley, 2253 (Bödeker, p. 134)	
762* 769–72	??? 605f 192f	??? I, 34		MS Douce 52, 91 *Wohunge of Ure Lord*, p. 277 *Cursor Mundi*, 4775f	
941*		? I, 299f [? II, 4]		Layamon, 17210–3 [cf. Wace 8057–62] *Ancrene Riwle*, p. 120 Giraldus Cambrensis, *Descriptio Kambriae*, . I, xii	
943f				MS Additional 35116	
963f				? *Handlyng Synne*, 2299f [cf. Wm. of Waddington]	
1039f	78f				Galatians, vi, 7f
1072; 1074*	?? 458–60				
1225f*			[I, 18]		
1271f*	?? 173–86	I, 17			
1273f*				MS Douce 52, 105	
1275–8*	?? 138–41			MS Faustina, A.x. *Riming Poem*, 67–9	

* Ascribed to Alfred in O&N

PROVERBS: WORKS OF REFERENCE

The Owl and the Nightingale	Articles on Proverbs	W. W. Skeat, Early English Proverbs (1910)	Oxford Dictionary of English Proverbs (1948)	M. P. Tilley, Dictionary of the Proverbs in England in the 16th and 17th Centuries (1950)	S. Singer, Sprichwörter des Mittelalters (1944–7)	W. Gottschalk, Die bildhaften Sprichwörter der Romanen (1935–8)
99f	J. G. Kunstmann, Southern Folklore Quarterly 3 (1939), 75–91	28	314	B377	i, 137	i, 211
135, 138		29	??? 250 ??? 670	??? T497	i, 134	i, 42
176		72	200f	D79	iii, 127	? iii, 42
236		30	587			
291f	C. T. Onions, MÆ 9 (1940), 86f		233	G. 33	i, 154f iii, 87	iii, 161
301		31	?? 667	?? P358		?? ii, 31
351f		25	?? 665 ?? 415	??? M792f ??? M804–6 ??? M1294 ??? T158 ??? V90	? i, 154	? i, 262 ? ii, 65, 95

529f			? 227	? F693-4	? iii, 53f	
571f		32				iii. 144
638			446	N79	ii, 11f	
658	C. Brett, *MLR* **14** (1919), 7f		275f	H209		
687f 699f		83	21	B59	iii, 130	
762 769–72		8	716	W527	i, 84f iii, 135	
941				? N307	? ii, 127	
943f		33				
963f			? 631	? S982		
1039f		36	608	S687	ii, 160	ii, 273–5
1072, 1074		34	612			
1225f		35				
1271f		81			iii, 130	

hawk that it was the buzzard's young that had defiled the nest, the hawk threw out the son of the buzzard, saying, ' Of a[n] ey *I* þe brohte, of kynde I ne moch[t]e ', that is, ' I have hatched thee out of the egg, but could do nothing to change thy nature.'—And he was broken in every way.

In the version (in Anglo-Norman) by Nicholas Bozon [p. 23; Latin translation p. 205] the owl asked the hawk to bring up his son. The owlet came, and the hawk told him to follow the ways of the hawk's chicks, and learn their nature. The hawk goes in search of food, and when he returns the nest has been fouled. ' What is all this I find, contrary to your breeding? Who has done it? ' he asks. His sons say, ' Your foster-child.' ' Indeed! ' says the hawk, ' It is truly said in English, *Stroke oule and schrape oule, and evere is oule oule.*' [The Latin translation quotes the ME proverb. ' Ah! ' said the hawk, ' *Hyt ys a fowle brydde that fyleth hys owne neste.*'] So it is with many people who are born of base lineage: whenever they are in high places, often instructed and informed in religion, or in the polite world, or in noble bearing, they always come back to their station and to their nature to which they are born. Therefore it is said in English : *Trendle the appel nevere so fer, he conyes fro what tree he cam.*

THE HAWK AND THE NIGHTINGALE

Æsop's fable of the hawk and the nightingale has been retold by Marie de France [Warnke, Bib. 88, pp. 215f]. The nightingale is commanded by the hawk to sing; but she says she could not sing as long as she sees the hawk so close. If the hawk were to fly on another tree she would sing more beautifully.

A related Middle High German fable [? by Stricker. Edited by F. Pfeiffer, *Zeitschrift für deutsches Altertum* 7 (1849), 331f] tells of how a song-bird was singing with such earnest concentration on a green bough that he forgot himself. A hawk got hold of him with his feet. The little bird's voice ceased to be sweet, and he sang as do those who wrestle with death.

A SUMMARY OF MARIE DE FRANCE'S FABLE OF
THE CAT AND THE FOX

A cat and a fox were companions. They talked of tricks to save themselves when hard-pressed. ' My friend,' said the fox, ' I have a hundred tricks [*other versions have other numbers*], and if those fail I still have a bag of tricks left.' The cat wished to part company with him, for he only had one trick, all his neighbours knew that. As they were speaking thus, they saw two hounds running towards them. ' I need your help,' cried the fox. ' Help yourself,' answered the cat; ' I only have one trick, and this is it.' With that he jumped on a thorn bush and was safe. He saw how the hounds were pulling the fox about, and cried, ' Comrade, why don't you untie your little bag? You are saving it up too long.' The fox, as he saw the cat free, would gladly have had the cat's one trick for his bagful. And the cat recalled the saying: ' Often the fox is caught, however wily his words may be.'

One word of an honest man is worth more than all a liar can say, however reasonable it may sound. [Warnke, Bib. 88, pp. 315–18.]

A SUMMARY OF MARIE DE FRANCE'S LAY OF THE AUSTIC

I will tell you an adventure of which the Bretons made a lay. It has the name of *The Austic*, and so they call it, I think, in their land, that is *russignol* in French, and *nihtegale* in plain English.

Two knights there were in the city of St Malo, and they were neighbours. The one had a wife endowed with every courtly virtue. The other was famed for prowess, for honour, and for liberality. The wife loved her neighbour, and he loved her; but all with discretion, for, being so near, they could see each other, talk and exchange gifts undisturbed, unobserved, and unsuspected. There was not much to displease them, except that a high wall of dark stone was between them, and they could not quite come together to their pleasure. For the lady was closely guarded when *he* was in the land. For a long time they loved each other, until summer came, and woods and meadows were green once more and the orchards in bloom. If a man is yearning for love, no wonder he is intent on it! I will tell you truly of this knight: with all his might he was intent on it, and the lady too, in word and glance.

In the nights, when the moon was shining and her lord had gone to rest, she often rose from his side, and put on her mantle. She came and stood by the window to see her lover, who she knew would be there, for he led just such a life as she, and used to watch for her the greater part of the night. They took delight in seeing, since they could have no more. She arose so often that her lord grew angry and questioned her. ' My lord,' she answered, ' he has no joy in this world who hears not the *austic* sing. It sings so sweetly out there by night that I rejoice in it and long for it. I cannot sleep, and therefore I stand here.' When her lord heard that, he laughed out with anger, and thought of ways of ensnaring the *austic*. Every servant in his house set traps, nets, and snares, all over the orchard. At length they took it captive, and handed it over alive to the lord of the house. He was very glad when he held it. He went to his lady's chambers, and said, ' My lady, I have ensnared the *austic*, for whose sake you have been awake so often. Now indeed, you can lie in peace. It will wake you no more.' The lady was angry and asked him for it, and he in his rage broke its neck with his own hands. That was a very base deed. He threw it at the lady so that it stained her smock with blood; and then he left her. The lady took the body and wept bitterly, and cursed all who had betrayed the *austic*, and put an end to her greatest joy. ' Alas,' she said, ' now I shall not be able to stand by the window and see my lover. He will think me false; I will make known to him what has happened: I will send the *austic* to him.'

In a piece of brocade embroidered with gold and all inscribed she enfolded the little bird, handed it to one of her servants, and sent him to her lover with a message. The servant gave the *austic* to the knight, and related all his message. The knight, when he had seen and heard it all, was sad. He had a vessel made of pure gold set with jewels, with a well-fitting lid. He had the *austic* placed inside, and the reliquary sealed. He had it carried with him, always.

The adventure was told—it could not long be concealed. The Bretons made a lay of it, and it is called *The Austic*. [Warnke, Bib. 87, pp. 146–151.]

A brief discussion of some other versions of this story

A fuller discussion is provided by Warnke, Bib. 87, pp. cl–clvi, which should be consulted for references. In *Le Renard Contrefait* the story is told by Renard of an old king of *Bretaigne* (which is now called *Angleterre*), his young queen and her lover, who was a young knight separated from the palace only by an orchard, in which the nightingale used to sing. The incidents are virtually the same, until the nightingale is taken and killed. Then the queen loved the knight even more. She spoke in secret to him and complained of the king. The knight gathered his friends and made war on the king, who lost his life; and the queen married the knight.

In the *Gesta Romanorum* [edited by H. Oesterley, 1872, chap. cxxi] the story is more complicated: An old, rich knight is married to a fair, young wife who is in love with a poor young knight married to an old rich wife. Outside the palace of the rich knight was a fig-tree; and there the nightingale sang so sweetly that the young lady, filled with longing, had to get up and listen. The old knight shot the nightingale. When the young knight was told of it he thought, ' Alas, if that cruel man knew what strong love there is between me and his wife he would treat me even worse.' He armed himself, and killed the old knight. Soon afterwards the young knight's old wife died, and he married the young lady.

In the English translation (of about 1440) of the *Gesta Romanorum* the young lady gets up to hear her lover, the nightingale's song being more of an excuse than a reason—whereas in the Latin version the song of the nightingale was the actual reason why she got up.

Alexander Neckam in the chapter of *De Naturis Rerum* devoted to the nightingale (pp. 102f), alluding to the story in which the nightingale has led the lady into illicit love, tells of how her husband had the nightingale drawn asunder by four horses.

A SUMMARY OF A PENYWORTH OF WYTT

Gentlemen, listen to my song, of how a merchant of this country was unfaithful to his excellent, loyal, and obedient wife. He loved another woman, lavishing on her clothes fit for a queen, while he spent nothing on his own true wife. The time came when the merchant had to go abroad; he went to his paramour and took leave with kisses and tears. When he took leave of his wife he asked her for any money she might wish to let him have, to buy things with for her abroad. ' Sir,' she said, ' you have all I possess. But take this penny, and buy for me a pennyworth of wit; and keep it safe in your heart.' He put the penny in his purse, and travelled to France. When he had finished selling and buying, he bought the best jewellery for his paramour, and wished to spend nothing on his wife, until his man said to him, ' Let us not forget the mistress's penny.' The merchant swore, ' That was a damned silly bargain: to buy a pennyworth of wit for her. I can't find it in all France.' He was overheard by an old man, who said he was ready to sell him a pennyworth of wit. ' But tell me, which have you, a paramour or a wife?' ' Sir, I have both; but I love my paramour best.' The old man then instructed him, ' When you get back, put on shabby clothes, and go to your paramour. Tell her you have lost everything. Then go to your wife. Whichever of the two helps you the best in your need, live with her.' ' Farewell,' said the merchant, ' here's your penny.' He did what the old man said. His paramour, when she saw from afar his shabby outfit, and heard from her maid that he was seeking refuge because he had murdered a nobleman, rejected him utterly. He went his way.

Listen, friends, for the better chapter is still to come. The merchant is now in his own hall. His wife joyfully welcomed him. He told her how he had lost everything, done murder, and now sought refuge in her chamber; and she stood by him in his need. She undertook to intercede on her knees for him with the king himself, and to work for him and to maintain him. All night he spent with her, and in the morning he put on his rich clothes and went to his paramour, who welcomed him with kisses. But he asked to see all the treasure that he had ever given her, for he had heard that she had given them to a new lover. His paramour said she had been maligned, and produced the riches he had lavished on her. He put everything in a bag, carried it away, and presented it all to his wife, saying, ' I bought all this with your penny.' And he explained to her why he had come so poorly clad. From that time on he lived happily with her. [E. Kölbing, *EStn* 7 (1884), 111–25.]

THE ROYAL WREN

Alexander Neckam [pp. 122f] tells how the wren, though the smallest of the birds, claimed to be their king: in Latin he is called *regulus*. When the birds were assembled to choose their king it was agreed that whichever bird could fly highest should be king. The wren hid in the eagle's wing, and when the eagle claimed his rightful title, the wren left his hiding-place and flew on to the head of the eagle himself. He claimed the title, and his claim was upheld.

The story of the royal rank of the wren was known throughout the Middle Ages and goes back to Antiquity. Pliny refers to it [*Naturalis Historia*, viii, 37]; and so does Aristotle [*Historia Animalium*, translated by D'Arcy W. Thompson, 1910, p. 615a], who says that one nickname of the wren is ' king ' [cf. Fr. *roitelet*, German *Zaunkönig*]; and the story goes that for this reason the eagle is at war with him.

There is evidence that the wren is at war with the owl. Cf. *Macbeth*, IV.ii.9–11:

> For the poore Wren
> (The most diminitiue of Birds) will fight,
> Her yong ones in her Nest, against the Owle.

Pliny, x, 95, refers to the strife between owls and the other, smaller birds immediately after a reference to the wren; and Aristotle [*op. cit.*, p. 609a] says, ' There is enmity also between the owl and the wren; for the latter also devours the owl's eggs.'

A SUMMARY OF THE DIALOGUE BETWEEN WINTER AND SUMMER

In autumn an old man and a youth are sitting in debate. The wind leads before them two kings, the one old and venerable, and stiff with ice, the other young and gay, full of flaming fire. They are Winter and Summer. Summer begins the debate with a partial account of the change of the seasons. Winter insists on his greater power: ' Your glory comes to nothing at my rough might. I practise science and cultivate wisdom.' He claims to be the father, the beginning of growth, whereas Summer, as mother and nurse, is inferior. Summer replies: ' You rage with tempest, hail, snow, and rain; days grow short, the birds are silent, the world is deprived of its strength through the cold. You are older, yet your merits are less than mine, for I restore to the world its strength and beauty.' Winter: ' My mighty tempests purge and heal the world. I advance hunting and navigation. You must sweat red in the face. The poor birds, neglected by you, are fed by me. You, like Phaeton, burn the world.' Summer: 'You are hated by all. The ocean is churned up by you, the sun shines less bright.' Winter: 'The evils which you have nourished, snakes, frogs, toads, flies, flees, locusts, wasps, and midges, I destroy. My snows restore wine. Your heat forces human beings to bare themselves indecently. While I, indoors, converse intelligently with the civilised, you hop like mad with boorish bumpkins in the open. You abandon yourself to fantastic imaginings, while I consort with the urbane, with men of learning and with prophets, and take delight in music.' Summer: 'Though I may produce these evils, I am still the consolation and the hope of the miserable. Your studies only extend to Epicurus and to Venus.' Winter: 'I feed you, beggar, by planting seeds. Frivolity and vice are unknown to me. Through you everything decays. The pauper is diligent with me, with you he is lazy and greedy.' Summer: 'All things mature in my time. What are your gifts? Brambles, thorns, hail, snow, rain, and clouds! The world sighs at your severity, and rejoices in my life-giving mildness. Flowers adorn my garments, and plays enhance joy.' Winter: 'You nourish fornication and adultery, and lead astray to jousts, round-dances, and amours; and filthy songs are heard, not the praise of God. You let loose all vices.' Summer wishes to submit the dispute to a judge, and so does Winter after trying to gain victory by a trick. Theologia comes to judge the case. She counsels peaceful reconciliation: the dispute of the seasons will destroy them both; together they would enter heaven. [Walther, Bib. 85, pp. 34–46, 191–211.]

GLOSSARY

GLOSSARY

In compiling the Glossary the aim has been to list every form; no attempt has been made, however, to parse every form, except in so far as was thought helpful for translating.

In this text many words occur in several spellings; and this has made necessary many cross-references and some divergence from the normal alphabetical arrangement: **k** will be found under **c**, **qu** under **cw**, **y** under **i**. In words of native origin, **f** when it represents *v* (e.g. initially) will be found under **v** (consonant). The vowel written **u** or **v** is kept distinct from the consonant also written **u** or **v**. **vv** and **u** when used for **w** are not kept distinct from **w**. **ʒ** follows **g**. **sh** will be found under **sch**. In the group **hw** or **wh**, the **h** has been ignored in the arrangement.

The prefix **i-** has been ignored in the arrangement when it comes before verbs, but not when it comes before nouns, or adjectives, or adverbs.

A line number in italics indicates that the word at that line is emended, a line number in square brackets indicates that the word is supplied. Where a line number is followed by *n* the Notes should be consulted (though not every note is referred to in the Glossary in this way).

&, *see* **and**
a, *see* **an**, **on**
abak, *adv.* back, backwards, 824, 877
abide, *v. tr.* wait for, stay for, endure; *inf.* 1695, 1706, be pursued by, 1215; **abideþ**, *pres. pl.* 1702. —*v. intr.* wait, stay, persist; **abid**, *pres.* 3 *sg.* 466, 1778n; **abide**, *pres. subj. sg.* 1389n; **abid**, *imp.* 747, 837 (*2*), 845 (*2*); **abod**, *p.* 3 *sg.* 41, **abot** 1175. Cf. **nabideþ**
abiten, *inf.* bite to death, 77
aboʒte, *p. pl.* paid for, paid the penalty for, 1060
abrad, *p.p.* dilated, 1044n
abute, *adv.* round about, all around, 16; **al abute**, on all sides, 645; **hire abute**, around her, 1593
ac, *see* **ah**
acursi, *v.* curse, anathematise; *inf.* 1704; **akursedest**, *p. 2 sg.* 1184
acoled, *p.p.* cooled down; **he is . . . acoled**, his ardour is . . . cooled, 205. Cf. **nacoleþ**
acorde, *n.* agreement; **at one acorde**, of one mind, 181
acwalde, *p.p.* killed, 1370

ad, *see* **at**
adel, *n., adj.* addle(d), 133
adiʒte, *pres. 1 sg.* order, set forth, 326
adrede, *v.* fear; *inf.* 1266, *refl.* 1484; *pres. subj. sg.* 1487
adun, *adv.* down, 208, 1454, 1458; **adune**, 920
adunest, *pres. 2 sg.* din into, 337
afoled, *p.p.* befooled, made a fool of, 206
after, *prep.* after, 140, 200, 468, &c.; in search of 591—*adv.* afterwards, later, thereupon, 469, 1040.—**after þan**, accordingly, 650, 1578
aginne, *inf.* begin, go about it, 1289
agon, *v.* go, vanish, pass, perish; *inf.* 355, 1280; **ageþ**, *pres. 3 sg.* 1453; **ago**, *p.p.* over, done with, 507, 508
agrulle, *inf.* annoy, trouble, 1110
aʒaf, *p. 3 sg.* returned; replied, 139
aʒen, *prep.* against, 7, 668 (*2*), 676, &c.; expecting, in expectation of, to meet, 436, 1153; **aʒeines**, contrary to, 1371.—**aʒen**, *adv.*

back, 454, 818; aȝein, 1788, see stont.—aȝen þet, ready for when, in anticipation of when, 499

aȝte, see aht

ah, conj. but, 1176, 1183, 1185, &c.; ac, 83, 177, 226, &c.—ac is, it is rather, 512

ah, pres. 3 sg. ought to, 1471. Cf. nah

ahene, see oȝe

aht, adj. worthy, valiant, 1479, 1481, 1500; aȝte, pl. 385, 389. Cf. noȝt

ahweneþ, see awene

aishest, v. ask; pres. 2 sg. 473, aisheist 995, axest 707, axestu do you ask 711; askedest, p. 2 sg. 1310

aiþer, see eiþer

ai-vvare, adv. everywhere, 216

al, adj. all, 65, 173, 220, &c.; alle, 222, 431, 433, &c. [771]; alre, gen. pl. (+superl. adj.) of all, very, 10, 121, 684, &c.—þu al, all (the rest) of you, 74; al . . . it, it all, 1090, al (. . .) hit 1216, 1256, acc. sg. 1060; ow alle, all of you, 1686, 1697; hi . . . alle, all of them, 1116, alle ho 66, alle heo 1677.—al, pron. everything, all, 78, 414, 630, &c.; pl. 1174.—al þat, as much as, 1086.—al, adv. quite, entirely, exactly, all, wholly, utterly, completely, 8, 27, 215, &c.; just, 855; alle, 331, 1391.— See mid alle

alamed, p.p. paralysed, grown lame, 1604

alde, see old

alegge, inf. set aside, refute, 394

almiȝti, adj. almighty, 1173

aloþeþ, pres. 3 sg. grows loathsome, 1277

al-so, adv. just so, just that, so, also, likewise, 129, 237, 298, &c.; al-swo, 891, 1243, 1323; al-swa, 1329, 1373, 1663.— al-so, conj. as, just as, 503, 550, 554, &c. as if 146, like 1012; al-swo, 1738

Alured, n. Alfred, 235, 294, 299, 349, 569, 761, 1074; Alfred, 942, 1223, 1269; Aluered, 685; Aluerid, 697

am, see beon

amanset, p.p. cursed, excommunicated, 1307

amis, adv. astray, wrong, 1365, 1434, 1540

among, prep. among, along with, amid, 506, 563, 593 (2), &c. amon 164.—adv. now and then, 6

an, prep. in, on, 299, 323, 467, 905, 1246, 1371, 1372, 1588 (second), 1651; after 1458; a, in, by (in adv. phrases of time), on, 20, 89 (2), 115, &c. at 323; to, into 1417; in, along 1428

an, pres. 1 sg. grant, 1739

an, see and, on

anan, see anon

and, conj. and, 4, 1240, 1270, &c.; &, 5 (2), 6, 8, &c. 1056, 1528; an, 7, 192, 278, 355, &c.

andsuare, andsware, andswere, see ondsware

ane, see on

anhoð, v. hang up, hang; pres. pl. 1646; anhonge, p.p. 1195

anne, see on

anon, adv. at once, straight away, 488, 522, 1554, anan 1658

ansuare, imp. sg. answer, 555

ansuare, ansuere, ansvere, ansvvare, answare, answere, see ondsware

ape, n. ape, 1325

appel, n. apple, 135

ar, conj. before, 552, 692, 859, &c.; by the time that, 1687; before, rather than that, 1698

aredde, pres. subj. 3 sg. rescue, set free, deliver, 1569

areȝ, adj. cowardly, 407

areȝþe, n. cowardice, 404, arehþe 1716

areme, see arme

aren, see harm

ariȝt, adv. right, properly, correctly, 400, 1552; ariht, 904, 1420, 1576

arise, v. rise, arise, get up; inf. 327; arist, pres. 3 sg. 1394, 1397; ariseþ up, pres. pl. 731

arme, adj. pl. wretched, poor, miserable, 537, areme, 1162

art(u), see beon

askedest, see aishest

aschewele, pres. 1 sg. scare away, 1613

aspille, inf. destroy, waste, 348

astorue, *p.p.* perished, dead, *1200*

aswinde, *v.* vanish, decay, wear out; *inf.* 1574; **aswunde,** *p.p.* feeble, 1480, **asvnde** 534

at, *prep.* at, in, by, close to, [86], 181, 293, 479, 527, &c.;˙ faced with, 750; **ad** 325.—**atte,** at the, 1513, **ate** 592

atbroide, *p.p.* snatched away, stolen, extorted, 1380n

ateliche, *adj.* terrible, loathsome, 1125

atholde, *v.* keep, retain, preserve, consider; *inf.* 695, 1420; **athold,** *p. 3 sg.* 392

atprenche, *inf.* elude, 248n, 814

atrute, *inf.* escape, 1168

atschet, *p. 3 sg.* shot away; drove out, 44; **atschote,** *p.p.* shot out of, 1623

atstonde, *inf.* withstand, 750

atte, *see* **at**

atter-coppe, *n. pl.* spiders, 600

attest, *see* **hoten**

attom, *adv.* at home, 1527. *Cf.* **hom**

atfliþ, *pres. 3 sg.* flees away, 37

atwende (+*acc.*), *inf.* escape (from), turn away (from), 1427

atwite (+*dat. of person+acc. of thing*), *v.* blame (someone) for (something), find fault with . . . for . . ., reproach . . . for . . ., upbraid . . . for . . .; *inf.* 1234; **atwist,** *pres. 2 sg.* 1332, **atuitest** 597; **atuitestu,** *v.* +*pron. 2 sg.* do ye blame (&c.), 751, **attwitestu** 1187; **atwiten,** *p.p.* 935

aþele, *adj. used as n., pl.* those of high birth, the nobility, 632

aualle, *inf.* fall, collapse, 1685

afere, *inf.* terrify, frighten, 221, **oferen** 978; **aferd,** *p.p.* afraid, 410, 472, **oferd** 399

auinde, *inf.* find out, discover, 527, 856

afonge, *v.* receive ; *inf.* suffer, 1196; **auoþ,** *pres. pl.* give ear to, hear, 843

auorþ, *adv.* forward, 824

awaiwart, *adv.* away, 376

awedeþ, *pres. pl.* go mad, rage, 509. *Cf.* **nawedeþ**

awei, *adv.* away, 33, 177, 1700; **awai,** 250, 1510

awene, *v.* trouble, vex, grieve, afflict; *pres. 1 sg.* 1258; **ahweneþ,** *pres. 3 pl.* 1564

a-wer, *adv.* anywhere; in any way *1342*n

awreke, *reflex. v. pres. subj. pl.* take vengeance, get (their) own back, 1562; *p.p.* avenged, 1105; **bon of þe awreke,** get even with you, 262

awroþeþ, *pres. 3 sg.* becomes angry, 1278

ax, *n.* axe, 658

axest(u), *see* **aishest**

baldeliche, *see* **boldeliche**

bale, *n.* calamity, 687, 699

banne, *n.* troop, mobilised army, 390

ibanned, *p.p.* called out, called up, 1668

bare, *adj.* mere, 547, 571; (*used as n.*) the open, 56, 150

bareȝ, *n.* barrow-pig; **of bore wrchen bareȝ,** lose his virility, 408

bataile, *n.* battle, 1197

be, *see* **beon**

bedde, *n.* bed, 967, 1047, 1492n, 1499, &c.

bedde, *n.* bed-fellow, husband, 1500. *Cf.* **ibedde**

bede, *see* **bidde**

bed-time, *n.* bed-time, 324

beire, *see* **bo**

belde, *see* **bold**

bende, *n. prepos. sg. or pl.* bond(s), 1428

beod, *see* **bode**

beon, *v.* be; *inf.* 932, 1195, 1198, &c. **beo** 1194, 1318, 1493, &c. **bon,** 262, 666, 724, **be,** 1151, 1768, **bo,** 190, 418, 979, &c. **boe** 1303; **am,** *pres. 1 sg.* 170, 276, 277, &c.; **art,** *pres. 2 sg.* 38, 61, 65, &c., **artu** +*pron.* are you, 541, 542, 1298, **hartu** 1177; **is,** *pres. 3 sg.* 73 (2), 74, &c., there is, 637, **his,** 1498, 1761; **boþ,** 296, 670, 848; **beoþ,** *pres. pl.* 1227, 1338, 1348, &c., **beoð** 911, **boþ,** 75, 88, 178, &c.; *pres. subj. sg.* **beo,** 1225, 1233, 1242, &c., **bo,** 128, 137, 151, &c., 295, **bo wuch ho bo,** let it be what it will, whatever it may be, 1378;

beon, *pres. subj. pl.* 1221, **bon**, 452, 740, 883, **bo**, 97, 181, 860; **beo**, *imp. sg.* 1638, **bo**, 261, 546; **beoþ**, *imp. pl.* 1735; **was**, *p. 1 sg.* 1; **were**, *p. 2 sg.* 1059, 1062, 1180; **was**, *p. 3 sg.* 5, 19, 27, &c.; **were**, *p. pl.* 16, 1104, **uere** 1306; **were**, *p. subj. sg.* 21, 23, 53, 85, &c., 1310, 1314; **weren**, *p. subj. pl.* 76, 976, **were**, 203, 427.— *impers. v.* **me is**, *pres. 3 sg.* I feel, 34; **þe is** (*see* unneaþe); **him beo**, *pres. subj. sg.* things may go with him, he may feel, 1271. *Cf.* nam

bere, *n.* behaviour, outcry, 925. *Cf.* ibere

bere, *v.* bear, carry, shoulder; *pres. 1 sg.* 1599, 1701; **berþ**, *pres. 3 sg.* 775, 403 (*see* ilete); **bereð**, *pres. pl.* 1372.—**ibore**, *p.p.* born, 716

berne, *n. prepos. sg. or pl.* barn(s), 607

berne, *inf.* (*used passively*), be set on fire, be burnt down, 1203

berste, *pres. subj. pl.* burst, 990

beseo, *reflex. v. pres. subj. 3 sg.* shall look **to** (himself), 1272

best, *n.* animal, 99

bet, *adv. compar.* better, rather, more easily, *21*, 23, 39, 172, &c.; **ne . . . þe bet**, no better, 1327; **best**, *superl.* best, 470.

bete, *inf.* make good, make amends, repent, 865

betere, *adj. compar.* better, 283, 712, 713, &c.; **betere is**, it is better, 931

bi, *prep.* (*adv.*), by, close to, near, along, alongside, close by, beside, at, 109, 241, 278 (2), &c., with 428 (2), from 816, in 1432; with, as regards, 46, 92, 93, 129, 245, 1243, 1373; helped by, through, because of, by means of, as a result of, 723, 871, 1361, 1449, 1463, 1465

bichermet, *pres. pl.* scream at, 279

bicloped, *p.p.* made a charge, brought an indictment, 550

biclopt, *p.p.* in an embrace, clasped, *1048*

bicome (to), *p. pl.* came (to), arrived (at), 1791; **bicume**, *p.p.* come (away), 137.—**bicumeþ** (to), *impers. v. pres. 3 sg.* is

proper (for), 271; **bicom**, *p. 3 sg.* came about, happened, 105

bidde (+*acc. of thing*), *v.* pray (for *something*), ask, beg; *inf.* 858; **bidde**, *pres. 1 sg.* 741n, 1221, 1253, &c.; (+ *dat. of person*) bid, 929; **bit**, *pres. 3 sg.* 445, 1352, **bid**, 441, 1437; **biddeþ**, *pres. pl.* 886; **bede**, *p. 2 sg.* 550; **bede**, *p. subj. sg.* 1678

biginne, *v.* begin; *pres. 1 sg.* 1456; **bigon**, *p. 3 sg.* 13

bigrede, *v.* cry out against, cry out at, caw at; *inf.* 1413; **bigredeþ**, *pres. pl.* 279, **bigredet** 67; **bigrede**, *pres. subj. sg.* 304; **bigradde**, *p. pl.* 1144

bigrowe, *p.p.* grown over, 27, 617

biȝete, *v.* obtain, procure, attain; *inf.* 1629; **biȝete**, *pres. subj. sg.* 726

bihalde, bihaltst, *see* biholde

bihede, *v.* watch over, protect; *inf.* prevent 635; **bihede**, *p. 3 sg.* 102; **bihedde**, *p.p.* 1048n

bihemmen, *inf.* hem (it) round, trim (it) up, 672

bihinde, *prep., adv.* behind, at the back (of), behindhand, 528, 594, 666, 937, &c.—*n.* behind, backside, 596

biholde, *v.* see, behold, look at, contemplate, gaze on; *inf.* 71, **bihalde** 1325; **biholde**, *pres. 1 sg.* 1566; **bihaltst**, *pres. 2 sg.* *1322*n; **bihold**, *p. 3 sg.* 30, 108

bihote, *p.p.* promised, 1745

bile, *n.* beak, 79, 269, 1675

bileck, *see* biluþ

biledet, *pres. pl.* pursue; mob 68

bilegge, *v.* wrap up, explain away, gloze over; *inf.* 672, 904; **bileist**, *pres. 2 sg.* 839

bileue, *inf.* remain, stay, hold back, 42, 464, **bileaue** 1688

biliked, *p.p.* made pleasing, 842

biluþ, *pres. 3 sg.* locks up, 1557; **bileck**, *p. 3 sg.* 1081

bineoðe, *prep.* under, 912

binimeþ, *pres. 3 sg.* takes away, 941; **binume** (+*dat.*), *p.p.* taken from, 1226

bireued, *p.p.* deprived, rid, 120

bischopen, *n. dat. pl.* bishops, 1761

bischricheþ, *pres. pl.* screech around, 67

bisemed, *p.p.* made decent, 842

bisemere, *n. prepos.* mockery, 1311; **hire a bisemar,** in mockery of her, 148

bisne, *adj.* blind, 97, 243

bispeke, *v.* speak about; *pres. subj.* 1561; *p.p.* determined 1738

bispel, *n.* moral tale, parable, fable, 127

bistant, *pres. 3 sg.* stands by, besets, harasses, 1438n

bisvvike, *v.* deceive, ensnare; *inf.* 158; **biswike,** *pres. subj. pl.* 930

bit, *see* **bidde**

bitelle, *inf.* defend, 263

bitide, *v.* happen, come to pass, turn out; *pres. optative sg.* 52; **bitidde,** *p. 3 sg.* 1107

biti3t, *p.p.* attired, clad, 1013

bito3e, *p.p.* covered; employed, made use of, 702

bituxen, *prep.* between, 1747

bitweone, *prep.* between, 1379

biþenche, *v.* (*usually reflex.*) bethink (oneself), ponder, take thought, bear in mind, collect (one's) thoughts; *inf.* 471, contrive it 828; **biþenchest,** *pres. 2 sg.* 1505; **biþencþ,** *pres. 3 sg.* 1509; **biþenche,** *pres. subj. sg.* 871; **biþo3te,** *p. 3 sg.* 199, 704, **biþohte** 939

biuore, *prep., adv.* before; the first of 776; in advance, beforehand 1235

biwepe, *v.* weep over, bewail; *inf.* 980; **biwepen,** *pres. subj. pl.* 974

biwerest (urom), *pres. 2 sg.* protect (against), defend (against) keep (from), 1126, 1517

biwro, *inf.* cover up, conceal, 673

bled, *n.* blossom, flower, 1042

blenche, *inf.* dodge, jump out of the way, 170, 1231

blenches, *n. pl.* tricks, dodges, 378

bleo, *n.* colour, complexion, face, 1547; **blo,** 152, 441

blete, *adj.* bare, 616.—(*used as n.*) being exposed, 57

blind, *adj.* blind, sightless, 243, 1237

blis, *n.* bliss, happiness, joy, 1280; **blisse,** 420, 422, 433, &c.

blisse, *pres. subj. sg.* shall rejoice, 478.—**blisseþ** hit, *reflex. pres. 3 sg.* rejoices, 435

bliþe, *adj.* happy, glad, 418, 740, 992, &c.; **bliþur,** *compar.* 1108

blo, *see* **bleo**

blod, *n.* blood, 945, 1127n, 1434, &c.; **blode,** *prepos.* nature 1350

blosme, *n. pl.* blossoms, 16, **blostme,** 437 '

blowe, *v.* blossom; *inf.* 1133, 1201; **iblowe,** *p.p.* in flower, flourishing, blossoming, 618, **blowe,** 1636

bo, *pron., adj.* both, 990; **boþe,** 381; **boþe we,** both of us, 1681; **þare beire,** *gen. pl.* of both, 1584.—**boþe . . . an** (*or* &), both . . . and; . . . and also; . . . as well as, 50, 225, 386, &c.

bo, *see* **beon**

boc, *n.* book, 1325; **bokes,** *gen. sg.* 1208; **boke,** *prepos. pl.* 350

bode, *inf.* offer, 530; **beod,** *pres. 3 sg.* commands, 1437

bodest, *v.* proclaim, foretell, prophesy; *pres. 2 sg.* 1152, 1157, 1160, **bodes** 1155; **bodeþ,** *pres. 3 sg.* 1170

bodi, *n.* body, 73

boe, *see* **beon**

bo3e, *see* **bov**

bold, *adj.* bold, daring, *317,* 405; **bolde** 410, **belde** 1715

boldeliche, *adv.* boldly, courageously, 401, **baldeliche** 1707

boldhede, *n.* valour, boldness, 514

ibolwe, *p.p.* swollen with anger, 145

bon, *n. pl.* bones, 1120

bon, *see* **beon**

bonde-man, *n.* peasant, 1577n

bor, *n.* beer, 1011

borde, *n.* table, board, 479, 1492n, 1579

bore, *n. dat. sg.* bear, 1021

bore, *n.* boar, 408

ibore, *see* **bere**

ibor3e, *p.p.* saved, 883

bote, *n.* relief, remedy, help, 688, 700, 858n

bote, *see* **bute**

boþ, *see* **beon**

boþe, *see* **bo**

bov, *n.* branch, bough, *242*n; **bo3e,** *prepos. sg.* 15, 816, 125, 1244; **bo3e,** *prepos. pl.* 616

breke, *inf.* break, 1080, 1334, 1693

breche, *n.* arable land, fallow field, 14n

ibred, bredde, *see* bretst

brede, *n.* breadth, 174

brede, *n.* plank, 965

brede, *n.* roast meat, 1630

breme, *adj.* wild, fierce, 202, 500

bretst, *v.* breed; *pres. 2 sg. 1633*n; bredde, *p. 3 sg.* 101; ibred, *p.p.* 1724

breþ, *n.* breath, fervour, passion, 948, 1454, 1461

brid, *n. sg.* little bird, chick, 124; briddes, *nom., acc., dat., prepos. pl.* 106, 107, 626, 654, &c.; bridde, *acc. pl.* 123; *prepos. pl.* 111, 644

bridel, *n.* bridle, 1028

briȝt, *adj.* bright, clear, 623; briȝte, *acc. sg.* 1681, sharp 240; þane briȝte, (the way of) light, 250; briȝter, *comp.* 152.— brihte, *adv.* clearly, 1245, 1656

bringe, *v.* bring, lead; *inf.* 710, 854, 1035, &c. persuade 1417, adduce 1478, ibringe 1539; bringe vrom, deflect from, dissuade from, 1029; bringe, *pres. 1 sg.* 433; bringþ, *pres. 3 sg.* 1534, bringeþ 1171; bringþ (on), brings (to), bestows (on), 1447; bringeþ, *pres. pl.* 524; ibringe, *pres. subj. sg.* bring . . . to it, induce 1023; broȝte, *p. 3 sg.* 107, brohte, 1726; ibroȝt *p.p.* 545; heo is þar-to broht, it is suggested to her, 1559

brod, *n.* brood, 1633; brode, *prepos. sg.* 93, 130.—a brode, hatching, brooding, 518; goþ to brode, goes and breeds 1386

brode, *adj.* broad, wide, big, 75

ibroded, *p.p.* extended, widespread, 1312

(i)broȝt(e), (i)broht(e), *see* bringe

broiden, *p.p.* plaited, woven, 645

broþer, *n.* brother, 118

brune, *n.* burning, fire, 1155

buc, *n.* belly, body, carcass, 1132, 1494

budel, *n.* beadle; budel in tune, town-crier, 1169

buggen, *inf.* buy, procure, 1368, bugge 1506

ibunde, *p.p.* tied, bound, 656, held responsible, 1354

bur, *n.* dwelling, 958; bures, *gen. sg.* 652; bure, *prepos. sg.* 649, 937, 957, &c. (inner) chamber 1081; bures, *acc. pl.* 1045

burȝ, *n. acc. sg.*, castle, citadel, 766

burne, *n.* brook, stream, 918

bute, *prep.* without, except (for), other than, but, 183, 357, 574, &c. outside 1386, bote 884.— n(e) . . . bute, only, 575, 576, 811, &c. ne . . . but 799.—bute, *conj.* unless, except that, but that, than that, other than, 558, 560, 566, &c. except when 1138; bute þat, except that, 1322

buue, *prep., adv.* above, over, on, on top (of), master over, 208, 1346, 1494, high 1052

can(st(u), kan, *see* con

kanunes, *n. pl.* canons, 729n

kare, *n.* care, sorrow, grief, 1590

cartare, *n.* carter, 1186

castel, *n. acc. sg.* castle, 175, 766

cat, *n.* cat, 831, kat 810

keie, *n.* key, 1557

kene, *adj.* bold, keen, warlike, 276, 681, 1705; (*used as n.*) 526

ikepþ, *v.* hold, keep; *pres. 3 sg.* is on the look-out, 1228.—ne kep ich noȝt, I have no wish, 154

certes, *adv.* indeed, certainly, 1769

chadde, *see* schede

chapmon, *n.* merchant, 1575

charpe, *see* scharp

chatere, *n.* chatter, jabbering, 284

chaterest, *pres. 2 sg.* jabber, 322

chaterestre, *n. fem.* chatterbox, 655

chatering, *n.* chatter, jabbering, 576; chateringe, 560, 744

chauling, *n.* jawing, 284, 296

chelde, *see* scheld

cheorles, *n. gen. sg.* (of a) boor, rustic, common fellow, 1494, chorles 512; chorles, *pl.* 509, common people, 632

cheose, *inf.* choose, 1343

cherde, *p. pl.* turned, 1658

cheste, *n.* contention, strife, brawling, 177, 183, 296, &c.

chide, *v.* scold, chide, rebuke, rail at; *inf.* 287, 297, 1696; chist, *pres. 2 sg.* 1331; chid, *pres. 3 sg.* 1533; chide, *pres. subj. sg.* 291; chidde, *p. 3 sg.* 112

child, *n.* child, girl, 1463; chil, 1315, 1440; childe, *dat. sg.* 782;

children, *nom. pl.* 631, monastery boys 1115n; **childre,** *acc. prepos. pl.* 1453, 1776

chinne, *n.* chin, 96

chirche, *n. prepos. sg. or pl.* church(es), 608, 721, 1211; **chircce** 902; **chirche** (*used attrib.*) church-, church's, 727, 984, 1036, 1428

chirme, *n.* uproar, clamour, 305

chist, *see* chide

chokeringe, *n.* choking sounds, squeaking, 504

chorles, *see* cheorles

king, *n.* king, 235, 942, 1091; **kinges,** *gen. sg.* 1095; **kinge,** *dat., prepos. sg.* [1731], **king** 1728

clackes, *pres. 2 sg.* clack, 81

clansi (**wiþ**), *inf.* purge (of), cleanse (of), 610

clawe, *n. pl.* claws, 153

clawe, *pres. subj. 2 sg.* claw, 154

cleine, *see* clene

clenche, *inf.* rivet, clinch, 1206

clene, *adj.* clean, pure, undefiled, 584, 590, 627, &c. **cleine** 302

clennesse, *n.* purity, chastity, 491

cleopeþ, *pres. 3 sg.* calls, 1315

clerkes, *n. pl.* clerics, clerks in orders, 722, 729; *gen. sg. used attrib.* scholarly, 1328

climbe, *inf.* climb, 833

clinge, *v.* wither away, shrivel up; *inf.* 743; *pres. subj. 2 sg.* 1619

cliures, *n. pl.* claws, talons, 84, 1676, 1701; **cliuers,** 155, 270; **cliure,** *prepos. pl.* 78

cloþ, *n.* cloth, clothing, clothes, 1174; **cloþe,** *prepos. sg. or pl.* 1359, 1530

clowe, *n.* clew, ball, bundle, 578

cludes, *n. pl.* rocks, rocky hills, 1001

clute, *n. prepos. pl.* clods, 1167

knarres, *n. pl.* crags, 1001

kniȝt, *n.* knight, 1087, 1093, 1100, **cniht** 1575; **kniȝtes,** *pl.* 768

icnowe, *v.* recognise; *pres. subj. 3 sg.* shall acknowledge, shall cherish 477

coc, *n.* cock, 1679

codde, *n.* belly, carcass, 1124

cogge, *n.* cog-wheel, [86]

col-blake, *adj.* coal-black, 75

cold, *adj.* cold, cool, 622

com(e(n), **comest,** **comeþ,** *see* **cumen**

con (**of**), *v.* can, know, know (about, of), know how to, be skilled (in), can do; *pres. 1 sg.* 263, 1207, 1208, &c. **kon** 708, **can,** 170, 310, 603, &c. *1793*, **kan,** 757 (2), 759, 794; **const,** *pres. 2 sg.* 904, 1420, **canst,** 560, 805, 972, &c. **canstu,** *v.* + *pron. 2 sg.* do you know, 1321; **con,** *pres. 3 sg.* 1238, 1324, 1327, &c. **kon,** 680, 695, 774, **can,** 197, 249, 574, &c. **kan,** 720, 798, 816, &c.; **kunne,** *pres. pl.* 911, 1552; **cunne,** *pres. subj. sg.* 47, 48, **kunne,** 188, 811, 813, **conne,** 1268; **cuþe,** *p. 3 sg.* 1717, **kuþe,** 663, 697, 714; **cuþe,** *p.pl.* 1305

copenere, *n.* lover, 1342

corn, *n.* corn, grain, 1126; **cornes,** *pl.* 1202

coue, *adv.* swiftly, 379

cradele, *n.* cradle, 631

crafte, *n.* skill, ability, talent; *prepos. sg.* 787, 791; **craftes,** *pl.* 568, 711, 807.—**wiecche crafte,** *acc. sg.* witchcraft, 1308; **wicche crefte,** *prepos. sg.* 1301.—**kan craft,** have skill, am skilful, 757, 794

crei, *n.* crop, throat, 335n

crempe, *inf.* restrain; **do me crempe,** make me stop, 1788

Cristes, *n. gen. sg.* Christ's, 481 (*see* **masse**), 609, 886, 981, **Cristis** 1568

croked, *p.p.* crooked, bent, 80, **icroked** 1676

crope, *v.* creep; *inf.* 819; **cropþ,** *pres. 3 sg.* 826

crowe, *n.* crow, 126, 304n, 1130, 1613

croweþ, *pres. 3 sg.* crows, 335

cu-, *see also under* **cw-**

kukeweld, *n.* cuckold, 1544

kume, *n.* coming, arrival, 436

cumen, *v.* come, arrive, get, appear; *inf.* 1131, **kume,** 821, 859, **come,** 611, 1678; **cume,** *pres. 1 sg.* 435, **come** 1211; **cumest,** *pres. 2 sg.* 908, **comest** 585; **cumeþ,** *pres. 3 sg.* 302, 420, 459, &c. **kumeþ** 1462, **icumeþ** 456, **comeþ,** 1437, 1531, **kumed** 683; **cumeþ,** *pres. pl.* 523; **kume,** *pres. subj.* 1319, come 1015; **com**, *p. 1 sg.* 453, 462; **come**, *p. 2 sg.* 1058; **com**, *p. 3 sg.* 132, 133, 998, &c.; **come**, *p. pl.* 1671, 1690; **come**, *p. subj. sg.* 1300; **comen**, *p. subj. pl.* 1014; **icumen**, *p.p.* descended 130, **icume**, 138, 1225.—**cumeþ ut of**, *pres. 3 sg.* peers out of 444.—**comen on**, *inf.* attack, befall, 1199; **kumed (an)**, *pres. 3 sg.* 1246.—*impers. v.* **kumen**, *inf.* occur, happen, come, 1190; **comeþ . . . of**, *pres. 3 sg.* is caused by, 1236

kun, *n.* kin, kinsfolk, tribe, 714; **cunne**, *dat., prepos. sg.* 271, 1775, **kunne**, 1099, 1674; **kunne**, *gen. pl.* 888, 1396; **cunne**, *prepos. pl.* kinds, 20

cunde, *n.* nature, kindred, stock, 251, 273, 276, &c. **boþ þine cunde**, accord with your nature, 88. *Cf.* **icunde**

cundut, *n. acc. sg.* carol(s), 483n

cunne, kunne, *see* **con, kun**

kunrede, *n.* kindred, tribe, 1677

kursest, *pres. 2 sg.* curse, 1178

custe, *n. prepos. sg. or pl.* character, way, quality, 9, *115*, 1398

cuþe, kuþe, *see* **con**

cuþest, *v.* make known, reveal, show; *pres. 2 sg.* 90; **cuþ**, *pres. 3 sg.* 132, 138

cuuþ, adj. known, 922

quad, *see* **iqueþe**

cwalm, *n.* plague, murrain, 1199; **cualm** 1157

cwaþ, cwaðo, quaþ, *see* **iqueþe**

qued, *adj.* evil, wicked, 1137.—*n.* ill luck, misfortune, 1152

icwede, *see* **iqueþe**

queme, *inf.* please, 209, **icweme** 1784

cwesse, *inf.* crush, suppress, 1388

iqueþe, *v.* say; *inf.* 502; **cwaþ**, *p. 3 sg.* 1729, 1751, 1769, &c. **cwaðo**, 1186, 1739, **quaþ**, 117, 187, 189, &c. **quad** 117; **icwede**, *p.p.* 1653

quide, *n.* saying, 685

dahet, *n.* ill luck; **dahet habbe . . .**, may . . . have ill luck, 99.—*interj.* **dahet euer**, a curse for-ever on, 1169; **dahet þat**, woe to any who, 1561

dai, *n., often used as an adv.*, day, by day, 89, 103, 219, &c. 336 483, 736; **daie**, *prepos.* 241, 372, 384, &c.; **daies**, *gen.* 1431 (*used as adv.*) by day, 1590

dai-liȝt, *n.* daylight, 332

dai-rim, *n.* daybreak, 328

dai-sterre, *n.* the morning star, 328

dale, *n.* valley, 1

dare, *v. pres. 1 sg.* stay hidden, 384

darr, *v.* dare; *pres. 1 sg.* 1106; **darst**, *pres. 2 sg.* 853, 1695; **dar**, *pres. 3 sg.* 1110, 1131, 1135, &c.; **durre**, *pres. subj. sg.* 1706

dead, *see* **ded**

deale (mid), *inf.* deal (in); bandy 954

deaþe(s, *see* **deþ**

ded, *adj.* dead, 1138, 1732, **dead** 1619.—**be ded**, die, 1151

dede, *n.* deed, doings, activity; *sg.* 513, 708; *prepos. sg. or pl.* 232, 1376, 1580, &c.

del, *n.* part, bit,; **ech del**, *adv.* every bit, altogether, 1027

deme, *n.* judge, 1783

deme, *v.* judge, condemn; *inf.* 1747; **demþ**, *pres. 3 sg.* 1777, **demeþ** 1755; **deme**, *pres. subj. sg.* 201.—**riȝt us deme**, pass just sentence upon us, 188; **dom deme**, shall give judgment, 210

deoulene, *n. gen. pl.* of devils, 932. —**deouel** *n. used attrib.* devils', devil's, 1412

derne, *n.* dark, 608.—*adv.* in the dark, in secret, 1353

dernliche, *adv.* secretly, 1423

dest, deþ, *see* **don**

deþ, *n.* death, 1196, 1620; **deaþe**, *prepos. sg.* 1617; **deaþes**, *gen. sg. used as adv.* dead, 1632, 1634

diche, *n.* ditch, 1239

diȝele, *adj.* hidden, secluded, 2

diht, *pres. 3 sg.* composes, sets down 1756; **dihte**, *pret. 3 sg.* attuned 1655; **idiȝt**, *p.p.* appointed, 641, **wel idiht**, well-proportioned, of good build 1547

dim, *adj.* dim, dark, lustreless, 369, 577

disputinge, *n.* disputation, debate; **gest . . . to disputinge**, enter upon a disputation, 875

dom, *n.* judgment, trial, sentence, 210, 1061, 1692, &c.; **domes**, *gen. sg. (object of **abide**) 1695;

dome, *prepos. sg.* 179, 193, 545, &c.—**hit is a . . . dome,** it is the opinion of . . . 289

don, *v.* do, perform, render, contrive, act, behave, bring it about, achieve; +*inf.* cause to, make; *inf.* 159, 382, 1053, **do,** 548, 603, 997, &c. 1070; do, *pres. 1 sg.* 298, 329, 447, &c. succeed 789; **dest,** *pres. 2 sg.* 49, 321, 977, &c. **dost,** 237, 429; **dostu,** *pres. 2 sg.* +*pron.* 218, 411, 563; **deþ,** *pres. 3 sg.* 564, 779, 783, &c. **doþ,** 156, 157, 322, &c. **doð** 917; **doþ,** *pres. pl.* 95, 218, 251, &c. 630, 633]; put 1118, commit 1734; do, *pres. subj. sg.* 1092; do, *pres. subj. pl.* 1010; do, *imp. sg.* 1788, put 807; **do we,** *imp. 1 pl.* +*pron.* let us do so, 1781; **dude,** *p. 3 sg.* 1016, 1637, put, bestowed 1089; **idon,** *p.p.* done, finished, 115, 1094, **ido,** 113, 453, 463, &c. had 521

dor, *n.* animal, 493, 1323; *nom. pl.* 1012, 1200; **dore,** *prepos. pl.* 1126

Dorsete, *n.* Dorset, 1753

idorue, *p.p.* stricken, 1158

drahe, *v.* draw, draw near, approach, entice, lead on, attract; *inf.* convert 1375; **draȝst,** *pres. 2 sg.* 589, 895; **draȝþ,** *pres. 3 sg.* 776, **draheþ** 1399, **draȝeþ,** leads 1434; **drah,** *imp.* 1186n; **idraȝe,** *p.p.* drawn together 586.— *reflex. v. pres. 1 sg.* **ich me draȝe** (to), I take after, 273, 970

drede, *n.* dread, jeopardy, 684

dreim, *n.* joyous sound, melody, harmony, 21; **dreme,** *prepos. sg.* 314

drenche, *inf.* drown, founder, 1205

drinkeþ, *pres. pl.* drink, 1009

driue, *v.* drive, hunt, run (*tr.*); *inf.* bring . . . (to do something) 1475; **driueþ,** *pres. pl.* 66, 809n

drunnesse, *n.* drunkenness, 1399n

dude, *see* **don**

duȝeþe, *n.* manhood, maturity, 634

dumb, *adj.* dumb, 416

dune, *n.* hill, hill-country, 832, 919

duntes, *n. pl.* blows, 1227

dure, *n.* door, 778

durre, *see* **darr**

dusi, *adj.* foolish, 1466

dweole, *n. dat. sg.* error; devious way 1239.—*adj.* heretical, perverse, 926

dwole, *n.* error, mad course, 825, 1777n

e, *see* **he**

ear, *see* **er**

earding-stowe, *n.* dwelling-place, 28

earen, *n. pl.* ears, 338

east, *adv.* east, 923

eauar, eauer(e, *see* **euer**

eauer-euch, eauere euh, *see* **euer-euch**

ech(e, *see* **euch**

eche, *adj.* everlasting, eternal, 742, 1279

eft, *adv.* again, once more, 818, 1063, 1110, 1326; after, afterwards, 1106, 1429; back 1531. —**eft sone,** again, 821; **eft . . . noȝt ne,** no more, 1486

eȝe, *n. pl.* eyes, 144, 381, 426, 990; **eȝen,** 364, 1044; **eȝene** 75

ey, *n.* egg, 104; **eye,** *prepos. sg.* 133; **eyre,** *prepos. pl.* 106

eiȝte, *n. gen. sg.* of property, 1153

eine, *pron., num.* one; **mani eine,** many a one, 759n

eiþer, *pron.* each (of two) 9, 796, **aiþer** 7; **hure eiþer,** each of us, 185.—*adj.* either, 887

ei-wat, *pron.* everything, all kinds of things, 1056

elles, *adv.* else, otherwise, in some other way, 662, 1010, 1196

elles-hwar, *adv.* elsewhere, 932

ende, *n.* end, far side, limit, 652, 826, 1132n, &c.

endi, *pres. 1 sg.* end, 1456

ene(s, *see on* **on**

engeles, *n. pl.* angels, 916

Engelonde, *n.* England; **for Engelonde,** for all England, for all the world, 749

eni, *adj.* any, 557, 708, 720, &c. some 1015; **eni mon, eni man,** *see* **mon**

eorne, *v.* run; *inf.* 1204n; **urneþ,** *pres. pl.* 375

er, *adv.* before, formerly, (*often used with past to form plu-*

perfect); 866, 1144, 1432; **ear,** 1216, 1560, 1637; **ere** 1309 (*see* lutel); **her** [1225].—**erur,** *comp.* earlier, 1738; **erest,** *superl.* first; **þanne erest,** only then, 525, 683; **ȝif . . . þanne . . . erest,** once . . . (*conj.*), 1121f

erde, *n.* own country, 460

erede, *adj.* devoid of counsel, not sure what to do, 1295

ereming, *n.* wretch, poor thing, *1111*

erende, *n.* task, mission, 463

erendeð, *pres. 3 sg.* intercedes, *943*

erest, *see* **er**

erien, *inf.* plough, 1039

erne, *inf.* ride, 1204n

erur, *see* **er**

este, *n.* grace, gratification, pleasure, delight, 353, 1504, 1506.— *adj.* gracious, pleasant, 999, 1031

ete, *v.* eat; *inf.* 108; *pres. 1 sg.* 598; **etestu,** *pres. 2 sg.*+*pron.* 599; **eteþ,** *pres. pl.* 1007

eu, *see* **þu**

euch, *adj.* each, every; **ech,** 315, 434, 477, &c. *1592*; **eche,** 195, 800, 814, &c.—**euch mon,** *see* **mon; eauere euh,** *see* **euer-euch**

eue, *n.* evening, 323, 332, 432, &c. **eve** 41

euening, *n.* peer, equal, 772

euer, *adv.* always, ever, at any time, forever, at all times, 132, 362, 370, &c.; **eauer** 1272, **eauere** 1282; **euere** 359; **eure,** 333, 335, 358 (2), &c.; **ȝaure** 1180. —**so eauar,** whatever, 1474; **euer mo,** for ever more, at all times,. 238, 1108; **eure forþ,** for ever more, 356. *Cf.* **neuer**

euer-euch, *adj.* every, 1316, 1642, **eauer-euch** 1315; **eurich,** 194, 229, 231, &c. **evrich,** 422, 426.—**eurich** *pron.* everyone, 494. —**euer-euch mon, euer-euch man, evrich monnes,** *see* **mon; eauere euh þing,** *see* **þing**

efne, *adv.* plainly, smoothly, 313

(*For* **f** *in words of native origin see under* **u, v.**)

fals, *adj.* false, 210

faucun, *n.* falcon, 111, 123, **faukun** 101

flockes, *n. pl.* flocks of wool, 427. *Cf. under* **v**

flores, *n. pl.* flowers, 1046

foliot, *n.* foolish snare, 868n

gabbinge, *n.* falsehood, lies, 626

gale-gale, *n.* chatterbox, 256n

Galeweie, *n.* Galloway, 910

game, *see* **gome**

gan, *see* **gon**

gelus, *adj.* jealous, 1077

genge (+*dat.*), *adj.* convenient (for), prevalent, effective, 804n, 1065; **hom is genge,** is what they know, 1002

gengþ, *pres. 3 sg.* goes, 376

gente, *adj.* high-born, elegant, 204

gest, geþ, *see* **gon**

gideliche, *adv.* foolishly, madly, stupidly, 1282

gidie, *adj. used as n. prepos. sg. or pl.* foolish, 291

ginne, *n.* cunning, ingenuity, 669, 765

ginneþ, *pres. pl.* begin, 437, 722n, 1700

glad, *adj.* glad, happy, joyful, 434, 1278, 1511; **glade,** *pl.* 424, 451. —**gladur,** *comp.* 19, **gladdere** 737

gleu, *adj.* prudent, 193

go, god, *see* **gon**

God, *n.* God, 1173; **Godes,** *gen. sg.* 357, 361, 855, &c.—**God hit wot!** God knows! 867, **Godd hit wot,** 1543

god, *adj.* good, 175, 477, 621, &c. effective 800, virtuous 1374; **gode,** 270, 307, 368, &c.—**gode . . . to** (+*inf.*), good for (+*pres. part.*), 1369.—**god,** *n.* good, good thing, virtuous man, benefit, good purpose, 329, 565, 1040, &c.; **gode,** 246, 720, 739, &c.; **godne,** *acc. sg. masc.* 812. —**wat . . . godes,** what good, 563.—**mon is gode,** for the good of mankind, 1631

godd-spel, *n.* gospel, 1270; **god-spelle,** *prepos. pl.* 1209

godhede, *n.* goodness, excellence, virtue, 351, **godede** 582

gold, *n.* gold, 1366

gol-finc, *n.* goldfinch, 1130

golnesse, *n.* lechery, wantonness, lasciviousness, 492, 498, 899, &c.

gome, *n.* game, sport, match, 521, 1443, 1666, **game,** 1649

gon, *v.* go, walk, move; *inf.* 214, **gan** 1510, go, 653, 1431; **geþ,** *pres. 2 sg.* 875, 1651; **geþ,** *pres. 3 sg.* 528, 1462, **goþ,** 522, 877; **goþ,** *pres. pl.* 588, 795, 1013, &c. **goó** 938, **god** 647; go, *pres. subj. pl.* 745.—**gon to,** go about it, get to work; *inf.* 669; **gest . . . to,** *pres. 2 sg.* 838n; **goþ to,** *pres. 3 sg.* goes for, assails, 305. —**uorþ þu go!** go your way! 297; **go so hit go,** come what may, 1285

gore, *n.* triangular piece of cloth, gore; (*by synecdoche*) dress, 515

gost, *n.* spirit, being, 1111, 1401, 1408; **gostes,** *gen. sg.* 1398

(i)grad(de), *see* **grede**

grame, *see* **grom**

igramed, *see* **igremet**

granti, *pres. 1 sg.* grant, consent, undertake, 201, **graunti** 745

gras, *n.* grass, 1042

grede, *v.* cry, cry out; *inf.* 308, 975, 979, &c.; *pres. 1 sg.* 474, 1220, 1252, &c.; **gredest,** *pres. 2 sg.* 566; **gred,** *pres. 3 sg.* 1533, 1665; **gredeþ,** *pres. pl.* 1671; **gradde,** *p. sg.* 936, *p. pl.* 1662; **igrad,** *p.p.* 1149

greie, *adj.* gray, 834

igremet, *p.p.* vexed, angered, grieved, 933, **igramed** 1603

grene, *adj.* green, 18, 456, 617, &c.

gret, *adj.* great, big, large, 754, 1488; swollen, 43; **grete,** 3, 119, 318, &c.—**grettere,** *comp.* 74

grimliche, *adv.* fiercely, 1332

grine, *n.* snare, 1059; *pl.* 1056

grislich, *adj.* grim, ghastly, horrible, frightening, 224, 312, 315, &c. **grisliche** 1140

griþ, *n.* peace, 1005, 1369

griþ-bruche, *n.* breach of the peace, 1734n

grom, *adj.* angry, grieved, 992

grome, *n.* harm, injury, grief, 1090; **grame,** 49, 1484.—**hadde . . . grame,** suffered, 1076; **þe seolue . . . to grome,** to your own harm, to your own discomfiture, 1284

gromes, *n. pl.* boys, lads, 1645, lads in service 1115n

groni, *pres. subj. sg.* may groan, 872, 874

gropeþ, *pres. 3 sg.* gropes, touches, 1496

groue, *n.* grove, 380

growe, *inf.* grow, 1134, 1202; **growe,** *p. pl.* 136

grucching, *n.* grumbling, grousing, 423

grulde, *p. subj. sg.* were stirring; were strumming, 142

grunde, *n.* ground, 278, 506, 801

Gulde-forde, *n.* Guildford, 191

gult, *n.* guilt, offence, sin, 1410, **guld** 1427; **gulte,** *prepos.* 874

gulte, *pres. 3 sg.* commits an offence, sins, 1523

ȝaf, *see* **ȝiue**

ȝal, *see* **ȝollen**

ȝare, *adj.* ready, at hand, in readiness, 215, 296, 488, &c. **ȝarre,** *pl.* 1222; **ȝarewe,** *acc. pl.* 378

ȝaure, *see* **euer**

ȝe, *adv.* yes, indeed, 1732

ȝe, *see* **þu**

ȝelpst, *see* **ȝeolpest**

ȝef, *see* **ȝif, ȝiue**

ȝeme, *n.* heed, care; **nime(þ) ȝeme of,** watch closely, observe, take note of, 649, 727, 1469

ȝene, *v.* meet, oppose, counter; *inf.* 845; *pres. 1 sg.* 893

ȝeolpest, *pres. 2 sg.* boast, 1299, **ȝelpst** 971, **ȝulpest** 1641, 1650, 1652

ȝeoneþ *pres. 3 sg.* gapes; **ȝonie,** *pres. subj. sg.* 292.—**ȝeoneþ after,** longs with mouth wide open for, 1403

ȝeorne, *adv.* eagerly, 1352, 1581; **ȝorne,** 538, 661

ȝep, *adj.* clever, nimble, 465, 829

ȝephede, *n. nom. sg.* cunning, astuteness, 683

ȝer, *n.* year; (*used as adv.*) 101, 790, 1259.—**a ȝere,** in spring, 1133n

ȝerd, *n.* stick, rod, 777

ȝet, *adv., conj.* yet, also, furthermore, besides, still, 299, 309, 505, &c. *1417, 1697, 1748;* **ȝut,** 363, 541, 679, &c.; even then 1143; **ȝete** 747, **ȝette** 1307.— **þe ȝet,** even then, 1624

ȝeue, *see* **ȝiue**

ȝif, *conj.* if, as long as, 51, 56, *59,*

116, &c.; ȝef, 347, 1180, 1181,
&c.; yif 284.—ȝif þat, if, 693;
ȝif . . . n(e), unless, 382

ȝiue, v. give, render; inf. 1767,
ȝefe 1710; ȝiue, inf. used pas-
sively, be given, 1692; ȝiue,
pres. 1 sg. 1686; ȝiueþ, pres. pl.
1773, ȝeueþ 1776; ȝaf, p. 3 sg.
55, 149, 1101, ȝef 1176; iȝiue,
p.p. 551

ȝoeþe, n. youth, 633

ȝoȝelinge, n. wailing, hooting, 40

ȝollen, v. yell, scream; inf. 977,
989; ȝolle, 972, 987; ȝolst,
pres. 2 sg. 985, ȝollest 223; ȝal,
p. 3 sg. 112

ȝomere, adv. dolefully, 415

ȝond, dem. pron. yonder; þe ȝond,
that one over there, 119

ȝongling, see ȝunling

ȝonie, see ȝeoneþ

ȝorne, see ȝeorne

ȝulinge, n. yelling, screaming, 1643

ȝulpest, see ȝeolpest

ȝunge, adj. young, 1134, 1434

ȝunling, n. young thing, child,
youngster, 1433, ȝongling 635;
ȝunglinge, prepos. sg. 1447

ȝut, see ȝet

habbe, v. have; inf. 258, 260, 281,
&c.; pres. 1 sg. 174, 269, 368,
&c.; hauest, pres. 2 sg. 153, 155,
240, &c.; hauestu, pres. 2 sg.
+pron. 1668; haueþ, pres. 3 sg.
301, 378, 513, &c., haued, 119,
suffers 167, hauet, 113; habbeþ,
pres. pl. 431, 1032, 1197, &c.
1681, habbet 651, habeþ 1611,
haueþ 1675; habbe, pres. subj.
sg. 99, 515, 1274; pl. 1222;
hadde, p. 1 sg. 1083; p. 3 sg.
146, 216, 395, &c.; p. pl. 1008,
1103. Cf. nauestu

hacche, n. hatch, gate; casement,
1058

hadde, see habbe

haȝe, n. prepos. sg. or pl. en-
closure(s), hedge(s), 585, hahe
1612

haȝel, n. hail, 1002

haȝte, p. 3 sg. (had) hatched, 105

hahe, see haȝe

hald(e), see holde

hale, n. nook, 2

halt, see holde

halter, n. nom. sg. halter, 1028

halue, n. side, case, 109, 887

ham, see hom

hard, adj. hard, severe, difficult,
1694; harde, 530, 602, 706.—
harde, used as n. hard time,
difficult circumstances, severe
season; nom. sg. 459; prepos.
sg. or pl. 527, 703

hardeliche, adv. bravely, 402

hare, n. hare, 373, 383

harm, n. harm, injury, disaster,
affliction; nom. sg. 1246, [1254]
1733; harem 1260; aren, harm-
ful thing, 1498n; harm, acc. sg.
1235; hareme, prepos. 1161

harpe, n. harp, 22, 24, 142, 343

hartu, see beon

hatiet, pres. 3 sg. hates, 230

haueck, n. hawk, 303, hauec 307;
haukes, gen. sg. 271

haued, hauest(u), haueþ, haued,
hauet, see habbe

he, pron. 3 pers.; masc. nom. sg.
he, 102, 105, 109, &c. 120; it,
21, 22, 23, &c. 1374, a man 236;
e, he, 1475; hine, acc. sg. him,
873, 1544, 1749, &c.; it, 680,
1374, 1375; (used refl.) him-
self, oneself, 236, 471, 828, 871,
1272; him, dat. and prepos. sg.
him, 194, 209, 212, &c. for him,
with him, 1090, 1173; (used
refl.) himself, 122, 211, 1484;
hin, him, 890.—heo, fem. nom.
sg. she, 934, 1295, 1296, &c.
1661; it, 948, 950, 1380; ho,
she, 19, 33, 42, &c.; it, 318, 342,
1378; he, she, 141, 396, 401,
469, 936, 953, 1389, 1509 (2nd),
1560; hi, she, 10, 185, 306,
1439; hi, acc. sg. her, 29, 30, 32,
&c. 308; used refl. herself, 199;
heo, her, 1438, 1530, it 1232;
used refl. herself, 939; hire, dat.
and prepos. sg. her, 148, 395,
397, &c. for her, to her, 1082,
1296, 1570, 1600; (used refl.)
herself, 704.—hit, neuter, nom.
sg. it, 28, 41, 52, &c. (used
expletively) 414; (used as formal
subject) there, 906; hit, acc. sg.
it, 92, 96, 116, &c. 126, 1008,
1224, 1248 (2), 1365; so, 290, 942,
1476; this 1467; him, dat. sg.
with it 682, for it, 1448.—hi,
all genders, nom. pl. they, 12, 95,

96, &c.; **heo**, they, 929, 931, 1306, 1351, &c. 1662; **ho**, they 66, 76, 97, &c.; **hi**, *acc. pl.* them, 108, 843, 854, &c.; (*used refl.*) themselves, 1257, *1562*; **heo**, them, 926, 1258; **heom**, *dat. and prepos. pl.* t'hem, 930, 960, 1254, &c.; (*used refl.*) themselves, 1253, 1764; **hom**, them, 62, 94, 285, &c. for them, to them, for their benefit, 868, 1026; **hon**, *used refl.*, 881

heare, *see* **here**

hecst, *see* **heh**

hegge, *n.* hedge, 17, 59, 587

heȝe, *adv.* high, loud, 989, **heie** 1646.—**herre**, *comp.* 1637

heh, *adj.* high; **on heh**, high, high up, 1456, **on heþ**, up high, 1405. —**hexst**, *superl.*; (*used as n.*) *970*n.—**alre hecst**, at its highest, 687, 699

heie, *see* **heȝe**

heie, *n.* hedge, 819

hei-sugge, *n.* hedge-sparrow, 505

helle, *n.* hell, 1014

helpe (+*dat. of person*), *v.* help, be of use; *inf.* 664, 1719; *pres. 1 sg.* 484, 606, 735, &c.—**ne helpþ**, *pres. 3 sg.* used impersonally, it is no use, 171

heme, *n. pl.* villagers, 1115n

hen, *n.* hen, 413

Henri, *n.* Henry, 1091

heo(m), *see* **he**

heonne, *adv.* from here, away, away from here, 1673; **honne**, 66, 850, 864, 881

heore, *possess. adj. 3 pl.* their, 1612, 1775, 1777; **here**, 739, 938, 978; **hore**, 280, 330, 390, &c.; **hire**, 1520, 1566

heorte, *n.* heart, 947, 1475, 1565, 1604; **horte**, 37, 43, 670, &c.; memory, 686; *gen. sg.* 945.— **on horte**, essentially, radically, 808n

heouene, *n.* heaven, 916; **houene**, 728, 897.—**houene** (*used attrib.*) heavenly, of heaven, 717, 732

hepe, *n.* heap.—**ful bi hepe**, full and heaped up, 360

her, *see* **er**

her, *adv.* here, 462, 680, 882, &c.

her-among, *adv.* in this, 744

her-bi, *adv.* apropos of this, 127, 1497

herdes, *n. pl.* herdsmen, shepherds, 286

here, *see* **heore**

here, *n. prepos. sg. or pl.* hair(s), 428, **heare** 1550

here, *n.* army, 1702n, 1709, 1790

(i)here, *v.* hear, listen to; **ihere**, *inf.* 224, 544, 748, &c., **ihire** 312; **ihereþ**, *pres. pl. 222*; **herde**, *p. 1 sg.* 293, **iherde** 3; **iherde**, *p. 3 sg. 1635*, 1657, 1667; **iherd**, *p.p.* 1317, **ihert**, 1763

herest, *pres. 2 sg.* praise, 1518

her-gonge, *n. prepos. sg. or pl.* military expedition(s), invasion(s), 1191n

heriinge, *n.* praise, glorification, 981

her-of, *adv.* about this, 875, 1563; because of it, for it, 1076

herre, *see* **heȝe**

her-to, *adv.* to this, to this point, 487, 657, 665

her-uore, *adv.* for this.—**her-uore hit is þat**, that is why, 1165

hete, *n.* hate, 167

heþ, *see* **heh**

heued, *n.* head, 74, 119

hexst, *see* **heh**

hi, *see* **he**

hider, *adv.* here, 462, 955, 1671

hiderward, *adv.* here, 1690

hiȝte, *n.* hope, delight, joy, 272, 1103

hiȝte, *v.* hope; **hiȝte me**, *pres. 1 sg. refl.* rejoice, 532.—**hiȝteþ aȝen**, *pres. 3 sg.* looks with hope forward to, 436

him, *see* **he**

himward, *adv.*; **to himward**, towards him, 375

hin(e), *see* **he**

hine, *n. pl.* monastics, 1115n

hire, *possess. adj. 3 sg. fem.* her, 26, 43, 44, &c. *1341*, its 949, **hure** 1599, **hore** 305

hire, *see* **he**, **heore**

ihire, see **(i)here**

his, *possess. adj. 3 sg.*; *masc.* his, 102, 106, 107, &c. *1576*; **is**, 403, 571, 1483.—**his**, *neuter*, its, 100, 122, 351, &c.

his, *see* **beon**

hit, **ho**, *see* **he**

hoked, *adj.* hooked, hook-shaped, 79. *Cf.* **ihoked**

hokeþ, *pres. 3 sg.* turns this way and that (along), 377

ihoded, *p.p.* ordained, 1177; **to preost ihoded**, ordained priest, 1311

hoȝe, *n.* care, anxiety, trouble, 701

hoȝeþ, *pres. 3 sg.*; (+*acc.*) is mindful of, is intent on, 1602; **hoȝeþ of**, takes thought of, turns his thoughts to, 455

hohful, *adj.* thoughtful, anxious, 1292, **hoþful**, 1295; **hoȝfule**, *pl.* 537

holde, *v.* hold, keep, maintain; *inf.* 3, 1552, **halde** 1369; **hald**, *pres. 3 sg. 1576*, **halt**, keeps on with, 356; **hold**, *p. 3 sg.* 144; **holde**, *p. pl.* 12; *p. subj. sg.* 51.—**halt**, *pres. 3 sg.* considers, thinks, 32; **iholde**, *p.p.* 1723.—**me holde**, *pres. 1 sg. refl.* remain, 59.—**holde mid** (*or* **wiþ**), hold with, side with, be of the party of; *inf.* 1419, 1680; **holdest mid**, *pres. 2 sg.* 1517.—**þar-to holde**, *inf.* abide by that, 1691

hole, *n.* hole, 826

hole, *adj.* hollow, with a hole, 965n

holȝ, *adj.* hollow, 643, 1113

holi, *adj.* holy, 721, 1382

holinesse, *n.* holiness; purity of the spirit 900

hom, *n.* home, 1751; (*used adv.*) 457, 460, *1534*, **ham** 1531. *Cf.* **attom**

hom, hon, *see* **he**

honde, *n. prepos. sg. or pl.* hand(s), 1372, 1757n.—**þu me gest an honde**, you are placing yourself under my control; you are submitting to me 1651

hongi, *inf.* hang, 816; **hongest**, *pres. 2 sg.* 1142; **hoþ**, *pres. 3 sg.* 1123, **hongeþ** 1132; **hongeþ**, *pres. pl.* 1612; **hong**, *imp. sg.* 658; **ihonge**, *p.p.* 1136.—**þat þer hongeþ**, his virility, 1485

honne, *see* **heonne**

hord, *n.* hoard, store.—**hit . . . legge on hord**, store it up, 1224; **leide an hord**, stored up, 467

hore, *see* **heore, hire**

horne, *n.* horn, 318

hors, *n.* horse, 773; *nom. sg. or pl.* 629; **horse**, *prepos. pl.* 1062, **horsse** 768

horte, *see* **heorte**

hose, *adj.* hoarse, 504

hot, *adj.* hot, 1275; **hote**, *wk.*, 1454

hoten, *v. passive*, be called; *inf.* 256; **attest**, *pres. 2 sg.* 255.—*v. active*, command; **hot**, *pres. 3 sg.* 779

hoþ, *see* **hongi**

hoþful, *see* **hohful**

hou, *n. acc. sg.* colour, hue, 619; **howe**, *prepos. sg.* 152, 577

houdsiþe, *n.* departure, journey, 1586n

houene, *see* **heouene**

houen-kinge, *n.* king of heaven, 862

houen-tinge, *adj.* reaching to the skies, 1001

houle, *see* **ule**

howe, *see* **hou**

hu, *adv., conj.* how, 46, 263, 294, &c.

hude, *n.* hide, skin, 1114

hude, *v. refl. or tr.* hide, conceal (oneself *or* a thing); *inf.* 1113; *pres. 1 sg.* 265; **hud**, *imp. sg.* 164

huing, *n.* hooting, 1264

hule, *see* **ule**

hunke, *see* **þu**

hund, *n. nom. sg.* dog, hound, 817; **hundes**, *gen. sg.* 822; **hunde**, *dat. sg.* 814; **hundes**, *pl.* 375, 809

hundred, *n.* hundred, 1101

hunger, *n.* hunger, 1191n

hupþ, *v.* hop, dart; *pres. 3 sg.* 379; **hupte**, *p. 3 sg.* 1636

hure, *see* **hire, ich**

hure, *adv.* at least, at any rate; least of all 1483n.—**hure & hure**, especially, 11, 481

hurne, *n.* corner, 14

hus, *n.* house, 623, **huse** 1528; **huses**, *gen. sg.* 1155; **huse**, *prepos. sg.* 479, 609; *prepos. sg. or pl.* 1333; **huses**, *pl.* 1203

hw-, *see* **w-** (*the h has been ignored in the alphabetical arrangement*)

(*For verbal forms prefixed by* **i-** *see the stem*)

i, *see* **ich, in**

ibedde, *n.* bed-fellow, consort, wife *or* husband; *acc. sg.* 968, 1490, 1570. *Cf.* **bedde**

ibere, *n. sg. or pl.* behaviour; noise, cries, 222, 1348. *Cf.* **bere**

ich, *pron. 1 pers.*; *nom. sg.* 1, 1, 3, 34, &c. *1698*, **ih** 868, **ic** 1049; **i**, 293, 448, 592, &c.; **me**, *acc.*, *dat.*, *or prepos. sg.* me, 34, 38, 39, &c. *280*; (*used refl.*) myself, 263, 265, **mi** 835 *see* **sulfe.**—**unker**, *gen. dual*, of us two, 151.—**we**, *nom. pl.* we, 177, 179, 181, &c.; **hure**, *gen. pl.* of us, 185; **us**, *acc.*, *dat. or prepos. pl.* us, 187, 188, 201, &c.

ikunde, *n.* nature, instincts, 1383. —**ov . . . icunde**, your natural way, 114. *Cf.* **cunde**

icundur, *adj. comp.* more natural, 85

icundeliche, *adv.* naturally, by natural instinct, 1424

ydel, *adj.* useless, 917.—**on idel**, uselessly, 920

iduȝe, *adj.* of use; **him beo iduȝe**, might do him good, 1582

Iesus, *n.* Jesus, 1092

igrede, *n. prepos. sg. or pl.* clamour, cries, 1643

ih, *see* **ich**

ihende, *adv.* near, near at hand, close, 1131.—**heom is ihende**, is upon them, 1263

ihoked, *adj.* hook-shaped, 1675. *Cf.* **hoked**

ihold, *n.* stronghold, 621

yif, *see* **ȝif**

ilke, *adj.* same, very, 99, 742

ilete, *n.* noisy behaviour, 1715; face 1446.—**berþ grete ilete**, puts on a great show, 403. *Cf.* **lete**

iliche, *adj.*, *adv.* (the) same, 358, 362; **ilich** (+*dat.*) like, 316, 318, 319, **iliche** 1460; **iliche**, alike, without change, 618, 718; **ilike** (*used as n.*), **þine ilike**, the like of you, 157

ille, *adj.* bad, evil; *used as n.* evil man, man of ill-will, 421.—**is him ille**, annoys him, pains him, 1536

ilome, *adv.* often, 49, 290, 1211, &c.—**ofte & ilome**, time and again, 1521.—**ilomest**, *superl.* most often, 595. *Cf.* **lome**

iloue, *n. pl.* lovers, 1047. *Cf.* **leof**

imene (+*dat.*), *adj.* common (among), shared (by), 234, 628;

used as n. companion, 1412.—**haueþ imene**, has dealings with, 301

imunde, *n.* thought, 252.—**of þine imunde**, what you think of, 1516

in, *prep.* in, on, into, within, at, 1, 2, 14, &c. in the way of 1208; **i**, 1340, 1416; **ine**, 350, 438, 495, &c.

innoþ, *n.* (the) inside, womb; inner source 1319n

inoȝe, *adj. pl.* enough, 16.—**inoh**, *adv.* 1182, 1208, 1252, &c. **innoh** 1220

insihte, *n.* insight, wisdom, 1187. —**wot insiȝt**, has deep understanding of, 195

in-to, *prep.* into, 150, 996, 1583, as far as in 1758

ire, *n.* iron. 1030

iredi, *adj.* ready, 488

Irish, *adj.* Irish, 322

Irlonde, *n.* Ireland, 907

is, *see* **beon**, **his**

isene, *adj.* visible, obvious, evident, manifest, clear, 166, 275, 367, &c. *Cf.* **sene**

isome, *adj.* united, reconciled, peaceable, 1735, **ysome** 180

isunde, *adj.* sound, healthy, 1102

iui, *n.* ivy, 27, 617

iuo, *n.* foe, enemy, 1716. *Cf.* **uo**

ifurn, *adv.* formerly, long ago, long past, of old, 1306.—**of olde ivvrne**, from distant days long past, 637

iwar, *adj.* aware, vigilant, 147, **iwarre** (? *comp.*) *1221*. *Cf.* **war**

iwarnesse, *n.* vigilance, 1228

iweld, *n.* control, power; **nah iweld**, is not responsible, 1543n

iwende, *n. prepos. pl.* alternatives, contrivances, 651n

iwis, *adv.* certainly, indeed, for certain, 35, 118, 1189, &c.

iwit, *n.* wisdom, 1188; **iwitte**, *prepos.* 1217.—**non iwit ne kon**, is not wise, 774. *Cf.* **wit**

iwune (+*dat.*), *n. or adj.* usual (with), the custom (with), 1320, **iwone**, 475

la, *interj.* ah, 1543

lacche, *inf.* seize, 1057

iladde, *see* **lede**

laȝe, *n.* law, custom 969, sentence 1061, dictum 1037n.

laȝe, *see* **loȝe**

lahfulnesse, *n.* respect for law, lawfulness, 1741

lai, *see* **ligge**

lame, *see* **lome**

lasse, *adj., adv. comp.* less, smaller, 370, 1227, 1410; (*used as n.*), *sg.* less exalted, low, humble man, 1406, *pl.* 482

(i)last, *see* **ileste**

lat, *see* **leten**

late, *adv.* late, 1147; **later,** *comp.* later; less punctually, 963

lateþ, *see* **leten**

lauedi, *n.* lady, 959, 1569, **lefdi,** 1051; **lauedies,** *pl.* 1338, 1519, 1563

lauerd(es, *see* **louerd**

leches, *n. pl.* looks, 1140

lede, *v.* lead, conduct, bring out; *inf.* 1684; **ledest,** *pres. 2 sg.* 1672; **ledeþ,** *pres. pl.* 280; **iladde,** *p. 3 sg.* 398; *p.p.* 1294

legge, *inf.* lay, place, 1224; **leiþ,** *pres. 3 sg.* brings down 801; **leidest,** *p. 2 sg.* 104; **leide,** *p. 3 sg.* 467, **lede** 1057.—**me adun legge & þe buue,** *pres. subj. sg.* should cast me off and set you up, 208

ley, leie, *see* **ligge**

leist, *see* **ileste**

leng, *see* **long**

lengþe, *n.* length, 174

lenst, *pres. 2 sg.* lend, bestow on, 756

leof, *adj.* dear, beloved, agreeable, 1277; **lof,** 572; **loue,** 968, welcome 1035.—**me is lof to,** I like to, 281, I hold dear, 609; **þat leof is,** who likes, 1524, **þat is lof** 231; **lof him were,** may have been dear to him, 203. *Cf.* **iloue**

leof-mon, *n.* lover, 1430

leorni, *see* **lorni**

lepe, *n.* basket, 359

lere, *adj.* empty, 1528

lere (to), *v.* teach, instruct (in); *inf.* 1017, 1050; *pres. 1 sg.* 1347; **lerdest,** *p. 2 sg.* 1053

lese, *adj.* untrue, lying, 756

lesing, *n.* falsehood, 848

ileste, *inf.* last, endure, 341; **ilest,** *pres. 3 sg.* 851, 1451, **lest,** 1450,

leist 333, **ilast** 1038, **last,** 516, 1466, **ilesteþ** 347

lete, *n.* behaviour, uproar, 35. *Cf.* **ilete**

leten, *v.* let, leave, leave off, leave alone, abandon, allow to, cause to; *inf.* 1018, **lete** 1445, 1471; **lete,** *pres. 1 sg.* 1457; **let,** *pres. 3 sg.* 919, 1093, 1097, &c. **lat** 308; **leteþ,** *pres. pl.* 1771; **lat,** *imp. sg.* 258, 260, 261, &c.; **lateþ,** *imp. pl.* 1729, 1737; **lete,** *p. 2 sg.* 1308; **lette,** *p. 3 sg.* 952. —**leteþ beo,** *imp. pl.* let be, cease, 1699, **lateþ beo** 1735; **let ...ut,** *p. 3 sg.* let loose, 8; **lete we awei,** *imp. 1 pl.* let us refrain from, let us have done with, 177; **lat awai,** *pres. 3 sg.* leaves alone, 250; **leteþ (of),** *pres. pl.* consider, hold in esteem, 1774

ilefde, *p. 3 sg.* believed, 123 (*see* **liueþ**)

lefdi, *see* **lauedi**

leue, *n.* leave, 457

leues, *n. pl.* leaves, 1046, leaves (of a book) 1326; **leue,** *prepos. pl.* 456

libbe, *inf.* live, 1192; **libbeþ,** *pres. pl.* 1012; **libbe,** *pres. subj. pl.* 1006

liki, *inf.* please, 342

licome, *n.* body, 1054

liest, *see* **liȝe**

lif, *n.* life, 988, 1127, 1137, &c.—**liues,** *gen. sg. used adv.* alive, 1632, 1634.—**lif an lime,** life and limb, capitally, 1098; **for his liue,** for the life of him, 1078

lif-daȝe, *n. prepos. pl.* days of life; **on lif-daȝe,** alive, 1141

ligge, *inf.* lie, 1200; **list,** *pres. 2 sg.* 1502; **liþ,** *pres. 3 sg.* 430; **liggeþ,** *pres. pl.* 959, 1048; **ligge,** *pres. subj. sg.* 1619; **lai,** *p. 3 sg.* 1509, **ley** 1494; **leie,** *p. subj. sg.* 134.—**liþ bihinde,** falls behind, 528

liȝe, *inf.* lie, tell lies, 853; **liest,** *pres. 2 sg.* 367, 1335; **iloȝe,** *p.p.* 847.—**þat þu ne liȝe,** *pres. subj. sg.* and don't you lie! 599

liȝt, *n.* light, 230, 734, **liht,** insight, discernment, 949; **liȝte,** *prepos. sg.* 163, 198, 252, &c., **lihte** 1431

lihtlich, *adj.* easy, 1185, 1759.—
  liʒtliche, *adv.* easily, 854, **liht-
  liche,** indifferently, 1774
liim, *n. acc. sg.* bird-lime, 1056
lilie, *n.* lily, 439
lime, *n.* limb, 1098 (*see* **lif**)
linde, *n.* limetree, 1750
linnene, *adj.* linen, 1174
list, *see* **ligge**
liste, *n.* art, cunning, 172, 763,
  767.—**kan liste,** am artful, am
  shrewd, 757
litle, *see* **lutel**
liþ, *see* **ligge**
liue(s, *see* **lif**
liueþ, *pres. 3 sg.* believes; **him
  sulue liueþ,** trusts in himself,
  810n (*see* **ilefde**)
loke, *n.* lock, 1557
loki, *inf.* look, see (to it), keep
  watch over, 604, 641; **lokeþ,**
  pres. 3 sg. 1555; **loke,** *imp. sg.*
  166, 295.—**me loki wit,** guard
  myself against, 56
lodlich, *adj.* loathsome, 32, 71, 91
lof, *see* **leof**
loʒe, *adv.* low, 1052, **laʒe** 1456
iloʒe, *see* **liʒe**
lome, *adv.* often; **lome & ofte,**
  time and again, 1545. *Cf.*
  ilome
lome, *adj.* lame, crippled, 364,
  lame 1732
lond, *n.* land, country, 999, 1003,
  1031; **londe,** *prepos. sg. or pl.*
  922, 996, 1095, &c.—**upe londe,**
  in the country, 733n.—**cumeþ
  to londe,** is here, 420
lond-folc, *n.* population, people,
  1158
long, *adj.* long, tall, long-lasting,
  334, 344, 562, &c.; **longe,** 140,
  270, 523, &c.—**alle longe niʒt,**
  all night long, 331.—**longe,** *adv.*
  long, for long, for a long time,
  45, 81, 253, &c.—**leng,** *adv.
  comp.* longer, any longer, 42,
  493, 502, &c. 516 (*see* **more**)
longeþ, *impers. v. pres. 3 sg.*; **him**
  (*or* **hin**) **longeþ,** he longs, he
  yearns, he has desire, 890, 1486;
  hon longeþ, they long, 881
longinge, *n.* longing, yearning,
  869, 889
lore, *n.* learning, skill, instruction,
  1471, 1640, suggestion 1351.—
  bokes lore, book-learning,

scholarship, 1208; **clerkes lore,**
  scholarship, 1328
lorni, *v.* learn; *inf.* 642; **leorni,**
  pres. 1 sg. 1212.—**ho hadde
  ilorned,** she had gained her
  knowledge, 216
losen, *inf.* lose, 351; **lost,** *pres. 3
  sg.* 830, 1159, **luste** 1193n
loþ (+*dat.*) *adj.* repulsive (to),
  hateful (to), loathsome (to), 65,
  72, 115, &c.; **loð** *1607*.—**loþe,**
  used as n. hated man, 943
loþe, *n. prepos. sg. or pl.* troubles,
  injury, harm, 1146
loue, *see* **leof**
louerd, *n.* lord, husband, 968,
  1055, 1076; **lauerd,** 959, 1479,
  1491, &c.; **louerdes,** *gen. sg.*
  1589, **lauerdes,** 1586
lud, *adj.* loud, 6, 983, **lude** 314.—
  lude, *adv.* loud, loudly, 112, 141,
  982, &c.
lugge, *n. prepos. sg. or pl.* stick(s),
  pole(s), 1609
lure, *n. prepos. sg.* loss, 1153
luring, *n.* scowling, louring, 423
lust, *n.* lust, desire, pleasure, 507;
  luste, *prepos. sg. or pl.* 895,
  1397; **lustes,** *acc. pl.* 1388, 1390,
  1414
lust, *impers. v. pres. 3 sg.* pleases;
  me lust, it pleases me, 613, **ne
  lust me,** I have no wish, 287;
  lust him . . . to, he takes pleasure
  in, 212, **him . . . lust,** he desires,
  213; **me luste bet,** *pres. subj. 3
  sg.* I would rather, 39
luste, *see* **losen**
luste (+*acc.*), *inf.* listen (to), 896;
  lust, *pres. 1 sg.* 1594; **lust,** *imp.
  sg.* 263, 267, 546, &c.; **lusteþ,**
  imp. pl. 1729; **luste,** *p. 3 sg.*
  143, 253, 467
lute, *adj.* little, 763
lutel, *adj.* little, small, slight, 561,
  578, 582, &c.; **lutle,** 631, 765,
  782, &c.; **litle** 1776.—**lutel,** *adv.*
  little, 911, 1404.—**nu lutel ere,**
  just now, 1309
luteþ, *pres. 3 sg.* lies hidden,
  skulks, 373
lutli, *inf.* reduce, lessen, 540
luþer, *adj.* worthless, bad, poor,
  1137
luue, *n.* love, 207, 446, 511, &c.
  love-affair, sweetheart, 1343.—
  habbe . . . luue, am loved, 461

N

luuien, *inf.* love, 1341, luuie, 1345, 1357; luueþ, *pres. 3 sg.* 230, 232, 1423, &c.; luuieþ, *pres. pl.* 791, 1355

make, *n.* mate, husband, 1159, 1193, 1429

makest, *v.* make, produce; *pres. 2 sg.* 339; makeþ, *pres. 3 sg.* 354, 638, 1444; *pres. pl.* 650, 1390, makeð 1648; makie, *pres. subj. sg.* 1544

mai, *v.* can, may; *pres. 1 sg.* 366, 383, 448, &c.; miȝt, *pres. 2 sg.* 64, 221, 348, &c. may be, 1122, miȝst 642, mist 78, myht [771]; miȝtu, *pres. 2 sg.* +pron. 502; mai, *pres. 3 sg.* 185, 248, 274, &c. can avail 762; muȝe, *pres. pl.* 62, 1117; muhe, *pres. subj. sg.* 1581; miȝte, *p. 1 sg.* 371, 1086; miȝtistu, *p. 2 sg.* +pron. 1504; miȝte, *p. 3 sg.* 42, 393, 394, &c. could . . . bear to, 1078; mihte 953; miȝte, *p. pl.* 978, mihte 1749; miȝte, *p. subj. 2 sg.* 601.—wel mai, I have good reason, 228, miȝte wel, wel miȝte, had good reason (to), 570, 1104, ful wel miȝte had very good reason 1292; muȝe bet, shall rather, 182, miȝtest bet, should rather, 256.—to hwan þu miȝt, what use you are, 1621; hwat mai . . . þah, how can . . . help it . . . if, 1440

maide, *n. sg.* maiden, virgin, girl, 1064, 1343, 1418, &c.; maidenes *pl.* 1516, maide 1338

maine, *n.* strength, 760n

maister, *n. nom. sg.* master, 191, 1746, maistre 1778

man-kunne, *n. dat., prepos. sg.* mankinde, 973, for mankind 849, man-kenne 1725

man, *see* mon

mani(e), *see* moni

manifolde, *adj.* numerous, 1551

mannes, *see* mon

mansing, *n.* cursing, excommunication, 1312; mansinge, *prepos.* 1182

masse, *n.* mass, 1181; Cristes masse, Christmas, 481

me, *see* ich, mon

mede, *n.* field, 438

meinþ, *v.* mix, stir up, intersperse, confuse; *pres. 3 sg.* 945; imeind, *p.p.* 18, 428; meind, brought together, 131; imend 870, imeinde 823

men, *see* mon

imend, *see* meinþ

mene, *v.* mean, complain (of), say, refer (to); *refl. inf.* 1257; *pres. 1 sg.* 583; menst, *pres. 2 sg.* 755, menest 648; meneþ, *pres. pl.* 1563.—bi . . . ich hit mene, I refer to . . . in particular, 92

meoster, *n.* trade, profession; do . . . mi meoster, follow my calling, 924

merci, *n.* mercy; do merci (+dat.), have mercy (on), 1092

mere-wode, *adj.* mad after the mares, 496

mershe, *n.* marsh, 304

meshe, *inf.* crush, 84

mest, *adj. superl.* greatest, 852; *adv. superl.* most, 684

mete, *n. acc. sg.* food, 107, 597; *prepos.* 1530, 1630

mi, *see* min, ich

mid, *prep.* with, by, through, among, 18, 27, 76, &c. in 954, armed with, clad in 1030 (2), mit 616.—mid, *adv.* also, 136.—mid hom, in themselves, 536; heom . . . mide, with them, 1768.—mid alle, altogether, 666, 1458, for all 827; mid alle þan þat, by every means that, 1436

midde, *n.* middle, 124, 643

middel-niȝte, *n.* midnight, 325, midel-niȝte, 731

miȝte, *n. acc. sg.* strength, ability, 1188, 1670, miȝtte 536

miȝt(e(st), miȝst, miȝtu, miȝtistu, myht, mihte, *see* mai

milc, *n.* milk, 1009

milce, *n.* grace, mercy, 1404.—hadde milse an ore (of), took kind pity (on), 1083

milde, *adj.* mild, lenient, 1032.—mildre, *comp.* 1775

mile, *n.* mile, 1592

milse, *see* milce

min, *possess. adj. 1 sg.* my, 37, 272, 460, &c.; mi, 37, 272, 311, &c. 869; mine, 36, 46, 51, &c. 1457; mire, *dat., prepos. sg. fem.* 1741

misbeode (+dat.), *inf.* ill-use, ill-treat, 1541

misdede, *n. sg. and pl.* wrong-doing(s), misdeed(s), 231, 980, 1356

misdon, *v.* do wrong (to), misbehave, err; *inf.* (+*dat. of person*),1489; **misdeþ,** *pres. 3 sg.* 636, 1401, 1537; **misdoð,** *pres. pl.* 1770; **misdɔ,** *pres. subj. sg.* 1353; **misdo,** *p.p.* 1393

misȝenge, *inf.* go astray, miss the mark, 1229n

mishap, *n. acc. sg.* disaster, ill-luck, 1249

mislikeþ, *pres. 3 sg. or pl.* displease(s), 344

misliche, *adv.* variously, indiscriminately, irregularly, 1773

misnume, *p.p.* made a mistake, gone wrong, 1514

misrede, *inf.* give bad advice, lead astray, 1063; **misraddest,** *p. 2 sg.* 160

misreken, *inf.* go astray, 490, **misreke** 675

misrempe, *pres. 1 sg.* go wrong, go astray, 1787; *pres. subj. sg.* 1353

misstorte, *inf.* start off wrong, 677

mist, *see* **mai**

miste, *inf.* miss, fail, 764n; **mist,** *pres. 3 sg.* 1640.—**mist of,** *pres. 3 sg.* escapes from, 825; **hauest imist al of,** are quite devoid of, lack altogether, 581

mistide (+*dat.*), *impers. v. pres. subj. sg.* it may turn out badly (with), 1501

misfonge, *inf.* misapply, go wrong, 1374; *pres. subj. sg.* 1440

mit, *see* **mid**

mo, *adj. comp.* greater, 803.—*adv. comp.* more; **euer mo,** at all times, for ever after, 238, 1108; **neauer þe mo,** for all that, 1330; **na mo,** no more, 564, (*after neg.*) any more, 568

mod, *n.* mind, spirit, mood, thoughts, temper, anger, 8, 952, 1032; **mode,** *prepos. and dat. sg.* 517, 661, 740, &c.; *pl.* griefs, 1520n.—**of nesche mode,** tender-hearted, 1349; **mid mode,** in spirit, through pride, 1412n

mod, *see* **mot**

modi, *adj.* full of spirit, bold, 500

modinesse, *n.* pride, 1405, 1416

mon, *n.* man, mankind, human being, *indef. pron.* one; 455, 691, 773, &c. anyone 1110; **man,** 477, 573, 671, &c. anyone, 1079; **me,** *indef. pron. only,* one (**me** +*v.* often=*passive in* MnE), 32, 142, 291, &c. 845, 1023, 1374, 1625, 1629 (*1st*), 1657; **monnes,** *gen. sg.* 338, 490, 786, &c., **mannes,** 1476, 1499; **men,** *dat. and prepos. sg.* 1246, **manne,** 800, 1556, 1665, **mon** 1631n; **men,** *pl.* men, people, 98, 127, 244, &c.; **monne,** *gen., dat. and prepos. pl.* 131, 289, 475, &c. **manne,** 234, 389, 585, &c.; **men,** *dat. pl.* to the men, 910.—*In various pronominal phrases*: **eni mon,** anyone, anybody, someone, 1215, 1474, **eni man** 1233; **euereuch man,** everyone, everybody, 1271, 1608, **evrich monnes,** *gen. sg.* 426; **euch mon,** everyone, everybody, 975, 1224; (ne) **no mon,** no one, nobody, (with neg.) anyone, anybody, 1273, (ne) **non mon,** 1413, 1553, **nan mon** 1539, (ne) **no man,** 248, 274, 571, &c., **na man** 901

moni, *adj.* many (a), 1393, 1411, 1575 (2), &c. **mani,** 759, 1323, 1756; **monie,** 72, 257, **manie** 1755

more, *n.* moorland, waste land, 818

more, *n.* root, 1328, 1392, 1422

more, *adj. comp.* greater, 690, 786, 906, 1548.—(*used as n.*) **more & lasse,** high and low, 482.—**more,** *adv. comp.* more, 448 (2), 539, 861 &c.—(ne) **na more,** no more, (with neg.) any more, 213, 1639, 1793, &c.—**habbe he . . . ne . . . ne leng more,** once he has . . . . . . no longer, 515f

moreȝeninge, *n.* morning, 1718

morȝe, *n.* morning, 432

mose, *n.* titmouse, 69, 503

most(e), *see* **mot**

mot, *n.* assembly; argument 468

mot, *v.* must; most, *pres. 2 sg.* 1304, **moste** 1302; **mot,** *pres. 3 sg.* 471, 669, 671, &c., **mod** 636; **mote,** *pres. pl.* 857; **mote,** *pres. subj. sg. and pl.* may, might, 52, 859, 987, &c. **moten,** *pl.* 741; **moste,** *p. 3 sg.* had to, 665 mowe, *inf.* mow, 1040

muche, *adj., adv.* great, greatly, much, 764, 1212, 1770

muchel, *adj., adv.* much, great, 847, 1094, 1207, &c. muchele, 906, 1217

muȝe, muhe, *see* mai

mulne, *n.* mill; *prepos. sg.* [86]; *gen. used attributively,* 778

munekes,ᵢ*n. pl.* monks, 729

murȝþe, *n.* joy, mirth, delight, bliss, pleasure, 341, 718, 725, &c. mureȝþe 355, murhþe 1402

murie, *adj.* joyous, sweet, 345, 728

murninge, *n.* mourning, lament, *1598*

mus, *n. nom., acc. pl.* mice, 87, 607; muse, *prepos. pl.* 591, 610

muþ, *n.* mouth, 673, 676, 678, &c.; muþe, *prepos. sg. and pl.* 234, 698, 713, &c.

na, *see* non

nabbed, nabbeþ, *see* nauestu

nabideþ, *pres. 3 sg.;* none . . . no . . . nabideþ, not one . . . ever holds back . . . 493. *Cf.* abide

nabuȝþ (+*dat.*), *v. pres. 3 sg.* does not submit to, does not obey, 782

nacoleþ, *pres. 3 sg. (after neg.)* cools off, 1275. *Cf.* acoled

nadde(st), *see* nauestu

nah, *pres. 3 sg.* has not, 1543 (*see* iweld). *Cf.* ah

naht, *see* noȝt

nai, *adv. (n.),* no, 266, 464; nai nai, oh no! no indeed! 856, 1670; nay nay, 543

nam, *pres. 1 sg.* am not, (*with neg.*) am, 534, 753, 754, &c.; nart, *pres. 2 sg.* are not, (*with neg.*) are, 407, 559, 575, &c. nard 1138; nartu, *pres. 2 sg.* + *pron.* you are not, 1330; nis, *pres. 3 sg.* is not (*with neg.*) is, 120, 206, 313, &c. *1539;* nere, *p. 2 sg.* (*with neg.*) you have . . . been, 656; nas, *p. 3 sg.* was not (*with neg.*) was, 114, 1336; nere, *p. subj. sg.* were not, would not be, (*with neg.*) were, 22, 283, 549, &c. *Cf.* beon

nan(ne), *see* non

narewe, *adj.* narrow, 377; *adv.* closely, 68

nart(u), nas, *see* nam

naþt, *see* noȝt

nauestu, *v.* have not, (*with neg.*) have; *pres. 2 sg.* +*pron.* 1670, neuestu, 898; naueþ *pres. 3 sg.* 772, 948, 1265, &c.; nabbeþ, *pres. pl.* 252, 1005, 1011, nabbed 536; naddest, *p. 2 sg.* 1061; nadde, *p. 3 sg.* 1560, *subj. sg.* 1708. *Cf.* habbe

na-þe-les, *see* no-þe-les

nawedeþ, *pres. pl.* do not go mad, 1384. *Cf.* awedeþ

nawiȝt, *see* noȝt

ne, *adv.* not, (*often used pleonastically with another neg.*), 42, 47, 48, &c. [770]; ne ne, not at all, 1358n.—ne, *conj.* nor; n(e . . . ne . . . ne, neither . . . nor, not . . . nor, 242, 266, 292 (*1st*), &c.

neauer, *see* neuer

necke, *n.* neck, 122

necst, *see* neȝ

nede, *see* neode

neȝ, *adj., adv.* near, close to; neh (+*dat.*), 1220, 1252, neþ 1267. —wel neȝ, almost, 44, 419, 660; wel neh, 1226, 1565, 1604.— neor, *comp.* nearer, near, 923, ner, 386, 1260, 1657; necst, *superl.* nearest, next, 688, nest 700

nele, nelle(þ), neltu, *see* nulle

neode, *n.* need, necessity, time of need, urgency, 906, node, 529, 638.—on þare beire nede, to provide for both of them, 1584; to here neode, to do their business, 938, to hore node, 588, 647; do wule hire ahene neode, will satisfy her own needs, 1542; don gode node, do good service, 388; him nod nis, he need not, 466.—nede, *adv.* needs; hit mod nede, it is forced to by necessity, 636

ne(o)r, *see* neȝ

neo-þe-les, *see* no-þe-les

nere, *see* nam

nesche, *adj.* soft, delicate, frail, tender, 1349, 1387, 1546

nest, *see* neȝ

nest, *n.* nest, 100, 102, 108, &c; neste, *prepos.* 92, 282, 640, &c. nest 964, 1386

netle, *n. prepos. pl.* nettles, 593

neþ, *see* neȝ

neuer (*often with adv.* **ne**), *adv.* never; (*with neg.*) at all, ever; 60, 114, 283, &c. [770]; **neauer**, 907, 1308, 1336, &c.; **neure**, 209, 611, 1631; **neuere**, 691.— **neauer þe mo** 1330, *see* **mo**; **ne . . . neuer so**, no matter how . . ., however . . ., 345, 1026. *Cf.* **euer**

neuestu, *see* **nauestu**

nich, *adv.* not I; **nich ne nai**, no and no again, 266. *Cf.* **ich**

Nichole, *n.* Nicholas, 191, 1746, 1778

niȝt, *n.*, *often used as adv.* night, by night, 89, 219, 227, &c. 336, 483, 736; **niȝte**, *prepos.* 365, 388, 390, &c. **nihte** 1432; **niȝtes**, *pl.* 523.—**niȝtes**, *adv.* by night, 238, 591, 1590

niȝtingale, *n*, nightingale, 4, 13, 29, &c.; **niȝtegale**, 1711, 1719, 1739, &c.; **nihtegale**, 1512, 1635; **niȝtingale**, *nom. pl.* 203

nimen, *v.* take, seize, take hold of, catch; *inf.* 607, 1764n, **nime** 1469; **nime**, *pres. 1 sg.* 457; **nimeþ**, *pres. pl.* 649; **nime**, *pres. subj. sg.* 359, 727; **nom**, *p. 3 sg.* 124, 1073; **inume**, *p.p.* 1059, refuted 541n, undertaken 1197. —**let . . . nime**, had . . . seized, 1097

nis, *see* **nam**

niso, *pres. subj. sg.* shall not see, 674; **niseȝe**, *p. subj. sg.* did not see, 382. *Cf.* **iseo**

nisvicst, *pres. 2 sg.* do not leave off, 406n. *Cf* **swike**

niþ, *n.* malice, hatred, envy, 1194; **niþe**, *prepos. sg.* 417, 1088, 1096, &c. 1401n

no, *see* **non**

nod(e), *see* **neode**

noȝt, *adj.* worthless, good for nothing, 1127, **naht** 1480.— **noȝt**, *adv.* (*often with* **ne** *or with v. with initial neg.* **n-**), not, not at all, by no means; (*where the neg. is otherwise expressed in translation*) at all; 58, 102, 154, &c. 340, **nout** 1426, **noþt**, 1391, 1395, 1552, **naþt** 1470, 1740, **nowiht** 928.—**noȝt**, *pron., adv.* nothing, 246, 458, 491, &c. 574, 1452, **nout** 1275, **naþt** 1620,

nowiȝt 884, **nawiht** 1324. *Cf.* **aht, oȝt**

nolde, *see* **nulle**

nom, *see* **nimen**

nome, *n.* name, 1762

non, *adj., pron., adv.* (*often with* **ne** *or with v. with initial neg.* **n-**), no, none, not any, not one, (*where the neg. is otherwise expressed in translation*) any, 369, 534, 559, &c., **nan** 1389, **none**, 212, 246, 252, &c. **no**, 42, 190, 516, &c.; **nanne**, *acc. sg. masc.* 1238, so godne ne . . . **nanne**, . . . none so good, 812.— **no**, and not at all, 579; **no!** 153, 997.—**no þing**, *pron.* nothing, (*with neg.*) anything, 624, 948, 1247; **none þinge**, *prepos. sg.* any creature, 1620; **no þing**, *adv.* not at all, in no way, (*with neg.*) at all, 562, 616.—**non mon**, *pron.* no one, nobody, (*with neg.*) anyone, anybody, 1553; **no mon, no man**, 248, 274, 571, &c.; **nan mon** 1539, **na man** 901.—**no þe**, *adv.* none the, (*with neg.*) any the, 283, 1260.—**na more**, *adv.* no more, no longer, (*with neg.*) any longer, 213, 1639, 1793, &c. **na mo**, 564, 568. [*Forms both* <*OE* nā, nō, *and* <*OE* nān *are listed together here.*] *Cf.* **on**

Noreweie, *n.* Norway, 909

norþ, *adv.* north, 921

not, *v.* do not know; *pres. 1 sg.* 1180, 1181, 1507, &c.; **nost**, *pres. 2 sg.* 755, 1112; **not**, *pres. 3 sg.* 780, 823, 1247, &c.; **nute**, *pres. pl.* 1010; **nustest**, *p. 2 sg.* 1300; **nuste**, *p. 3 sg.* 1441; **nuste**, *p. pl.* 175ln

note, *n.* use, usefulness, 557.—**to note**, of use, of service, 1122; **to . . . note**, to . . . advantage, 330.—**do gode note**, be of good use, do good work, 1034, 1624

noti, *pres. 1 sg.* use, 1033

no-þe-les, *adv.* nevertheless, even so, yet, nonetheless, 149, 374, 401, &c. **na-þe-les**, 827, **neo-þe-les**, 1297, 1314, 1370, &c.

noþer . . . ne, *conj., adv.* neither . . . nor, (*with neg.*) either . . . or, 465, 754, 832, &c. *1011*, **nouþer . . . ne** 1732 noþerward, *adv.* downwards, *144*

noþt, nout, *see* noȝt

nowe, *adj. pl. or adv.* new, newly, 1129

nowiht, *see* noȝt

nu, *adv.* now, 46, 205, 212, &c. *846, 1421, 1515*

nulle, *v.* will not, do not wish; *pres. 1 sg.* 1639, nelle 452; nule, (*in comp. construction*) will 1210; nultu, *pres. 2 sg.+pron.* 905, 909, 913, neltu 150; nele, *pres. 3 sg.* 1482; nulleþ, *pres. pl.* 1764, nelleþ 653; nolde, *p. 1 sg.* 159, 1742; *p. 3 sg.* 1080. *Cf.* wille

inume, *see* nimen

nuste(st), nute, *see* not

o, *see* on

oder, *see* oþer

odwite, *n.* reproach, shame, 1233

of, *prep.* of, from, out of, concerning, about, 9, 11, 14, &c. *48, 713, 1448, 1469*; by, by means of, through, 727, 1306, 1483; endowed with, 152 (*2*), 1547; in, 192, 193; made of, 320; at, 1402; as regards, with, in the way of, 31, 1212, 1411; because of, 40; on account of, for, 858

ofchamed, *p.p.* put to shame, ashamed, 934

ofdrad, *p.p.* afraid, terrified, 1150, 1744; ofdradde 1143

ofligge, *pres. subj. 3 sg.* lies with, 1505

oflonged, *p.p.* seized with longing, 1587

ofne, *n.* oven, 292

ofslahe, *p.p.* killed, slain, 1611

oft, *adv.* often, 36, 81, 539, &c. ofte, 1217, 1521, 1541, &c.

oftoned, *p.p.* vexed, 254

ofþuȝte, *impers. v. p. 3 sg.* it displeased. 397

oȝe, *adj.* own, *118*, 1650, owe 100; oȝene, 1089, 1341, 1652, ahene, 1286, 1542.—þes dai bo þin oȝe, the day is yours, 259

oȝt, *pron.* anything, 662, 663. *Cf.* noȝt

old, *adj.* old, 25, 638; olde, 207, 1037, alde 1183.—of olde, long ago, from days long past, 637, 685

on, *prep.* in, on, 51, 94, 174 (*2*), &c. one 613; on, with, 517, on me, in my case, 275, 367; on, at *808*

on, *num., adj., indef. art., pron.* one, the one, a, an, 25, 82n, 90, &c., an, 4, 54, 80, &c., o, 103, 333, 713, a, 45, 94, 98, &c.; one, 1, 2, 4, &c. ane 1021; anne, *acc. sg. masc.* 794, 799, 802, &c.; ore, *dat., prepos. sg. fem.* 17, 1750, 1754.—in on, without break, 356; at one, united in one, 785.—one, *adv.* alone, 1594; ene, once, 1107; ones (*historically gen. sg.*) of one kind, 1395, enes, once upon a time, 1049. *Cf.* non

onde, *n.* ill-will, malice, envy, spite, 419, 1096, 1401n

ondsware, *n.* answer, 1185, answare 399, ondswere 1573, andsware 639, 657, andsware 665, andsuere 705, answere 1710, ansvvare 55, ansuare, 487, 551, ansvere 470.—ȝaf andsuare, *p. 3 sg.+n. acc.* answered, *149,* ȝef ondsware 1176. *Cf.* ansuare

ongred, *p.p.* afflicted, grieved, 1588

onsene, *n.* look, face, 1706

op, *see* up

ope, *adj.* open, 168

opeliche, *adv.* openly, 853

orde, *n.* point, 1068, 1712.—ende of orde, from beginning to end, 1785n

ore, *see* on

ore, *n.* mercy, grace, 886, 1083, 1404, &c.

orþliche, *adj.* earthly, of the earth, on earth, 788

orfe, *n.* cattle, 1199, oreue 1157

oþer, *adj.* other, another, second, 54, 101, 204, &c. oðer 1184, oder 905; oþres, *gen. sg.* 1499, oþers 1476; oþre, *prepos. sg. or pl.* 1376.—oþer, *pron., adj. used as n.* the other (one), another, another thing, other matter, 7, 117, 494, &c., oder 903; oþer, one (of two), 1477; each other 286; oþeres, *gen. sg.* 9, *11*; oþer, *nom. pl.* 136, oþre 1593.—on oþer, differently, otherwise,

671.—oþer, *conj.* or, 243, 486, 666, &c.—oþer . . . oþer, either . . . or, 328, oþar . . . oþer 1479f

oþþan, *prep.* +*def. art. or dem. adj.* from that, 359

oure, *see* ure

ov, *see* þu

over, *prep.* over, on top of, 1524; 64 (*see* tukest)

ouerkumeþ, *v.* overcome, defeat, prevail over, dominate; *pres. 3 sg.* 788; ouerkome, *p. subj. sg.* 1743; ouercume, *p.p.* 542, ouerkume 1198, ouercome 1662

ouerquatie, *inf.* glut, 353

oferd, oferen, *see* afere

ouerdede, *n.* excess, intemperance, 352

ouergan, *v. intr. inf.* pass over, 952; ouergo, *p.p.* past, spent, 567.—ouergeþ, *v. tr. pres. 3 sg.* overwhelms, 947

ouerhoheð, *pres. 3 sg.* despises, scorns, 1406

ouer-longe, *adv.* for too long, 450

ouerseӡ, *p. 3 sg.* looked down at, 30

ouersid, *pres. 3 sg.* neglects, 1438

ouer-swiþe, *adv.* overmuch, excessively, 1518

oueruareþ, *pres. pl.* overrun, 387

ouer-fulle, *n.* overfulness, surfeiting, 354

oure, *see* ure

ow, *see* þu

ovvel, *n.* hook, 80

owe, *see* oӡe

ower, *poss. adj.* your, 1685, 1699, 1736

oxe, *n.* ox, 629

paþes, *n. pl.* paths, 377, 380, 815

ipeint, *p.p.* painted, 76

pes, *n.* peace, 1730n

pie, *n.* magpie, 126, 1613

pine, *n.* suffering, torment, pain, 1116, 1566

pinnuc, *n.* hedge-sparrow, 1130

pipe, *n.* pipe, whistle, fife, 22, 24, 319, &c.

pipest, *pres. 2 sg.* whistle, pipe, 503

piping, *n.* whistling, piping, 567; pipinge, *dat., prepos. sg.* 316, 337, 901

plaidi, *inf.* plead, litigate, 184, 1639; plaideð, *pres. 3 sg.* 944

plaiding, *n.* law-suit; holde plaiding, held plea(s), 12

plait, *n.* law-suit, pleading, 5, plaid 1737; plaites, *gen. sg.* of pleading, procedural, 472

pleien, *inf.* play, have a gay time, 486, pleie, 213, 1359; pleie, *pres. 1 sg.* 531; *pres. subj. sg.* 1425

pope, *n.* pope, 746

Portes-hom, *n.* Portesham, 1752, Portes-ham 1791

poure, *adj. used as n.* poor, 482

preost, *n.* priest, 902, 1311, 1313, prest 1180, prost 322, *978*; prestes, *gen. sg.* 1179, 1306; prostes, *pl.* 733; preoste, *dat. pl.* 913n

prude, *n.* pride, *1685*

pulte, *inf.* thrust, assail, 1524; *pres. 1 sg.* 873

punde, *n. gen. pl.* (*after num.*), pounds, 1101

(*For* q *see under* cw)

rad (to), *adj.* quick, ready (for), eager (for), 1043.—him boþ rade, come readily to him, 423. —raddere, *comp.* 738

raddest, *see* rede

raþe, *adv.* early, soon, quickly, 1086, 1147, 1700.—raþere, *comp.* 1242

reades, *see* red

readliche, *adv.* readily, 1281

recche (of), *inf.* care (about, for), set store by, take thought of, mind, 803; *pres. 1 sg.* 60, 458, 533, reche 58; rehþ, *pres. 3 sg.* 1404, recþ 491; reccheþ, *pres. pl.* 1006; roӡte, *p. subj. sg.* 427

reke, *inf.* go, proceed, 1606

red, *n.* advice, counsel, good sense, a sound plan, good idea, 396, 680, 682, &c.; rede, *dat., prepos. sg.* 307, 660, 702, &c.; reades, *pl.* 1222.—nom red (of), went to . . . for help, 1073; nimen heom to rede, adopt as their plan, resolve, decide, 1764n

rede, *inf.* read, advise, 350, 1697, 1782 (*see* speche); *pres. 1 sg.* 860; raddest, *p. 2 sg.* 159

rede, *adj.* red, 830

redles, *adj.* helpless, 691

red-purs, *n.* bag of good ideas, 694

reȝel, *n.* garment, dress, mantle, 562

rehte, *see* **riȝt**

rehþ, *see* **recche**

rem, *n.* outcry, hue and cry, 1215n

rente, *n.* income, revenue, 1767, 1773, 1776

reoþe, *n.* pity, compassion, 1445

res, *n.* rush, assault, violent impulse, 512

rest, *pres. 3 sg.* rests; rests for a moment, 1452

reste, *n.* rest, quiet, 281

reue, *n. prepos.* plunder, spoils, *458*

riche, *adj.* rich, 1770; (*used as n., pl.*) 482

riche, *n.* kingdom, 357, 361, 717, &c.

rideþ (upon), *pres. 3 sg.* rides, mounts, 494

riȝt, *n.* right, justice, truth, 188, 229, 396, &c., **riht**, 950, 1371, 1526.—**mid riȝte**, properly, justly, rightly, 184, 186, 470, &c.—**boþ . . . þine riȝte**, are your due, 88.—**riȝt**, *adj.* right, proper just, honest, rightful, lawful, straight, true, 549, **riht**, 958, 1692; **riȝte**, 179, 214, 264, &c., pure, downright, 1088, 1096; **rihte**, 1345, 1428, 1640, wholesome 1383, **riȝtte** 962, **rehte** 1602; **rihtne**, *acc. sg. masc.* 1238; **riȝte**, *prepos. sg. or pl.* (*used as n.*) (what is) right, upright men, 164, 197.—**riȝt**, *adv.* just, exactly, 76, 80, 142, &c. **riht**, straight 1736

rind, *n.* bark, 242n; **rinde**, *prepos.* 602

ripe, *adj.* mature, ripe, 211

ris, *n.* twig, bough, branch, 1636; **rise**, *prepos. sg.* 19, 53, 175, &c.; **ris**, *pl.* 586; **rise**, *prepos. pl.* 1664

rodde, *n.* slender shoot, rod, 1123, 1646

rode, *n. nom. sg.* cross, 1382

roȝte, *see* **recche**

rok, *n.* rook, 1130

Rome, *n.* Rome, 746, 1016

rorde, *n.* voice, 311

rose, *n.* rose, 443

rude, *n.* red hue, red complexion, 443n

rugge, *n.* back, 775

ruȝe, *adj.* rough, 1013

rum, *adj.* spacious, 643

rum-hus, *n.* privy, 652; **rum-huse**, *prepos. sg.* 592

rune, *n.* course, running; **þoues rune**, hue and cry for a thief, 1156

rune, *n. sg. or pl.* secret(s); news 1170

rure, *n.* downfall, ruin, 1154

sake, *n.* strife, contention, 1160; offence, blame, 1430; **sake** 1589

sade, *adj.* sated, weary of it, 452

salue, *n.* salve, balm; **haueþ tweire kunne salue**, has balm of two kinds, 888

sat, *see* **sitte**

skente, *pres. 1 sg.* entertain, delight, 449; *p. 1 sg.* 1085

skentinge, *n.* entertainment, delight, song(s) of delight, 446, 532, 613, &c.

skere, *inf. reflex.* free (oneself), clear (oneself) from a charge, 1302

shafte, *n. pl.* creatures, 788

schal, *v.* shall, must, to be about to (do something), to be going to (do something), to be destined to, ought to, am (art, is, &c.) to (do something); *pres. 1 sg.* 960, 1354, 1684, **shal** 547; **schalt**, *pres. 2 sg.* 956, **shalt**, 544, 748, 1066, **schald** 1572; **schaltu**, *pres. 2 sg.*+*pron.* 209, 1290, 1377, **shaltu** 749; **schal**, *pres. 3 sg.* 187, 611, 979, &c. **shal**, 342, 346, 530, &c.; must go, 724, **scal** 1199; **schule**, *pres. pl.* 1192, 1201, 1202, &c., **shulle**, 856, 1133, **schul** 1200, **schal** 1206n; **shulle**, *pres. subj. sg.* 442, 445, **schille** 1683; **schulde**, *p. 1 sg.* 1417, **sholde**, 464, 965, 997; **soldich**, *p. 1 sg.*+ *pron. 1025*; **sholdest**, *p. 2 sg.* 54; **schulde**, *p. 3 sg.* 1224, 1747; **scholde** 1728, **sholde**, 381, 764; would be sure to, 1020, **solde** 975; **schulde**, *p. pl.* 1262, **scholde** 1691, **solde** 977

schame, *see* **schome**

schamie þe, *refl. v.*, 3 *sg. pres. subj.* shame on you, 161

scharp, *adj.* sharp, 79, 270; **scharpe,** 153, **charpe** 1676.— **scharpe,** *adv.* shrill, 141

schawles, *see* **shueles**

schede, *inf.* tell apart, distinguish, 197; **chadde,** *pres. 1 sg.* shed, 1616

sheld, *n.* shield, 1022; **chelde,** *prepos. sg.* 1713

schende, *inf.* put to shame, scold, revile, 274, 1287; *pres. 1 sg.* 285; **ischend,** *p.p.* put to shame, harmed, violated, 1336

sheue, *n. prepos. pl.* sheaves, 455

schilde, *inf.* protect (oneself), shield, 62, **ishilde** 781; **schilde,** *pres. 1 sg.* 57; *pres. subj. pl.* 1253; **schild,** *imp. sg.* 163

schille, *adj.* resounding, shrill, sonorous, resonant, 142, 558, 1721.—*adv.* 1656

schille, *see* **schal**

shine, *n. pl.* shins, 1060

shine, *v.* shine; *pres. subj. sg.* 963

schipes, *n. pl.* ships, 1205

schirchest, *pres. 2 sg.* shriek, 223

ischire, *inf.* utter, speak, 1532

schirme, *inf.* fight, 306

schit-worde, *n. prepos. pl.* mucky words, 286

scholde, sholde(st), *see* **schal**

schome, *n.* shame, disgrace, 167, **schame,** 1290, 1650.—**schame** (+*dat.*), disgrace (to), 1761.— **for mine shome,** to put me to shame, to confound me, to disgrace me, 1075, **me . . . for schame** 1283; **do . . . schame,** bring . . . shame on, inflict . . . injury on, 1731; **don shome (of),** corrupt, defile, 1053; **do him schame (of),** bring shame on him (through), 1483; **dude me his oʒene shome,** brought on me his own shame, 1089; **goþ . . . to shome,** is ruined, is done for, 522; **gred þe manne a schame,** shouts with derision at the man, 1665; **scist me . . . schame,** speak to . . . disgrace me, 50; **me seist on oþer shome,** re-proach me with another piece of disgrace, 363

schonde, *n.* shame, shameful thing, disgrace, 1498, *1652*, 1733, **shonde,** 1402

short, *adj.* short, 73

ishote, *p.p.* shot, shot at, shot down, shot forth, 23, 1121

ischrud, *p.p.* clad, *1529*

shueles, *n. sg. or pl.* scarecrow, 1128, **schawles** 1648

schul(e), schulde, s(c)hulle, *see* **schal**

schunest, *tr., pres. 2 sg.* shun, avoid, shy away from, shrink from, 590; **shuneþ,** *pres. 3 sg.* 1165, **schuniet** 229; **shunieþ,** *pres. pl.* 792.—**schunet,** *intr. pres. 3 sg.* shrinks away, keeps out of the way, 236

sckile, *n.* reason, discrimination, 186

Scot-londe, *n.* Scotland, 908, 1758n

screwen, *n. prepos. pl.* black-guards, 287

sea, *see* **see**

sechen (for), *inf.* seek (out), 1508, **seche,** find 1759, **iseche,** attain to, 741; **secheþ,** *pres. 3 sg.* 380; **secheþ (to),** *pres. pl.* 538

sed, *n.* seed, 1041; **sedes,** *pl.* 1129, 1134

(i)sed(e), *see* **segge**

see, *n.* sea, 1754, **sea** 1205

segge, *n. prepos. sg. or pl.* sedge, 18

segge, *inf.* say, tell, speak, 186 393, 671, &c. *[1024]*; *pres. 1 sg.* 266, 835, 1421; **seist,** *pres. 2 sg.* 50, 265, 309, &c. (+*dat.*), say to, 1283; **seistu,** *pres. 2 sg.* + *pron.* 1075; **seiþ,** *pres. 3 sg.* 176, 1072; **segget,** *pres. pl.* 98, 127, 244, &c.; **segge,** *subj. sg.* 60, 844; **sei,** *imp. sg.* 1407, **seie,** 217, 556; **segget,** *imp. pl.* 113, *116*; **seide,** *p. 1 sg.* 1309; *p. 3 sg.* 9, 235, 299, &c., **sede,** 33, 217, 294, &c.; **sede,** *p. subj. sg.* 1296; **iseid,** *p.p.* 1037, **ised** 395

iseʒ(e), iseʒþ, *see* **iseo**

sehþ, *see* **sihð**

selde, *adv.* seldom, *943*, 944

sele, *n.* joy, happiness, a happy mood, 953

seme, *inf.* reconcile, 187

semes, *n. pl.* loads, 775

sende, *pres. 1 sg.* send, send out, direct, 1264; **send,** *pres. pl.* 1520; **sende,** *pres. subj. sg.* 1570

sene, *n.* sight, vision, 240, 368. *Cf.* **isene**

iseo, *inf.* see, [771], 1268, **ison,**

383, 529, iso, 366, 371, 374, &c.;
iseo, *pres. 1 sg.* 1219, 1235, 1241,
&c. iso, 327, 370, 451, &c. so 34;
isihst, *pres. 2 sg.* 1225, 1230,
1232, sichst 242; isiþ, *pres. 3 sg.*
407, siþ 950; iseʒþ, sees, under-
stands, 1465, isoþ 424, suþ 246;
soþ, *pres. pl.* 884; iseo, *pres.
subj. sg.* 1237, 1329; iseʒ, *p. 3
sg.* 29, 108, 109; iseʒe, *p. subj.
sg.* 425. *Cf.* niseʒe

seolliche, *adj.* marvellous, strange,
1299

seolfe, seolue *see* sulfe

seoluer, *n.* silver, 1366

seorhe, *n. prepos. sg. or pl.*
sorrow(s), 1599

seoþþe, *adv.* after that, next, then
again, for ever after, 1402,
soþþe, 324, 1103

serueþ, *pres. 3 sg.* serves, 1579

seten, *see* sitte

setle, *n.* seat, *594*

sette, *inf.* set, put, 1626; *p. 3 sg.*
1057

sewi, *inf.* show, 151

sh-, *see* sch-

sibbe, *n.* peace, 1005

sikerhede, *n.* assurance, certainty,
1265

sikerliche, *adv.* for certain, without
doubt, 1139

sikeþ, *see* sihð

(i)si(c)hst, *see* iseo

side, *n.* side, part, 429.—bi hire
side, beside her, by her side,
1502; an oþer side, on the other
hand, 299n

isihst, *see* iseo

sihð, *v.* sigh; *pres. 3 sg.* 1587, sehþ
1439n, sikeþ 1352; siʒte, *p. 3
sg.* 1291

singen, *inf.* sing, +*dat.* sing to,
for, 709, singin 910, singe, 39,
47, 54, &c.; singe, *pres. 1 sg.*
313, 321, 323, &c.; singst, *pres.
2 sg.* 505, 594, 899, &c. singest,
331, 412, 413, &c. singist, 219,
849, 1146, &c.; singþ, *pres. 3
sg.* 721, singeþ 414, singeð 916,
singet 196 (2); singeþ, *pres. pl.*
483, 732, 733; singe, *pres. subj.
sg.* 226, 876, 902; singe, *pres.
subj. pl.* 861; sunge, *p. 2 sg.*
1049, 1052; song, *p. 3 sg.* 20,
26, 141, &c.; sungen, *p. pl.*
1663; sunge, *p. subj. sg.* 1026

singinge, *n.* used as *adv.* by singing,
855

sitte, *inf.* sit, perch, 282, 743, 960,
&c.; *pres. 1 sg.* 384, 1218, 1244;
sittest, *pres. 2 sg.* 89, 518, 594,
&c.; sit, *pres. 3 sg.* [86], 1587;
sitteþ, *pres. pl.* 97, 1682; site,
imp. sg. 655; sat, *p. 3 sg.* 15,
145, 936, &c.; seten, *p. pl.* 1102

(i)siþ, *see* iseo

siþe, *n.* time, 293, 325, case 993.—
one siþe, once, 1163; oðer siðe,
once more, 1184

siueþ, *pres. 3 sg.* follows, 1526

islaʒe, *p.p.* slain, 1142

slepeþ, *pres. pl.* sleep, 1593

isliked, *p.p.* smoothed over, 841

slide, *inf.* slip, slide, escape, 1390;
islide, *p.p.* 686

slider, *adj.* slippery, 956

slitte, *n. prepos. sg. or pl.* slit(s),
pocket(s), 1118

slo, *n.* mire, morass, 1394

smak, *n.* taste, sense of taste, 823

smal, *adj.* thin, slender, little, 73;
smale, 64, 277, 320, &c.; grace-
ful, 204

smel, *n.* smell, sense of smell, 822

smiten, *inf.* strike, 78

smiþes, *n. pl.* smiths, armourers,
1206n

snailes, *n. pl.* snails, 87

snel, *adj.* quick, active, vigorous,
bold, 531, 829, 918; snelle, *pl.*
768.—snelle, *adj.* used as *n. nom.
sg.* 526

snepe, *adj.* used as *n. prepos. pl.*
fools, 225

sniuþ, *pres. 3 sg.* snows, 620

snou, *n.* snow, 1002, snov 430;
snowe, *prepos. sg.* 413

so, *see* swo

(i)so, *see* iseo

softe, *adj.* soft, gentle, 6, 1350,
1546; softest (+*dat.*) *superl.*
softest (for), 644

solde, soldich, *see* schal

soleþ, *pres. 3 sg.* is defiled, gets
dirty, 1276

solue, *see* sulfe

ison, *see* iseo

sone, *adv.* soon, before long, easily,
at once, 675, 677, 1055, &c.—
eft sone, again, 821.— (so) sone
so, as soon as, 501, 518

song, *n.* song, 36, 220, 315, &c.;
343; songes, *gen. sg.* 1358;

songe, *prepos. sg.* or *pl.* 11, 46, 82, &c.; songes, *pl.* 722, 896, 1457, &c.—chirche song, hymn, hymn-singing, 984; chirche songe, *prepos. sg.* or *pl.* 1036n

song, *see* singen

sor, *n. acc. sg.* injury, harm, suffering, sorrow, grief, trouble(s), 1234; sore, *prepos. sg.* or *pl.* 540, 689, 690, &c.

sore, *adj.* sad, severe, 1472, 1595. —*adv.* sorely, bitterly, 885, 1150, 1352, &c.

sorȝe, *n.* sorrow, trouble, care, 431, sorwe 884

sori, *adj.* sorry, sad, 994, 1084, 1162

sori-mod, *adj.* sad at heart, 1218

sot, *adj.* foolish, 1435

sottes, *n. gen. sg.* (*used attributively*), fool's, foolish, 1351, 1471; sottes, *pl.* fools, 297

sothede, *n.* folly, 1375, 1488

soti, *adj.* sooty, 578

soþ, *adv.* south, 921

soþ, *n.* truth (*often used as adv.*) truly, the truth, (*or in complementary constructions indistinguishable from the adj.* true) 217, 668, 844, soð 950, sooþ 1407; soþe, *prepos.* 264, 1258. —soþ, *adj.* true (*in complementary constructions indistinguishable from the n.* the truth) 313, 349, 570, &c., soð 1769; soþe, *prepos. sg.* truthful, 698

(i)soþ, *see* iseo

soþ-saȝe, *n.* true saying, truth, 1038

soþþe, *see* seoþþe

soule, *n. dat. sg.* soul, 1092

sowe, *inf.* sow, 1039; soweþ, *pres. 3 sg.* 1041; isowe, *p.p.* 1129, 1614

spac, *see* speken

spale, *n.* break, rest, 258n

spanne, *inf.* allure, urge, entice, 1490

speken, *inf.* speak, talk, make a speech, 678, 953, speke, 261, 553, 676, &c.; spekest, *pres. 2 sg.* 1282; specþ, *pres. 3 sg.* 1072, 1074, 1172, spekeþ, 1536, 1556; speke, *pres. subj. sg.* 1079; speke, *p. 2 sg.* 554; spac, *p. 3 sg.* 396, 401, 410, &c.; speke, *p. subj. sg.* 1513; ispeke, *p.p.* 1293

speche, *n.* speech, law-suit, plea, 13, 398, 480, &c.—unker speche rede, bring forward our pleas, 1782

spedde(stu), *see* spet

spel, *n.* story, narration, 128; spelle, *prepos. sg.* or *pl.* 1794; talk 264, sayings 294

spene, *v.* spend, expend; *inf.* put to use 165; spenþ, *pres. 3 sg.* 362, speneþ 1525; spene, *pres. subj. sg.* 1549

spere, *n.* spear, 1022; speres, *gen. sg.* 1068, 1712

spet, *v.* succeed; *pres. 3 sg.* 763; speddestu, *p. 2 sg.*+*pron.* 169; spedde (of), *p. 3 pl.* succeeded (in), 1792

speten, *inf.* spit, 39

spille, *inf.* destroy, waste, 1020; ispild, *p.p.* 1027

spire, *collective n.* reeds, 18

sprede, *inf.* spread, unfold, 437

sprenge, *n.* snare, 1066

springe, *inf.* spring, sprout (forth), grow, rise, 437, 1134; sprinþ, *pres. 3 sg.* 1042, springeþ, 734, 918; isprunge, *p.p.* spread, current, 300

spure, *n.* spur, 777

spuse, *n.* spouse, wife, 1527.— wedlock, the marriage vow; breke spuse, commit adultery, 1334

spus-bruche, *n.* adultery, 1368

spusing, *n.* wedlock, marriage, 1336, 1340.—tobreke ... spusing, commit adultery, 1554f; is spusing ... tobroke, adultery is ... committed, 1558

spusing-bendes, *n. pl.* marriage-bonds, 1472

sputing, *n.* disputation, contention, 1574

stable, *n.* stable, 629

stal, *n.* stall, place; stalle, *prepos.* 629.—stal ne stode, were of no use, 1632n

stal, *see* stele

starc, *adj.* violent, strong, fierce, 5, 1473; starke, 524, 1176

stard, *pres. 3 sg.* leaps, 379n

stare-blind, *adj.* quite blind, stone-blind, 241

starest, *pres. 2 sg.* stare, glare, 77

staue, *n. prepos. pl.* sticks, 1167

steape, *n.* step, 1592

stede, *n.* place, 590n, 966. *Cf.*
  stude

stele, *n.* steel, 1030

stele, *inf.* steal, go stealthily, 1499;
  stele, *p. 2 sg.* 103; **stal**, *p. 3 sg.*
  1432

steorre, *n. pl.* stars, 1329, **storre**
  1321

sterne, *adv.* sternly, 112

steuene, *n.* voice, 727, 898, 915,
  &c., **steune**, 504, 522, **stefne**,
  314, 317

sticke, *n.* stick, 1625

stif, *adj.* stiff, hard, stubborn, 5,
  79, 269

stiȝþ, *pres. 3 sg.* mounts, rises,
  1405

stille, *adj.* still, quiet, 261, 546,
  979.—*adv.* still, softly, low, 282,
  655, 1019, &c.

stoc, *n.* tree-trunk, stump, 25,
  stok 1113

stode, *n.* stud, 495

stod(e), **stond**, *see* stont

stones, *n. pl.* stones, 1118; **stone**,
  prepos. pl. 1609, **stoone** 1167

stont, *v.* stand; *pres. 3 sg.* 618,
  623, 778; **stode**, *p. 2 sg.* 1632
  (*see* stal); **stod**, *p. 3 sg.* 25.—
  stond aȝein, *imp. sg.* offer op-
  position, 1788

stor, *adj.* violent, severe, 1473

storre, *see* steorre

storre-wis, *adj.* skilled in astrology,
  1318

stottes, *n. pl.* horses, jades, 495

strenge, *n.* string, 1230

strengþe, *n.* strength, 173, 764,
  765, &c. **strencþe**, *1226*, 1713,
  strenþe, 781, 1674.—**ne mai no
  strengþe**, strength cannot avail,
  762

strengur, *see* strong

strete, *n.* road, 962

strong, *adj.* strong, fierce, hard, 5,
  579, 667, &c. 1388n; **stronge**,
  155, 269, 524, &c.; **strengur**,
  comp. 773.—**stronge**, *adv.* 972,
  much 254; (*or adj.*) 12

stubbe, *n.* stubble, 506

stude, *n.* place, 936, 1654; *prepos.
  pl.* 1767. *Cf.* stede

stumpeþ (at), *v.* stumble (over);
  pres. 3 sg. 1424; *pres. pl.* 1392

stunde, *n. prepos. sg. or pl.* time(s),
  706, 802.—**summe stunde**, some-
  times, 1353

istunge, *p.p.* stung, 515

sulied, *pres. 3 sg.* is defiled, gets
  dirty, 1240

sulfe, *adj.*, *pron.* very, self; very
  one 746n; **sulue** 495; **þe sulue
  mose**, the titmouse itself, 69;
  þe seolfe coc, the cock himself,
  1679.—**þu sulf**, you yourself,
  497; **þe seolue**, *dat.* to yourself,
  1284; **him sulue**, himself, 810;
  heom seolue, themselves, 930,
  hom solue, 883; **mi solue**,
  myself, 835

sum, *adj.*, *pron.* some, certain,
  some part, 6, 540, 1040, &c., a
  certain one 1016, **sun** 1397;
  sume, 293, 478, 879, &c.;
  summe, 1154, 1246, *1353*, 1648;
  sumne, *acc. sg. masc.* 1152

sum-del, *adv.* a little, 870, 934, 939,
  sun-del 1598

sumeres, *n.* summer; *gen. sg.* 489;
  sumere, *dat. or prepos.* 416, 509,
  622; *used attributively*, summer-,
  1n, *709*

sun, **sun-del**, *see* sum, sum-del

sunegeþ, *v.* sin, commit sins; *pres.
  3 sg.* 1416; **sunegi**, *pres. subj. pl.*
  928

sunge(n, *see* singen

sunne, *n.* sun, 912, 963

sunne, *n. sg. or pl.* sin(s), 863, 974,
  1395; **sunnen**, *prepos.* 858

sunfulle, *adj. used as n. dat. sg.*
  sinner, 891

sur, *adj.* sour, bitter, 866; **sure**,
  1082

su-, sv-, *see* sw-

suþ, *see* iseo

suþe, *see* swuþe

swa, *see* swo

sval, *p. 3 sg.* swelled; **sval . . .
  aȝen**, became puffed up with
  rage against, 7

sweng, *n.* stroke, blow, 799;
  swenge, *prepos. sg.* 803 *sg. or
  pl.* 1286; **swenges**, *pl.* 797

swete, *adj.* sweet, 866, **svete** 358

swete, *inf.* sweat, 1716

swike, *pres. 1 sg.* stop, cease, 1459;
  swikeþ, *pres. 3 sg.* is silent, 336;
  iswike, *pres. subj. pl.* 929. *Cf.*
  nisvicst

svikeldom, *n.* deceitfulness,
  treachery, 163, **svikedom**, 167

svikelhede, *n.* deceitfulness,
  treachery, 162, **swikelede** 838

suich(e), swiche, *see* swuch

suiþe, sviþe, swiþ(e), *see* swuþe

swo, *adv.* so, thus, in such a way, in that way, in this way, such a, 804, 1107, 1293, &c., swa, 1577, 1627, 1629, so, 43, 52, 141 (2), &c.—swo, *conj.* as, as if, 1777, svvo 76, swa 1665, so, 77, 80, 97, &c.—so . . . so, as . . . as, 334, 383

isuolȝe, *p.p.* swallowed, 146

swonk, *p. 1 sg.* toiled, 462

sworde, *n.* sword, 1068

swore, *n.* neck. 73, *1125*

swuch, *adj., pron.* such, such a, such a one, like that, of that kind, 1307, 1415n, 1453, &c. that sort of 1433, suich, 1169, the very man 405, swucch 1450; swuche 1511; swiche 1347; swucche, *prepos. sg. or pl.* 1540, 1711, such matter(s), *1324*; swucche, *pl.* 1551, 1562, suiche 178.—swuch, *conj.* as if, 1533, suich, 566, 976, 1008, 1014

swuþe, *adv.* very, much, strongly, 1561, 1591, swiþe, 1245, 1269, 1274, &c. *1567*, suiþe, quickly 376, sviþe 377, suþe, 2, 12, 155, &c. swiþ 1175

itache, *see* teche

tacninge, *n.* presaging, 1213n

tale, *n.* speech, discourse, debate, 3, 140, 410, &c. long tale 190; *pl.* 257

taueleþ, *pres. 3 sg.* plays at dice, gambles, 1666n

teche (+*dat.* of person), *inf.* teach, show, 914, 1021, 1766; *pres. 1 sg.* 892, teache, 1334, *1449*, itache 1347; techest, *pres. 2 sg.* 850

iteid, *p.p.* tied, 778

telen (of), *inf.* reproach (with), blame (for), *1415*, tele 1377; telst, *pres. 2 sg.* make the charge, bring the accusation, 310, calumniate, accuse falsely, 625

telle, *inf.* tell, speak, 293, 1210, 1571, &c.; *pres. 1 sg.* 267, 715; telstu, *pres. 2 sg.* +*pron.* do you think, 793.—telþ . . . wrþ, sets great store (by), 340

teme, *inf.* breed, bring forth young, 499; *pres. 1 sg.* 1470

temes, *n. pl.* teams, 776

teo, *v. intr. inf.* proceed, go, 1232. —tihþ, *v. tr. pres. 3 sg.* draws, entices 1435; itoȝen, *p.p.* brought up, reared, nurtured, 1725

teres, *n. pl.* tears, 426, 865

teþ, *n. pl.* teeth, 1538

tide, *n.* time, 489, 709; *pl.* (canonical) hours, 26

itide (+*dat.*), *inf.* happen (to), come upon, 1733; itit, *pres. 3 sg.* 1521, 1545, itid 1256; itide, *pres. subj. sg.* 1216

tihþ, *see* teo

time, *n.* time, 323n, 984

itit, *see* itide

tiþinge, *n. acc. sg. or pl.* news, tidings, 1035, 1171

to, *prep.* to, towards, 38, 71, 96, &c., *1476, 1489*; for, 232, 717, 739, 1630; as, 1311, 1429; at, 481, 731, 1579 (2); against 83; when it comes to 85; near 611; to produce 606; him to, to-(wards) him, 1627.—to, *adv.* too, there, 1432; 171, 257, 344, &c. 653

toberste, *v.* burst to pieces; his necke him toberste, *pres. subj. sg.* he break his neck, 122

tobeteþ, *pres. 3 sg.* beat to pieces, 1610

tobreke, *inf.* break, break to pieces, shatter, 1554, 1730, 1737; tobroke, *p.p.* 1558 (*see* spusing)

tobrode, *p.p.* torn apart, rent, 1008

tobuneþ, *pres. 3 sg.* beats severely, thrashes, 1166

tobusteþ, *pres. 3 sg.* pelt to bits, beat to pieces, 1610

tochine, *inf.* crack, split, 1565

todrowe, *v.* tear to pieces; *p. pl.* 126; todraȝe, *p.p.* 1062

togadere, *adv.* together, 807

itoȝen, *see* teo

toheneþ, *pres. pl.* stone to pieces, 1119

tohte, *adj.* taut, strained, 1446; toȝte (*used as n. prepos. sg. or pl.*) strained circumstances, 703

tolli, *inf.* entice, attract, allure, 1627

tome, *adj. used as n. acc. sg.* one that is tame, 1444

tone, *n.* vexation; seist me . . . tone, speak to . . . vex me, 50

tonge, *n. nom. sg.* a pair of pincers, 156

tonge, *see* **tunge**

toppe, *n.* top, 1422.—**top ne more,** from beginning to end, 1328

toppes, *n. pl.* tufts, tow, threads, 428

tort, *n.* dung, excrement; **a tort ne ȝiue ich,** I do not give a damn, 1686

toschakeð, *pres. pl.* shake to pieces, 1647

tosheneþ, *pres. pl.* break up, 1120

toslit, *p.p.* slit open, 694

tosvolle, *p.p.* puffed up, 145

totorueþ, *pres. 3 sg.* pelts to bits, 1166; **totorued,** *pres. pl.* 1119

totose, *inf.* tear to pieces, 70

totwichet, *pres. pl.* pluck to pieces, pinch utterly, 1647

touore, *prep.* before, 1728, 1783, **tofore** 746

toward, *prep.* to, against, 553, 554, 1254.—*adv.* onward; flying on its way 1229n

itrede, *p.p.* trodden, generated, 501

trendli, *pres. subj. sg.* may roll, 135

triste, *pres. 1 sg.* trust, 760; **truste (to),** *pres. subj. sg.* let . . . put his trust (in), 1273

trou, *n. acc. sg.* tree, 615; **tro,** *prepos. sg.* 438, **trowe** 135; **treon,** *pl.* 1201, **tron** 1133

truste, *see* **triste**

tukest, *pres. 2 sg.* tousle, pluck, torment; **tukest . . . over,** pluck . . . all over, tousle . . . all over, 63f n

tu-, *see* **tw-**

tune, *n.* village, town, 1169, 1753

tunge, *n.* tongue, 258, 1071, 1073, **tonge** 37

turf, *n.* turf, peat, 1167

turne, *inf.* turn, 820; *pres. 1 sg.* 1598; **turnþ,** *pres. 3 sg.* 818, **turneþ** 1284; **turnde,** *p. 3 sg.* turned out, 1090.—**turne amis,** pervert, 1365

tueie, *numeral, adj.* two; *nom.* 795, **two** 1047; **tweire,** *gen.* 888, 1396, **twere** 991n; **twom,** *dat., prepos.* 991n, **twam** 1477

twelue, *numeral,* twelve, 836

tuengst, *pres. 2 sg.* pinch, tweak, 156; **twengeþ,** *pres. 3 sg.* 1114

two(m), *see* **tueie**

þah, *see* **þeȝ**

þan(e), *see* **þon, þone**

þan(e), þanne, *see* **þe**

þanne, *see* **þonne**

þar, *adv., conj.* there, where, 16, 26, 97, &c. when, 676, 678, wherever 1399, in which, through which, 1692; **þer** 1485; **þare,** 295, 859, 913, &c.—**of þar,** of it, by it, 340.—**þar . . . þar,** where there . . . there, 981f

þar-after, *adv.* after that, then, next, 45, 393, 1296, &c.

þar-among, *adv.* among them, 497

þar-bi, *adv.* apropos of that, 98, 244

þar-biside, *adv.* close by, 25

þare, *see* **þar, þe**

þarf, *pres. 3 sg.* need(s), 803, **þaref,** there is need, 190

þar-in, *adv.* in it, on it, inside it, 621, **þar-inne** 95

þar-mid, *adv.* with it, with them, with that, 81, 156, 834, 1367, **þar-mide** 1370

þar-of, *adv.* of it, about it, of that, from that, about that, *120,* 190, 726, 1302, &c. at that 228, as regards that 1784; **þer-of,** 1247, 1305, 1348

þar-on, *adv.* in it, 104, **þar-one** 1240

þar-ouer, *adv.* above them, 1136

þar-rihte, *adv.* at once, 1246

þar-to, *adv.* to it, to that place, to that end, for it, 103, 589 *(2),* 647, &c. to do that 114, in answer to that 266, back to it 821, besides 1009

þar-þurh, *adv.* that way, that is how, 1558

þar-uore, *adv.* therefore, on that account, for that reason, that is why, *1236,* 1327, 1354, &c.; **þer-fore** 1260, 1523, **þare-uore,** 274, 758

þar-from, *adv.* from it, 137

þas, *see* **þe**

þat, *conj.* that, so that, 21, 23, 34, &c. *340,* [772], *970, 1319,* in such a way that 1475, till, until, 1791; **þet** 499 *(see* aȝen **þet).—þat . . . n(e),** but that, 1080, 1266, 1275, &c.—**þatte,** *conj.+def. art.* that the, 1512

þat, *see* **þe**

þe, *def. art.*, *dem. adj.*, the, that, 13 (*2*), 19 (*2nd*), 21, &c.; þat, 5, 8, 10 (*1st*), 101, &c. any 1478; þo, *nom. sg. fem.* 26, 199; þane, *acc. sg. masc.* 249, 250, 1097, &c. þene 1093, þanne 1406; þas, *gen. sg.* 338; þare, *gen. sg. fem.* 28; þan, *dat., prepos. sg.* 125, 129, 133, &c. *1731*, þon, 135, 801, þen, 1514, 1743; þare, *dat., prepos. sg. fem.* 31, 140, 529, &c., *1754*; þare, *gen. pl.* 1584; þan, *dat., prepos. pl.* 389.
—þe, *dem. pron.* that, 800; þat, 82, 313, 357, &c.; þes, *gen. sg.* about this, because of this, 748n, 882, þas, it 1442; þan, *dat., prepos. sg.* 200, 650, 1508, &c, þon 679; þan, *sg. or pl.* 1436; þare, *dat., prepos. sg. fem.* her, 1525, 1526, 1549; þeo, *nom. pl.* 1305, 1671, 1675, þo 843; þan, *dat., prepos. pl.* 1762.—þe +*comp.* (*historically instrumental sg. of dem. pron.*) the, any the, the . . . for it, 19 (*1st*), 283, 303, &c.; þe . . . þat, the . . . because, 34 (*1st*); þe . . . þe, the . . . the, 448, 1271 f.—þe, *rel. pron.* that, who, which, what, he who, those who, 1352, 1383, 1386, 1675; þat, 10 (*2nd*), 62, 78, &c. [86]. *506*, *918* (*2*), 1432; someone who, 188; to which, 231; þeo, *nom. pl.* 1324; þane þe, *dem. pron.* +rel., *acc. sg. masc.* him who, 1346; þan þe, *prepos. sg.* that which, what, 1614

þe, *conj.* that, 941n

þe, *conj.* or, 824n, 1064, 1360, 1362, 1408. See hwaþer (*under* w-)

þe, *see* þon, þo, þu

þeȝ, *conj.* though, even if, (*after neg.*) that, 48, 128, 134, &c. *813*, *1724*; þah, 1235, 1237, 1241, &c. *1544*; þoȝ 304.—þah, *adv.* however, though, 1779

þenche, *v.* think, consider, intend; +*inf.* intend to, have a mind to, think to; *pres. 1 sg.* 485; þencheþ, *pres. pl.* 1357, þencheþ (of), intend, plot, 1116; þenche, *pres. subj. sg.* 726, iþenche 723; þoȝtest, *p. 2 sg.* 157; þoȝte, *p. 3 sg.* 392, 469,

661, &c. þohte 1442; iþoht, *p.p.* 1560

þene, *see* þe

þenne, *adv.* from there, 1726, þonne 132

þenne, *see* þonne

þeo, *n.* thigh, 1496

þeo, *see* þe

þeode, *n.* country, nation, *prepos sg.* 1583, *sg. or pl.* 905; þode, *pl.* 387

þeostre, *see* þuster

þeos, *see* þis

þeoues, *see* þoues

þer(-), *see* þar(-)

þes, *see* þe, þis

þewes, *n. pl.* manners, 1017

þi, *adv.* therefore, 860

þi, *see* þin

þicke, *adj.* thick, stout, fat, dense, 17, 580, 587, &c.; (*used as n.*) dense growth, 1626.—*adv.* thick, 430

þider, *adv.* in that direction, there, 719

þiderward, *adv.* in that direction, 143

þilke, *def. art.* +*dem. adj.* the same, that same, 1038

þin, *poss. adj. 2 sg.* your, 74, 75, 161, &c. þi, 73 (*2*), 79, 104, &c.; þine, 35, 40, 53, &c.; þire, *dat., prepos. sg. fem.* 429, 914, 915, &c.—þin, *poss. pron.* yours, 319; þine, 624, 712

þinche (+*dat.*), *v.* seem (to); *impers. v.* it seems (to), things seem (to); *inf.* 346; þinchest, *pres. 2 sg.* 578; þincþ, *pres. 3 sg.* 541, 840, 1787, þingþ 1694, þuncþ, *1649*, 1651, 1672, þungþ 1473, þunþ 1592, þincheþ, *pres. 3 sg.* +*indirect object*, does it seem to you, 46; þuncheþ, *pres. pl.* 1472; þuȝte, *p. 3 sg.* 21, 23, 31, þuhte 1661

þing, *n.* thing, (*also used as pron.*) anything, something, 229, 231, 239, &c.; þinge, *dat., prepos. pl.* (*or sg.*) 309, 485, 625, &c., þing [771].—þing þat, what, 1582; wucche þinge, whatever, 1319; eauere euh þing, everything, 1279; no þing, nothing, (*with neg.*) anything, 948, 1247, none þinge, *prepos. sg.* (*with neg.*) any creature, 1620; an oþer þing, something else, 583, oþer þing

nis non, nothing else is, 784, **to** (. . .) **oþer þinge**, to anything else, for anything else, 559, 664; **for mine þinge**, in my cause, on my account, 434, **for hire þinge**, for her sake, 1597

þire, see **þin**

þis, *dem. pron., dem. adj.* this, the present, the (aforesaid), 113, 200, 392, &c., **þes**, 259; **þeos**, *nom., acc. sg. fem.* 1667, 1707, **þos**, 41, 143, 177, 253, &c.; **þis**, *gen. sg.* 1280; **þeos**, *nom., acc. pl.* 1653, 1770, **þos**, 139, 730; **þisse**, *dat., prepos. pl.* 659, 750, 1044, &c.

þo, *adv.* then, 25, 117, 187; **þe** 1624 (*see* **ȝet**).—**þo**, *conj.* when, seeing that, 105, 1070, 1653, 1667, 1690

þo, see **þe**

þode, see **þeode**

þoȝ, see **þeȝ**

þoȝt, *n.* thought, mind, 492; **þoȝte**, *prepos. sg. or pl.* 391, **þohte** 940

þoȝte(st), **(i)þoht(e)**, see **þenche**

þoleþ, *pres. 3 sg.* suffers, endures, 777

þon, *conj.* than, 505; **þan**, 22, 24, 74, &c., than that, 1023; **þane**, 39, 861, &c.; **þe** 564

þon, see **þe**

þonk, *n.* thought, 490.—**habbe . . . þonc**, am thanked, 461.—**hire þonkes**, *adv. phrase*, willingly, gladly, 70

þone, *conj.* when, seeing that, 684, 804; **þane**, 165, 482, 682, &c.; **þan**, 463, 809, 890

þonne, *adv.* then, 688, 694, 822, &c.; **þanne**, 508, 525, 531, &c.; **þenne** 1380

þonne, see **þenne**

þornes, *n. pl.* thorns, 586

þorne-vvode, *n.* thorn-bush, briar, 444

þorte, see **þrote**

þos, see **þis**

þoues, *n.* thief; *gen. sg.* 1156; **þeoues**, *pl.* 1372

þrete, *n.* threat, 58

þretest (to), *pres. 2 sg.* threaten, utter threats (against), 83; **þreteþ**, *pres. 3 sg.* 1609

þridde, *adj.* third, 325; (*used as n.*) 1478

þringe, *pres. subj. sg.* press hard, throw down, 796.—**þu art to me iþrunge**, you thrust yourself on me, 38

þriste, *adj.* bold, presumptuous, 171, 758

þroȝe, *n.* time, turn, 260.—**one þroȝe**, for a while, 1455; **sume þrowe**, for some time, 478

þrostle, *n. nom. sg.* thrush, throstle, 1659

þrote, *n.* throat, 24, 329, 558, &c. **þorte** 1721

þrowe, see **þroȝe**

iþrunge, see **þringe**

þrusche, *n. nom. sg.* thrush, 1659

þu, *pron. 2 pers.*; *nom. sg.* you, (thou), 33, 38, 47, &c. [771], *805, 1649*, **þv** 473; **þe**, *acc., dat., or prepos. sg.* you, (thee), 34 (*2nd*), 51, *62*, 66 &c. 210, 595, 1144, to you, 1300, 1309, 1618, with you *1320*; *used refl.* yourself, 353, 1113, 1302, for yourself 1506.—**hunke**, *dat. dual*, to the two of you, 1733n.—**ȝe**, *nom. pl.* you, 116, 1673 (*2*), 1702, &c.; **ow**, *dat., prepos. pl.* you, 1683, 1686, 1688, **eu** 1793, **ov**, to you, 114. 115

þuȝte, **þuhte**, see **þinche**

þule, see **ule**

þuncheþ, **þuncþ**, **þungþ**, see **þinche**

þunne, *adv.* thinly, 1529

þunþ, see **þinche**

þurȝ, *prep.* through, by, by means of, because of, throughout, 447, 765, *823*, 1162, **þurh**. [771], *1336*, 1715, 1757 (*2*), **þurþ**, 1256, 1405, 1428, **þurch** 1401

þurȝ-ut, *adv.* throughout, thoroughly, 879, 880

þurste, see **þuster**

þus, *adv.* thus, in this way, 758

þuster, *adj.* dark; *used as n.* darkness, 198, 230, 232; **þurste**, of darkness, 249; **þeostre** 1432

þusternesse, *n. nom.* darkness, 369

þuuele, *n.* thicket, 278

u, v—vowel

for **v, f, (u)**—consonant

see p. 204

ule, *n.* owl, 837, **vle** 26, **hule**, 4, 31, 41, &c. *411*, **houle**, 1662, 1785; **hule**, *gen. sg.* 28

unbliþe, *adj.* unhappy, 1585

unker, *possess. adj. 1 dual*, of the two of us, our, 552, 993, 1689, &c.

unker, *see* ich

unclene, *adj.* unclean, filthy, 91, 233

under, *prep.* under, underneath, 515, 1359, 1682, **vnder** [86]

underȝat, *p. 3 sg.* got to know, learnt, 1055, **underyat** 1091; **underȝete**, *p.p.* obvious, 168

understonde, *inf.* understand, 1262, 1497; **understond**, *pres. 3 sg.* 1463; **understod**, *p. 3 sg.* 951n, 1297, **understode** 662

ungod, *adj.* wicked, evil; *used as n.* evil, 1364; **ungode**, *prepos. sg.* 245, *used as n.* low-born man, 129

ungrete, *n.* want of size, 752

unhwate, *see* unwate

unihoded, *p.p.* unordained, 1178

unilike, *adj.* different; **þin unilike,** *used as n.* a very different person from you, 806

unisele, *adj.* unhappy, wretched 1004

unisome, *adj.* disunited, at variance, 1522

unlede, *adj.* miserable, vile, 976, 1644

unlengþe, *n.* want of tallness, 752

unmeþe, *n.* lack of moderation, excess, 352

unmilde, *adj.* ungentle, harsh, disagreeable, 61, **vnmylde** [1254]

unmurie, *adj.* dull, drab, 346

unneaþe, *adv.* hardly, only with difficulty, 1605.—*adj.* hard; **þe is wel unneaþe,** it is very hard for you, you are having a very difficult time, *1618*n

unorne, *adj.* wretched, mean, 317, 1492

unred, *n.* folly, wicked advice, foolish action, evil; *acc. sg.* 1464; **unrede**, *prepos. sg.* 161, 212; *acc. sg. or pl.* 1355

unriȝt, *n.* wrong, iniquity, wickedness, 165, 1094, 1368, &c. **unriht** 1548.—**don . . . vnriȝt of,** outrage (*v.*), do wrong with, 1053f

unrihtfulnesse, *n.* lawlessness, disregard of the law, 1742

unripe, *adj.* immature, half-grown, 320

unselþe, *n.* misfortune, disaster, ill luck, 1263

unsiþe, *n.* mishap, misfortune, 1164

unsode, *p.p.* uncooked, raw, 1007

unstrengþe, *n.* want of strength, 751

unstrong, *adj.* weak, 561

unþeu, *n. nom. sg.* vice, 194; **unþewes**, *pl.* vices, wicked ways, 1018

unuele, *adj.* bad, evil, wretched, 1003, **unfele** 1381

unwate, *n.* evil augury, ill luck, misfortune, **unhwate** 1267; **unwate**, *prepos. sg. or pl.*, 1148

unwerste, *see* unwreste

vnwiȝt, *n.* monster, evil being, 33, 90; **unwiȝtis**, *pl.* 218

unwille, *adj.* disagreeable, unpleasant; **him is unwille,** displeases him, 422, 1535.—**oure unwille,** *adv. phrase,* to our displeasure, till it displeases us, *347*n

unwrenche, *n. prepos. pl.* wicked tricks, wicked sins, 169, 872

unwreste, *adj.* miserable, sorry, evil, 1170, **unwerste**, petty, unavailing, 178.—**unwreste**, *adv.* badly, 342

vnwroȝen, *p.p.* revealed, exposed 162, **unwroȝe** 848

unwrþ, *adj.* worthless, 339, **vnwrþ** [770]

up, *prep., adv.* up, on, upon, 15, 96, 658, &c. **vp,** 851, 1422, **upe** 733n, **op** 1394.—**upe þon,** even so, 679n

upbreide (*+dat. of person +acc. of thing*), *inf.* reproach (someone) for (something), find fault with (someone) for (something), 1414

upbroȝte, *p. 3 sg.* brought forth, 200

upe, *see* up

uppon, *prep.* upon, on to, against, 1636, 1698, **uppen** 1683, **upon** 494

ure, *possess. adj. 1 pl.* our, 118, 420; **oure** *347.—possess. pron.* ours, 650, 958

urne, *inf.* run, 638

urneþ, *see* eorne

us, **vs,** *see* ich

ut, *prep. adv.,* out, 8, 121, 444, &c. aside 820, vt 53.—**ut of,** devoid of, 660; **vt of,** out of, 53

ute we, *imp. 1 pl.* let us, 1779

utest, *see* **utheste**

ut-halue, *adv.* on the outside, 110

utheste, *n.* outcry; **utheste uppon ow grede,** raise the hue and cry against you, 1698; **an utest uppen ow grede,** 1683

utlete, *n.* outlet, 1754n

utschute, *n. sg. or pl.* excess(es), gadding about, 1468

uu-, vv-, *see also* **w-**

uuel, *adj.* evil, wicked, bad, 1051; **uuele,** 1376, **vuele,** 247, 1171, 1172, **vvole,** offensive, 8.—**vuel strengþe,** brute force, 769.— **uuele,** *adv.* 1206, **vuele** 63

uuel, *see* **wel**

v, f, (u)—consonant

uaȝt, *see* **viȝte**

vair, *adj.* beautiful, fair, kind, civil, 584, **fair** 579; **vaire** 15, **faire,** 180, 439, 441, &c. specious 158, **fayre** 182.—**uairur,** *comp.* 152.—**faire,** *adv.* well, agreeably, courteously, 924, 1556

fairhede, *n.* beauty, 581

uale, fale, *see* **ueole**

falevv, *n.* loss of colour; **falevv icumeþ on grene leue,** green leaves fade, green leaves wither, 456

falle, *inf.* fall, drop, 630, 956; **fallest,** *pres. 2 sg.* 1286; **falþ,** *pres. 3 sg.* 1424, **falleþ** 1240; **ifallen,** *p.p.* fallen (off), 514, **falle** 1233.—**falle . . . adun,** *inf.* fall away, subside, 1457f; **falþ adun,** *pres. 3 sg.* 1454

falt, *see* **folde**

uare, *inf.* go, travel, go about it, behave, act, 640, **fare,** 658, 909, 1779, **ifare** 400; **fare,** *pres. 1 sg.* 454, 457, 460, &c.; **farest,** *pres. 2 sg.* 421, 520, 917; **farþ,** *pres. 3 sg.* 245, **fareþ,** 1243, 1437, 1584; **fareþ,** *pres. pl.* 386; **fare,** *pres. subj. pl.* 552; **fareþ,** *imp. pl.* 1736; **for,** *p. 3 sg.* 1474.— **ifare after,** *p.p.* gone to fetch, gone for, 1709

uaste, *adj.* firm, secure; impenetrable *17.*—**faste,** *adv.* tight,

firmly, 796; **uastre,** *comp.* more securely, 656

fast-rede, *adj.* steadfast in counsel, 211

uecche, *inf.* get, have, *1504*

fedest, *pres. 2 sg.* feed, nurture, 94; **iued,** *p.p.* 1529

uel, *n.* skin, 830, 834; **uelle,** *prepos. pl.* 1013.—**for þine felle,** to save your skin, 1572

uel, vel, *see* **wel**

felde, *n.* field, battlefield, 1714

fele, *adj.* good, proper, 1378

uele, fele, *see* **ueole**

felle, *inf.* knock down, 767

ueneð, *see* **wene**

fenge, *n.* round, bout, 1285

uenne, *n. prepos. sg. or pl.* fen(s), fenland, 832, **venne,** mud, mire, 962n

ueole, *adv., adj., used as n.* much, many, 1274; **uele** 1772; **uele,** 20, 535, 813; **feole** 1772; **fele,** 234, 387, 797, 805; **uale,** 1663, 1767; **fale,** 628, 1371, 1722.—**oþer feole,** many other, 1214

feor, *adv.* far, far away, far off, 923, 1426, 1657; **uor,** 646, 653; **for,** 398, 710; **feorre** 1322; **vorre** 327; **forre** 386

uerde, *n.* army, troops, 1790, **ferde,** 1668, 1672, 1684, military expedition, battle, 1156

ferden, *p. pl.* went, marched, 1789

fere, *n.* mate, companion, associate, 223, 932

uere, *see* **beon**

feþer, *n. nom. sg.* feather, 1688

vich, *see* **hwuch** (*under* **wu-**)

fiȝte, *n.* fight, 183

viȝte, *inf.* fight, 172, **fiȝte,** 667, 1069, 1669, &c.; **fiȝt,** *pres. 3 sg.* 176, 1072, 1074; **uaȝt,** *p. 3 sg.* 1071

fiȝtinge, *n.* fighting, 1704

fihs, *n.* fish, 1007

fiht-lac, *n.* fight, quarrel, 1699

uinde, *inf.* find, discover, devise, 470, 592, 665, **finde,** 595, 601, 1112, &c.; **uindestu,** *pres. 2 sg.* +*pron.* you will not find, 657; **uint,** *pres. 3 sg.* 696; **ifunde,** *p.p.* 705, 1515

uise, *see* **wis**

uisest, *see* **wisi**

fitte, *n.* equal, match, 784

flehs, *see* **flesch**

fleo, *inf.* fly, flee, escape, 1231, 1304, 1700, **flon** 150, **flo,** 406, 442; **fleo,** *pres. 1 sg.* 957, **flo,** 365, 372, 390, &c.; **fliȝst,** *pres. 2 sg.* 89, 227, 238, *405;* **fliȝt,** *pres. 3 sg.* 176, 308, **fliȝþ** 506; **floþ,** *pres. pl.* 278; **fleo,** *pres. subj. sg.* 1230; **fleo,** *pres. subj. pl.* 1673; **flo,** *imp. sg.* 33

flesch, *n.* flesh, meat, 1399, 1408, **flehs** 1007; **flesches,** *gen. sg. used attributively,* of the flesh, carnal, 1388, 1390, 1392, &c. **fleses** 895; **flesche,** *prepos. sg.* 1411, **fleshe** 83.—of **nesche flesche,** carnally frail, 1387

uliȝe, *n. pl.* flies, 600

fliȝst, fliȝt, fliȝþ, *see* **fleo**

flo, *n.* arrow, bolt, *1229*

flockes, *n. pl.* flocks, 280. *Cf. under* f

flod, *n.* flood, 946

flo(n, *see* **fleo**

floþ, *pres. 3 sg.* flows, *920,* **floweþ** 946

floþ, *see* **fleo**

fnast, *n.* breath, 44

uo, *n.* foe, opponent, 403. *Cf.* **iuo** (*n.*)

iuo, *inf.* catch, 612, 1628; **ifoð,** *pres. pl.* 1645.—**fo we on,** *imp. 1 pl.* let us begin, 179

uode, *n.* food, 606; **fode,** breed, race, offspring, 94

foȝe, *n.* propriety, *184n*

foȝle, *see* **fuȝel**

folc, *n. acc. sg.* people, nation, 1023

uolde, *n. prepos. sg.* pleat, fold, crevice, 696; *prepos. pl.* 602.— **in monie volde,** in many respects, 72

folde, *inf.* fold, shut, 1326.—**falt mi tonge,** my speech fails, 37

fole, *see* **ful**

folȝi (*+dat.*), *pres. 1 sg.* follow, 389; **folȝeþ,** *pres. 3 sg.* 307

fondi (*+gen. object*), *inf.* try, test, examine, 1442; **fondeþ,** *pres. 3 sg.* strives 1581; **vonde,** *imp. sg.* 1063

uonge (to), *inf.* catch, catch hold (of), seize (upon); **þar-to uonge,** ravage them, 1135

uor, *prep.* for, because, on account of, for the sake of, 19, 381, 404, &c. **vor,** 206, 276, 453, &c. **for,** 35, 161, 207, &c. *1351,* with, 419, 1716; **for** (*+inf.*), in order to, 540, 1287, 1766.—**for** (. . .) **to** (*+inf.*), in order to, 1017, 1018, 1057.—**vor,** *conj.* for, because, 43, 167, 178, &c. **for,** 32, 147, 170, &c. *1366*

for, *see* **uare**

uor, for, *see* **feor**

forbernest, *pres. 2 sg.* are burnt up, are consumed, 419

uorbisne, *n.* example, parable, proverb, 98, 244, 637

forbode (*+dat.* of person *+acc.* of thing), *pres. 1 sg.* forbid, 648

forbonne, *inf.* banish; **let forbonne . . .,** had . . . banished, 1093n

forbreideþ, *pres. pl.* pervert, corrupt, 1383, **uorbredeþ,** contort (themselves), 510; **forbrode,** *p.p.* 1381

uorcrempeþ, *pres. pl.* cramp (themselves) up, 510

fordeme, *inf.* condemn; **let . . . fordeme,** had . . . condemned, 1098

fordo, *p.p.* undone, rendered powerless, 822

fordrue, *inf.* dry up, 919

fore, *n.* track, trail, 817

foreward, *n.* agreement, 1693, **uoreward,** 822

uorȝete, *pres. subj. sg.* forget, 725

forhele, *inf.* conceal, 798

forleost, *pres. 2 sg.* lose, forfeit, 1649, **forlost** 897; **forleost,** *pres. 3 sg.* 949, 1666, **uorlost** 619, **forlost,** 519, 693, 817; **forleose,** *pres. subj. sg.* 1344, 1485; **forles,** *p. 3 sg.* 1100; **forlore,** *p.p.* 1391

forlere, *pres. subj. sg.* may misinstruct, may misguide, 926

forles, *see* **forleost**

forleten, *inf.* leave, forsake, leave off, give up, 988, **forlete** 966; **forlete,** *pres. 1 sg.* 36; **uorleteþ,** *pres. pl.* 634; **forlete,** *pres. subj. sg.* 404, *pl.* 961n

forlore, uorlost, forlost, *see* **forleost**

forme, *adj.* original, former, 820

uorre, forre, *see* **feor**

forstes, *n. pl.* frosts, 524

fort, *prep., conj.* till, until, 41, 332, 432

uorþ, *adv.* forth, forward, ahead,

far, 297, 398, for**þ**, 528, 877, 1789; 356, *see* euer

vor-þat, *conj.* because, 653, **for-þat** 365

vor-þi, *conj.* therefore, for that reason, that is why, 65, 277, 691, &c. **for-þi**, 288, 409, 1269, &c. **vor-þe** 787, **for-þe** 69

vor-þon, *conj.* because, 1105, **for-þon**, 1100, **for-þan** 1396, 1661; **for-þan þat**, 780, 793f—**uor-þan**, *conj.* therefore, for that reason, that is why, 1662, **vor-þan** 1087, **for-þan** 1600

forþure, *adv.* further, 1606

forworþe, *p.p.* ruined, (made) useless, 548, 573, 575, **forwurde**, enfeebled, 1491

uote, *n. prep. sg. or pl.* foot, feet, *51*

ifoþ, *see* iuo

uox, *n.* fox, 819, 825, fox *812*; foxes, *pl.* 809

vram, *see* urom

freo-man, *n.* man of standing, 1507

fro, *adj.* noble, well-born, 131, 134

frogge, *n.* frog, 85, 146

urom, *prep.* from, 1126, **vrom**, 197, 646, 1029, **from**, 62, 198, 288, &c. **vram** 163, **fron**, 135, 1614

frome, *see* **frume**

frond, *n.* friend, 477; **frondes**, *gen. sg.* 1154

frost, *pres. 3 sg.* freezes, 620

frouri, *pres. 1 sg.* bring comfort to, 535

frume, *n.* beginning, 1513, **frome** 476

fuel-kunne, *n.* tribe of birds, 65

fuȝel, *n.* bird, 1097, 1135; **fuȝeles**, *gen. sg.* 343; **fuȝeles**, *pl.* 1144, **fuheles** 1660; **fuȝele**, *dat.,prepos. pl.* 64, **foȝle** 277

ful, *adj.* foul, nasty, evil, filthy, putrid, loathsome, repulsive, odious, 94, 612, 964, **vvl**, 31, 236; **fule**, 32, 40, 87, &c. base 130, mâlign, 417, 1096, **vvle** 35, **fole** 104; **fulne**, *acc. sg. masc.* 1196.—**fule**, *adj. used as n.* someone filthy, 301

ful, *adj.* full, 247, 360; **fulle** 314.—**ful**, *adv.* very, quite, 471, 704, 810, 1189, 1292

fuleþ, *v.* dirty, soil; *pres. 3 sg.* 100; *pres. pl.* 96; **ifuled**, *p.p.* 110

fuliche, *adj.* complete; full-length 128n.—**fulliche**, *adv.* completely, fully, quite, 1687

fulied, *pres. 3 sg.* follows, 1239

fulste (to), *pres. 1 sg.* help (with), 889

vvlt, *see* wille

ifunde, *see* uinde

fundeþ (to), *v.* set out (for); *pres. 3 sg.* 719; **fundieþ**, *pres. pl.* 850, **fundeþ** 862

vvndrie, vvrs, *see* wu-

vust, *n.* fist, 1538

wa, *see* hwo

wake, *n.* wakefulness, no sleep, 1590

wai, *interj.* alas; **wai þat**, what a pity that, 120

wai, *see* wei

wai-la-wai, *interj.* woe and alas, 220

walde, *see* wille

walles, *n. pl.* walls, *767*

(h)wan, *see* hwo, hwon

(h)wan(n)e, *see* hwon

wanene, *see* whonene

wanst, *see* vvonie

war, *adj.* cautious, careful, 170, 192.—**beo . . . wear**, beware, 1638. *Cf.* iwar

vvhar, *adv., conj.* where, wherever, 64; **hwar** 1727; **war**, 526 (2), 1031, 1109, &c.; **ware**, 892, 1049.—**ne . . . no war**, nowhere, 1168

ware, *see* hwaþer

warm, *adj.* warm, 622; **warme**, *used as n.* warmth, warm place, 538

warni, *inf.* warn, 925; *pres. 1 sg.* 330, 739, 1259

warp, *see* worpe

war-to, *adv.* what for, 464

hwar-uore, *adv.* why, what for, 1421, **ware-uore**, 267, 268, 715. —**war-uore**, *conj.* and that is why, 1618

was, *see* beon

wat, *see* wite

what, (h)wat, *see* hwo

hwatliche, *adv.* actively, quickly, 1708

hwaþer, *pron.* which, whichever (of two); which side, 1198; **weþer** 991.—**ware unker**, which

of (the two of) us, 151.—
hwaþer . . . þe, *pron., adv., conj.*
which . . . (either . . .) or, which-
ever . . . (either . . .) or, what
way . . . (either . . .) or, whether
. . . or, 1362, hweþer . . . þe
1408, waþer . . . þe 1064, weþer
. . . þe, 824, *1360*

we, *see* ich

wear, *see* war

vvede, *see* wode

weȝe, *inf.* bear, 1022

wei, *n.* way, road, course, 308,
956, 1238, wai, 249, 1602; weie,
prepos. sg. 214, 820, 1428.—ut
of þe weie, astray, 1426

wei, *n.* whey, 1009

wel, *adv.* well, very, much, very
much, 31, 36, 44, &c.; quite,
216, 546; virtuously, honestly,
1360, 1362; successfully, 943;
readily, 201, 1739; carefully
471; indeed, truly, 138, 856,
1056, 1318; vvel, 68, 94, easily
1231; uel 537; vel 95

wel, *n.* well, 917

wel-cume (+*dat.*) *adj.* welcome
(to), 1600. *Cf.* vvol-cumeþ

wenden, *inf.* turn, go, go away,
1326; vvend, *pres. 3 sg.* 1464;
wende, *pres. subj. sg.* 864;
wende, *p. 1 sg.* 288; iwend,
p.p. 1519

wene, *n.* thought.—a wene, in
doubt, 682; me is a wene,
comes to my mind, 239

wene, *inf.* think, suppose, expect
dare say, hope, 1266, 1501;
pres. 1 sg. 237, 1694, 1748;
wenst, *pres. 2 sg.* 47, wenest,
259, 371, 1241, (+*inf.*) think
(to) 854, wenist 315; wenstu,
pres. 2 sg. +*pron.* 961, wenestu
303; wenþ, *pres. 3 sg.* 1040,
(+*inf.*) expects (to) 814, wened
901, ueneð 1554; weneþ, *pres.
pl.* 844

weolkne, *n. prepos. pl.* clouds,
sky, *1682*

weole, *n.* prosperity, 1273

wepen, *inf.* weep, 987; wepe, *pres.
1 sg.* 876, 1567; wepeþ, *pres. pl.*
885; wepe, *pres. subj. sg.* 226;
wepen, *pres. subj. pl.* 931, wepe
861

wep-mon, *n.* man, 1379

wepne, *n. pl.* weapons, 1369

wercche, *see* wrecche

were, *n.* man, husband, 1341,
1522, 1523

were(n), *see* beon

wereþ, *pres. 3 sg.* defends, 834

werieþ, *pres. pl.* wear, 1174

wernen (+*gen. of thing*) *inf.* refuse,
reject, 614, werne, deny, 1358

west, *adv.* west, 923

west, *pres. 3 sg.* grows, prospers,
689

weste, *n., adj.* waste land, desolate,
1000, 1528

weþer, *see* hwaþer *under* wa-

wh-. *The h of* wh- *and* hw- *has been
ignored in the alphabetical ar-
rangement*

whi, *adv., conj.* why, 150; hwi,
909, 1257, 1356, &c.; wi, 218,
268, 411, &c.

wi, *interj.* why, 1548n

wicche, *n.* witch; *used attribut-
ively,* 1301, wiecche, 1308 (*see*
crafte)

wike, *n. sg. or pl.* office, func-
tion(s), service(s), duty, 530,
603, 605, &c.

wike, *n. pl.* dwellings, 604

wicke-tunes, *n. pl.* dwelling-places,
730n

wide, *adv.* wide, far, far and wide,
288, 300, 430, &c.

wider, *adv.* to what place, where,
724

wiecche, *see* wicche

wif, *n.* woman, wife, 638, 1064,
1159, &c. *1469*; wiues, *gen.*
1468; wiue, *dat., prepos.* 1077,
1476, 1483, &c.; wiues, *pl.*
1562; wif, *acc. pl.* (? *sg.*), ? *dat.
sg.* 1334n

wiȝt, *n.* creature, thing, being, 434,
556, 612, &c. wiht 1642; wiȝtes,
pl. 431, 598, wiȝte, 87, 204, 535,
&c.

wilde, *adj.* wild, 125, 496, 946, &c.;
used as n. wild creature, 1444

wildernisse, *n,* wilderness, desert,
1000

hwile, *n.* time, 1591, wile 1020.—
wile, *used as adv.* once, at one
time, 202, 1016.—þe wile, while,
1141; one wile, for a while, 199;
lutle hwile, for a short while,
1451, an lutle wile 1458; sum
hwile, for a while, 1425; sum
wile, at times, sometimes, 6

wille, *n.* will, pleasure, 1256.—
fale manne . . . a wille, to the
delight of many people, 1722
wille, *v.* will, wish (to); *pres. 1 sg.*
262, 553, **wulle**, 903, 1109, **wule**,
1467, 1606; **wult**, *pres. 2 sg.*
1064, 1303, 1409, &c. **vvlt** 499;
wilt 165; **wultu**, *pres. 2 sg.* +
pron. 1669, 1693, **wiltu** 640;
wile, *pres. 3 sg.* 185, 214, 408,
&c. **wule**, 630, 1362, 1365, &c.
wle 406; **wulleþ**, *pres. pl.* 1257,
wlleþ 896, **wulle** 1730; **wille**,
pres. subj. sg. 77, 188, 306, 1289,
&c.; **wolde**, *p. 1 sg.* 172, 1261,
1419, &c.; **woldest**, *p. 2 sg.* 84,
1050; **wolde**, *p. 3 sg.* 70, 425,
1069, &c., **walde**, 1710, 1727;
wolde, *p. pl.* 1024, **walde** 1678.
Cf. **nulle**
vvimman,   wimmon,   wimmen,
wimmane, *see* **wummon**
win, *n.* wine, 1011
winne, *n.* strife, agitation;   **on**
winne, agitated, troubled, 670n
iwinne, *inf.* win, gain, conquer,
766, 1290
winter, *n.* winter; *prepos. sg.* 412,
474, 622, **wintere**, 415, 533;
winteres, *gen. sg.* 458
wippen, *inf.* flap, dangle, 1066
wirche, *inf.* make, 722, **wrchen**
408; **wraȝte**, *p. 3 sg.* (had)
brought to life, 106
wis, *adj.* wise, 192, 233, 298, &c.,
wise, 289, 1071, **uise** 961.—
wisure, *comp.* 1250, 1330.—
wise, *used as n.* wise man, sage,
176; *dat. pl.* 225
wisdom, *n.* wisdom, 770, [772],
1726, wise thing 1756; **wisdome**,
prepos. sg. 1212, 1299, 1766.—
do wisdom, do what is wise,
exercise discretion, 454; **wisdon**
can, is wise, 1482
wise, *n. sg. or pl.* wav(s), habit(s),
way of life, 893, 1029; melody,
song(s), tune(s), 20, 54n, 519,
1663, 1703
wisi, *inf.* show, guide, direct, 915;
uisest, *pres. 2 sg.* 973
wisse, *pres. 1 sg.* show, guide,
direct, 927
wiste, *see* **wite**
wisure, *see* **wis**
wit, *n.* wisdom, reason, wit, in-
telligence, (good) sense, 681,

689, 693, &c.; **witte**, *prepos.*
783, 1243.—**kan wit**, am wise,
759; **no wit not**, lacks wisdom,
780. *Cf.* **iwit**
wit, *see* **wiþ**
hwit, *adj.* white, 1276
wite, *v.* know; *inf.* 1139, 1281,
1443, &c.; **wot**, *pres. 1 sg.* 61,
189, 205, &c. **wat**, 1179, 1193,
1194, &c. **wod**, 1049, 1190; **wost**,
pres. 2 sg. 1407; **wostu**, *pres. 2 sg.*
+*pron.* 95, 716; **wot**, *pres. 3 sg.*
195, 236, 867, &c.; **wite**, *pres.*
subj. 1319, 1467; **wiste**, *p. 1 sg.*
160; **wiste**, *p. 3 sg.* 147, 940,
wuste 10; **wiste**, *p. pl.* 116.—
þat þu hit wite, I would have
you know, *440*
wite (+*dat. of person* +*acc. of*
thing), *inf.* blame (something)
on (someone), blame (someone)
for (something), lay (something)
to (someone's) charge, 1248,
1249; **witistu**, *pres. 2 sg.* +
pron. 1356
witest, *pres. 2 sg.* guard, keep
watch over, 1045
witi, *adj.* wise, 1189
witles, *adj.* without sense, not
guided by reason, 692
witute, *see* **wiþ-ute**
wiþ, *prep.* against, towards, with,
at, 403, 800, 1079, &c.; of,
from, 610; **wið**, 1608, 1669,
1775; **vviþ** 62; **wit**, 56, 57, 111,
&c.
wiþ-ute, *adv.* outside, outwardly,
646, 673, **wiðþute** 1594.—
wiþ-ute, *prep.* without, 1430,
wit-ute, 183, 264, 863
wiue(s), *see* **wif**
wlate, *n.* disgust, 1506
vvlatie, *inf.* be disgusted, disgust,
354
wle(þ), *see* **wille**
wlite, *n.* beauty, radiance, face,
countenance, 439n
wlonc, *adj.* proud; wanton 489
vvlt, *see* **wille**
wnder, *see* **wunder**
vvndrie, *see under* **wu-**
wnest, *see under* **wu-**
wnienge, *see* **woning**
wnne, *see* **wunne**
wo, *n.* woe, misery, 882, 892;
wowe, *prepos. sg.* 414
hwo, *pron.* who, 1195, 1505, **wo,**

113, 196 (2), 528 (2), &c. **wa** 1782, **wu** 187; hwan, *dat., prepos. sg.* whom, 1509, **wan** 530.—**what**, *pron.* what, 60, **hwat**, 1296, 1321, 1433, &c. **wat**, 185, 393, 599, &c.; **what**, what, as much as, 484, **hwat** 1601, **wat** 735; **hwat**, how, 1440, **wat**, 635; **hwan**, *prepos. sg.* what, what end, what purpose, 1621, 1633, **wan**, 453 (2nd), 716. —**wat . . . godes**, what good 563.—**hwat**, *interj.* what, 1730, 1751, **wat**, 1075, 1177, 1298

wod, *adj.* mad, 566, 1041, 1298, &c.; **wode**, 512, *1029*, 1385

wod, *see* **wite**

wode, *n.* woad, 76

wode, *n. prepos. sg.* weed, 320; *prepos. sg. collective,* (*or pl.*) 587, 593, **vvede** 937

woȝe, *adj.* crooked, 815; *used as n.* crookedness, (what is) wrong, 164, 198

wo-la-wo, *interj.* woe and alas, 412

vvol-cumeþ, *pres. 3 sg.* welcomes, 440. *Cf.* **wel-cume**

wolde, *n.* woodland, forest, 1724n

wolde(st), *see* **wille**

vvole, *see* **uuel** (*under vocalic* **u-**)

hwon, *adv., conj.* when, whenever, as soon as, 1566, **won** 324, **wone**, 327, 687, 699, &c. **wonne** 38, **hwan**, 1264, 1470, 1537, **wan**, 453 (*first*), 459, 591, &c. **wane**, 420, 451, 455, &c. **hwanne**, 1244, 1251, 1418, &c. **wanne**, 430, 435, 1446, &c.

whonene, *adv.* from where, 138, **wanene** 1300

vvonie, *inf.* wail, lament, moan, 975; **wones**, *pres. 2 sg.* 985, **wanst** 1644

woning, *n.* lamentation, ululation, 311; **woninge**, *prepos. sg.* 870

woning, *n.* dwelling, 1760; **wninge**, *gen. pl.* 614

wonne, *see* **hwon**

wop, *n.* weeping, 878, 986; **wope**, *prepos. sg.* 857, 865

word, *n.* word, saying, speech, 45, 200, 233, &c. **worde** 1270; **worde**, *prepos. sg.* 547; **wordes**, *pl.* 178, 756, 839, &c.; **word**, *acc. pl.* 139, 1653; **worde**, *dat., prepos. pl.* 158, 180, 182, &c.—

word after word, word for word, 468, **word after worde** 1786

worlde, *n.* world; *gen. sg.* 476, **worldes** 1280; **worlde**, *prepos. sg.* 1363

wormes, *n. pl.* worms, 601

worpe, *inf.* throw, 768; **vvorp**, *imp.* 121; **worpeþ**, *pres. pl.* thrust out, 596; **warp**, *p. 3 sg.* 125; **iworpe**, *p.p.* hit, 1121.—**warp a word**, made a speech, 45

worre, *n.* war, 385

wors(t)e, *see* **vvrs** (*under* **wu-**)

worþ, *see* **wroþ**, **wrþe** (*under* **wu-**)

iworþe, *see* **wrþe** (*under* **wu-**)

wost(u), **wot**, *see* **wite**

wowe, *see* **wo**

wowes, *n. pl.* walls, 1528

wraȝte, *see* **wirche**

wrake, *n.* vengeance, enmity, ruin, 1194

wranne, *n.* wren, 564, 1717, 1723, &c.

wraslinge, *n.* wrestling-match, 795

wraþþe, *n.* wrath, 941, 945, 954

wrchen, *see* **wirche**

wrecch, *n.* wretch, miserable creature, 1377, **wrecche**, 534, 1302, 1314, &c. **wercche** 1503.— **wrecche**, *adj.* wretched, miserable, 335, 556, 1111, &c. **wreche** 1688, **wercche** 564

wrechede, *n.* misery, 1219, 1251

wrench, *n.* trick, 811, 831; **wrenches**, *pl.* tricks, 798; **wrenche**, *historically gen. pl.* 813; **wrenche**, *prepos. pl.* 247, 472, 827

writ, *v.* write; *pres. 3 sg.* 1756; **wrot**, *p. 3 sg.* 235

writelinge, *n.* chirping, warbling, 48, 914

wrong, *n.* wrong, injustice, 877.— **wronge**, *adv.* wrongly, wickedly, 196, 1362

wrot, *see* **writ**

wroþ (+**wiþ**, **wið**, *or* +*dat.*) angry (with), hostile (to), 111, 1043, 1087, &c. **wroð** 1608, **worþ**, 1218, 1642, **wroþe** 1145.—**wroþe** (*used as n.*), angry man, 944.— **wroþe**, *adv.* angrily, wickedly, cruelly, 415, 972, 1360, wretchedly 1529, **vvroþe** 63

wrouehede, *n.* peevishness, perverseness, irritability, 1400n vvrs, wrste, wrþ(e), wrþschipe, *see* wu-

wu, *see* hwo

hwuch, *pron., adj.* what, what sort (of), 1443, 1504, 1674, **wuch** 1378; **hwucche,** *prepos. sg.* 936; **wucche,** 1319 (*see* þing).—each, every, **vich** 1378n

wude, *n.* wood, forest, woods, 615, 1626

wude-wale, *n. nom. sg.* woodpecker, 1659n

wule, wulle(þ), wult(u), *see* wille

wulues, *n. pl.* wolves, 1008

wummon, *n.* woman, 1359, 1387, 1393; *prepos. sg. or pl.* 1524; **vvimman,** *acc. sg.* 1413; **wimmen,** *pl.* 1355, **wimmon** 1357, **wummon** 1350n; **wimmane,** *prepos. pl.* 1379

wunder, *n.* wonder, marvel, wonderful thing; **vvunder** 361, **wnder** 852, **wundere** 1473.—**nis wunder nan,** it is not surprising, no wonder, 1389; **wunder hit is,** it is surprising, *1384*

vvndri, *pres. 1 sg.* am amazed, 228

wnest, *pres. 2 sg.* dwell, (go and) live, 589, **vvunest** 338; **wuneþ,** *pres. 3 sg.* 1752

wunne, *n.* joy, delight, happiness, 1100n, **wnne** *272*

vvrs, *adj., adv. compar.* worse, 34, worse, 303, 505, **wurs** 793, **wurse** 1416, **vvurse** 1408.—**worste,** *adj. superl.* worst, 10, **wrste** 121

wurschipe, *see* wurþschipe

wurþ, *adj.* worth, worthy, honoured, 769, 1550, **wrþ,** 340, 572

wrþe, *v.* become, grow, be (*forming passive*); *inf.* 846; **wurþ,** *pres. 3 sg.* 1158, **worþ** 405, **wrþ,** *548,* [770]; **wurþe,** *pres. subj. sg.* 1382, **wrþe,** 1173, was going to 400; **iworþe,** *p.p.* 660

wurþ-ful, *adj.* honourable, 1481

wurþschipe, *n.* honour, 1344, **wurschipe** 1288.—**was wrþsipe** (+*dat.*), redounded to the honour (of), 1099

wuste, *see* wite